AFTER
NATIVE CLAIMS?

AFTER
NATIVE CLAIMS ?

*The Implications of Comprehensive
Claims Settlements for Natural Resources
in British Columbia*

by

Frank Cassidy and Norman Dale

co-published by

Oolichan Books

and

**The Institute for Research on Public Policy
L'Institut de recherches politiques**

1988

ISBN 0-88982-087-2   Oolichan Books
ISBN 0-88645-081-0   IRPP

Canadian Cataloguing in Publication Data

Cassidy, Frank.
   After Native claims?

   Bibliography: p.
   ISBN 0-88982-087-2.   ISBN 0-88645-081-0 (IRPP)

   1. Indians of North America—British Columbia
—Claims. 2. Indians of North America—British
Columbia—Land tenure. 3. Indians of North America
—British Columbia—Land transfers. 4. Natural
resources—British Columbia. I. Dale, Norman, 1948-
II. Title.

   E78.B9C37 1988   346.71104'32'08997   C89-091031-6

FIRST PRINTING DECEMBER 1988
SECOND PRINTING JUNE 1989
THIRD PRINTING FEBRUARY 1990
FOURTH PRINTING SEPTEMBER 1990

Published by
Oolichan Books
P.O. Box 10
Lantzville, B.C., Canada V0R 2H0

and

The Institute for Research on Public Policy/
L'Institut de recherches politiques
P.O. Box 3670 South
Halifax, Nova Scotia, Canada B3J 3K6

Printed and bound in Canada by
Morriss Printing Company Ltd.
Victoria, British Columbia

COVER SERIGRAPH: Mark Henderson

Foreword

This book describes an attempt to look beyond the apparent present impasse in settlement of comprehensive claims by native peoples in British Columbia. The aim is to address and clarify the underlying issues so that there will be greater certainty about what is at stake, and greater insight into how resolution of the issues that give rise to and result from such claims might affect the economic, political, and environmental dimensions of the natural-resource-centred activities on which the economy of the province is so dependent.

But of course the issues raised here go far beyond British Columbia, into central questions facing all of Canada. The concept of steward-ship of resources, the special relationship with the land which is said to characterize traditional native communities, are notions with which we all must grapple as we face the challenges of global change and sustainable development so dramatically articulated by the World Commission on Environment and Development (the Brundt-land Commission). The attitudes which native communities will bring towards questions of resource development, environment and community enterprise after native claims are settled are of concern not just to resource-based companies, but to all of us. The analysis provided by this study of these attitudes as revealed in present initiatives or current plans of native groups offers insights on which resolution of current disputes and more effective use of resources in the future might be based.

This project has been a complex undertaking, drawing financial support from a diverse group of project sponsors, and advice and guidance through extensive consultation with a diverse group of advisors. Financial supporters include the Government of Canada (Indian and Northern Affairs, Fisheries and Oceans, the Canadian Forestry Service, and Energy, Mines and Resources), industry (Placer Development Ltd., Teck Corporation, and Westmin Resources Ltd.), the B.C. Federation of Labour, the Cariboo Tribal Council, and the Honourable J. V. Clyne.

The project advisory panel, which included Grant Ainscough, Owen Anderson, John Batteke, Gary Bowden, Katie Cooke, Liz Fraiken, Larry Guno, Ron MacLeod, Darcy Rezac, Ron Scrimshaw, Neil Sterritt, and Paul Tennant, furnished the authors with thought-

v

ful advice and criticism and helped in identifying and getting access to several of those interviewed for the study.

The Institute wishes to acknowledge, with deep gratitude for their support over an extended gestation period, the contributions and encouragement of these sponsors and advisors.

The authors wish also to acknowledge the labours of many people. Nigel Bankes, a member of the Faculty of Law at the University of Calgary, provided advice and written contributions on several legal-constitutional matters. Maureen Cassidy developed materials for Chapter One and contributed extensive editorial assistance throughout the book.

D'Arcy Davis-Case, Ken Leghorn and Christine Scotnicki worked on documentary analysis and interviews for the forestry chapter. Ms. Davis-Case and Mr. Leghorn participated in the planning stages of the research as did Carol Anne Rolf who also conducted research on non-renewable resource issues and prepared a working paper for Chapter Five as well as providing help with project administration. Some background materials on resource sectors other than those which are the focus of Chapters Three to Five were developed by Gerry Thorne. Stephen Jacoby provided detailed information on the forestry experience in southeast Alaska. Heather Dickson contributed valuable assistance to the background research for the scenarios. Warren Weir and Sean Krieger also undertook many necessary research and administrative tasks.

Deborah Needley contributed valuable and steady typing assistance throughout the project. To her a special thank you is owed. Frances Snowdown and Jean Dragushan of Paper Chase Ltd. as well as Barbara Egan also provided typing assistance.

Appreciation is also in order for the Native Affairs Secretariat of the Province of British Columbia and in particular Ruth Montgomery, a Director with the Secretariat, for providing the authors with a summary of the comprehensive claims in British Columbia as prepared by the Secretariat. This material is included in Appendix II.

Many colleagues provided advice as the work progressed. The authors wish to note in particular the help received from Professor Robert Bish of the University of Victoria and from Dr. Evelyn Pinkerton of the University of British Columbia. Paul Tennant and Katie Cook, members of the project advisory panel, contributed very useful comments and ideas for editorial alterations in the final stages of the project.

To the very large number of people interviewed for the study, we owe deep gratitude not only for their information but for their kind hospitality.

Finally, I join the authors in expressing appreciation to Barbara Hodgins, the former Director of this Institute's Western Resources Program. Through her deep commitment to this study, the Institute was able to conceive the original vision and outline of the study, develop its scenario-based approach, bring the project team together and provide extensive financial support, organize the project advisory panel, and offer ready advice and assistance over the three year life of the undertaking. We all hope that the results will contribute to a more informed and more fruitful resolution of some of the outstanding questions facing Canadian society today.

Rod Dobell
President
Institute for Research on Public Policy

Introduction

1. The Problem

Most of British Columbia is subject to comprehensive claims by native peoples. A climate of uncertainty exists for everyone in the native claims question: governments, native peoples, and industry as well as other third party interests, including environmentalists, residents of claimed areas and the general public. This climate of uncertainty is particularly an issue for those who are concerned with and affected by natural resource use and governance in the province.

The comprehensive claims question has apparently reached an impasse. There is little agreement among concerned parties about the matter of aboriginal rights and title. The negotiating process established by the federal government has not been productive. The provincial government refuses to negotiate comprehensive claims at all, contending such claims have no basis in law and that, if they did, their resolution is the responsibility of the federal government. Third party interests feel excluded from an active role in resolving the question. Native peoples are disappointed and frustrated by the lack of progress, and they resort increasingly to direct action and litigation to obtain the rights they feel are their due.

This study is an effort to look beyond this impasse and picture what might happen to natural resource use and management in the province as the result of comprehensive claims settlements. It is not so much a study of comprehensive claims as it is a study of how a resolution of the issues that give rise to and result from such claims might affect the economic, political, and environmental dimensions of natural resource-centred activities. The aim of the study is to address and clarify the underlying issues which surround the comprehensive claims question so there will be greater certainty about what is at stake and greater insight into how native claims might be resolved.

The natural resource sectors that this study examines are the fishery, forestry and non-renewable resources. The fishery is fourth in terms of its aggregate economic impact on British Columbia but since it is, and has traditionally been, fundamental to the way of life of native peoples it is discussed first. Forestry and non-renewable resources are the province's first and second resource sectors in terms of aggregate economic impact. The uncertainty that surrounds the comprehensive claims question has a particularly strong impact on these resource groupings. Other resource sectors such as those concerning water, wildlife, and agricultural development are not examined because of limitations of space. Nonetheless these sectors are important areas of related concern.

2. Method

Initially the research for this book focussed upon documentary analysis to distill the major themes and concerns people held in regard to the resource implications of the comprehensive claims question. Materials consulted included: background documents prepared by major concerned groups; proceedings of pertinent conferences; testimony presented to various parliamentary committees, task forces, and Royal Commissions; and newspaper accounts of incidents and developments related to the topic. Extensive analysis was undertaken of issues and events relating to comprehensive claims settlement in Quebec and the western Arctic as well as the relevant activities and circumstances of aboriginal peoples in Australia, Greenland, Alaska, and other jurisdictions. The positions, past and present, of various governments within Canada on comprehensive claims and matters of aboriginal rights were also examined in depth. In addition, the historical background of the native claims question in British Columbia was investigated. This preliminary work yielded a framework of economic, political, and environmental issues, which in turn shaped the scenarios formulated as the basis for interviews, case studies, and analysis.

The core data for this study comes from an analysis of interviews with, and documentary materials by and about, the major participants in the fishery, forestry, and non-renewable resource sectors in British Columbia and elsewhere. Researchers travelled throughout the province and made field trips to Washington, Oregon, Alaska, Alberta, Ontario, and Quebec. They analyzed informative and related developments in the western Arctic, Australia, Greenland, and other jurisdictions. In total, over 150 people were interviewed, some on two or more occasions. A list of the affiliations of those interviewed is provided in Appendix I. An effort was made to interview people from as many of the claimant groups in British Columbia as possible. Representatives of industry-wide associations as well as provincial and federal agencies active in resource management and/or native affairs were consulted. Knowledgeable people from other jurisdictions where relevant events have taken place were also interviewed.

In addition, the researchers reviewed the background of the native claims question in detail as it reflects the positions, past and present, of various Canadian governments as well as historical developments in British Columbia.

Interviews were loosely structured. The researchers came to the interviews with a set of questions revolving around the major economic, political, and environmental uncertainties that mark the comprehensive claims question as it affects natural resources in the province. Most of those interviewed were anxious to focus their discussion of resource issues and comprehensive claims on selected and specific topics. Interviewers generally accepted the discussion priorities of those interviewed so that a better appreciation could be attained of the weight attached to particular concerns and developments. On the basis of the first round of interviews, particular cases that ultimately comprised the examples discussed in the sections on "current and emerging initiatives" within each of the chapters on the particular resource sectors were selected. Follow-up interviews were then conducted and further documentary research was done. A research focus on developments surrounding the comprehensive claims and aboriginal rights questions was maintained throughout.

To stimulate thought and lend some order to the current and emerging realities explored for this study, a scenario-based analysis is used. While many scenarios of what may happen if comprehensive claims settlements came about are possible, scenario-based analysis elsewhere has shown that consideration of no more than two or three scenarios at a time is useful.[1] Three are used in this study. Three scenarios, or three accounts of what might happen to the use and management of fishery, forestry, and non-renewable resources in the province as a result of comprehensive claims, are provided and used as organizing frameworks. Each scenario predicts what is likely to happen to the resource base if comprehensive claims were settled according to the pattern inherent in each scenario.

The scenario "Partners in Development" pictures what might happen if native claim settlements reflect a consensus that resource development and the generation of economic benefits is paramount. In this scenario all parties, including native peoples, would agree that a businesslike approach to natural resource use should be emphasized. Economic values would take a much higher priority than political objectives or environmental concerns. Economic imperatives rather than governments would determine the rate and direction of resource use. In a sense, native peoples would pursue resource development as the basis for providing other social and economic benefits.

The "Allies and Adversaries" scenario presents a different picture of what might happen in the wake of comprehensive claims settlements. Bureaucracies and intergovernmental coordinating committees would proliferate. Regulation, mediation, and coordination through a variety of co-management approaches would become a focal point for the concerned groups. Economic and environmental concerns would be resolved, or remain unresolved, as they were addressed in expanded governmental settings. In some instances various parties would work together as allies in resource development and management. In others they would be adversaries.

"Homeland and Hinterland" is the third scenario used in this study. In this scenario native peoples would be able to preserve and govern large parts of their claimed lands and resources through the exercise of well-defined and more or less autonomous jurisdictional powers within specifically defined land bases. Native "homelands" would be explicitly separated from the rest of the provincial land mass which would remain a "hinterland" for resource development in terms of provincial, national, and international markets. As a result, the province would become much more regionalized and decentralized. The economic, political, and environmental dimensions of resource use and management would vary greatly from region to region.

These scenarios were developed in the course of the first stages of the research for this study. They were refined into their present form as the research progressed. The starting point for their development was taken as the experiences and events that have resulted from the comprehensive claims settlements in the western Arctic and Quebec. This course of action was based on the premise that settlements in British Columbia might be similar to those recently concluded elsewhere in Canada. On this basis, as well as on the basis of an analysis of the economic, political and environmental dimensions of the native claims question and discussion with natives and non-natives, the scenario "Allies and Adversaries" was formulated. The scenario was intended to depict a post-land claims future in which matters of governance would be central to the resolution of most problems remaining after, and arising out of, settlements.

Such an outcome to the native claims dispute might not be greeted with great approval by many people in British Columbia. Given the history of the development of fish, forest, and non-renewable resources in the province, it is clear there would be forces which would not favour settlements such as those in Quebec and the western Arctic. There has always been an especially strong, if not universally accepted, view in the province that development must proceed without too much governmental interference. It is also clear that, if settlements are reached, the British Columbia provincial government might not assume the active role taken by the provinical government in pre- and post-settlement activities in Quebec. Nevertheless, unlike the western Arctic, there would be a provincial presence which would have to be considered.

As the scenarios were formulated, it appeared these tendencies might reduce the likelihood of the kind of developments pictured in the "Allies and Adversaries" scenario or, minimally, introduce other possibilities. These possibilities might also result from the federal government's recent emphasis on restraint and the generally critical view some of the key native governments in British Columbia have of developments in Quebec as the agreements there have been implemented. Careful study of some of the events accompanying the implementation of native claims legislation in Alaska also raised additional questions about what might happen if settlements were reached in British Columbia.

All of these considerations gave rise to another scenario, "Partners in Development." In this scenario the role of governments is reduced and that of commercial interaction around resource development is increased. As Chapters Three, Four, and Five indicate, there is a good deal of evidence to support the view that such a scenario is as possible as the "Allies and Adversaries" scenario in the province.

One other scenario seemed necessary. On the basis of discussions with many native leaders and an analysis of several recent documents issued by some of the more influential tribal councils in the province, it is evident that these parties to the native claims question see another possible future if comprehensive claims settlements are reached, a future such as that identified in the "Homeland and Hinterland" scenario. This scenario posits clearly demarcated territories in which native people could retain their view of the land as a home and not as a frontier or hinterland for development. Meanwhile, in such a scenario, other parts of the province's land and resource base would remain under the same conditions of ownership and control as they currently are.

The events pictured in the "Homeland and Hinterland" scenario might satisfy the needs of those other than native peoples. Resource developers might find increased certainty. Other third parties might find a basis for enhanced community development and decentralization efforts. In addition, events involving aboriginal peoples in Greenland, Australia, and other places indicate the aspirations of many native peoples in British Columbia are similar in important ways to those of aboriginal peoples elsewhere. All of these possibilities led to the formation of "Homeland and Hinterland" as the other scenario for this study. Taken together these three scenarios have guided the research and formed a basis for the conclusions reviewed in Chapter Six.

These scenarios are not intended to be a series of forecasts, ranging from the most to least likely. If and when comprehensive claims settlements occur then actual post-settlement resource development and management patterns will likely evolve on the basis of a mixture of approaches. One set of approaches might characterize one region of the province or one resource sector. Another might predominate in other regions or sectors. The purpose of scenario-based analysis is not to predict such developments, but to envision some of their implications for resource use and management.

This type of study of current resource initiatives involving native peoples in British Columbia and elsewhere suggests that such activities are most often part of more comprehensive strategies. For example, a band or tribal grouping may be found to be forging a partnership in the development of forest resources while, at the same time, it is arguing for reasonably autonomous powers, such as those pictured in the "Homeland and Hinterland" scenario, in relation to another resource. This is just one example of a general tendency on the part of many native groups to achieve their fundamental goals through a variety of means.

3. Scenario-based Analysis

The context, in a public policy sense, surrounding the comprehensive claims question and its effects upon resource development and management in the province of British Columbia is turbulent and complex. There is a great deal of information on the views of the interested parties and their fears as well as hopes for the future. In fact, there is so much information that it has, to a significant extent, deteriorated into noise, into a loud clamour of contending opinions. Uncertainty itself has become an issue. This atmosphere is the starting point for the present work. One of the key goals is to identify the core of uncertainty so that the real issues surrounding the comprehensive claims question and its implications for natural resources can be viewed in an informed and productive manner by all — native peoples, government representatives, business leaders, other third parties, and the general public.

Clarifying critical uncertainties is one objective; there are others. A central purpose of this book is to understand and yet look beyond current debates on the comprehensive claims and natural resources in the province and to speculate, in an informed and disciplined manner, about what might happen if claims agreements were reached. One major way of doing this, as indicated previously, is by documenting current and emerging resource development and management initiatives involving native peoples, in the province as well as elsewhere, in the resource sectors of fisheries, forestry, and non-renewable resources. Settlements would change the economic and political landscape of British Columbia to some extent, but an examination of such current initiatives should give an informed glimpse of what might happen if settlements were reached on comprehensive claims.

Such an effort needs to be structured so that some sense can be made out of varied and unevenly-developed initiatives. This is a role which may be fulfilled by the generation of scenarios. Scenario-based analysis is central to this study. Scenarios are a device for stimulating thought and lending some order to complex and emerging realities. A scenario is an account of a possible course of action or events. It is a picture, a story that illuminates multiple aspects of a perplexing question, a discrete image of the future. Scenario-based analysis is based on the perspective that decision-makers need frameworks within which they can make a series of judgements about the most productive, and most unproductive, efforts to solve difficult problems.

There are two main ways in which policy analysis concerning possible futures may be undertaken: by a process of forecasting and by an exercise in scenario building.[2] Forecasting is founded on the premise that the future can be predicted if enough information and data are available. On the basis of this assumption, the forecaster provides a set of prognostications which form the basis for a coherent view of a more, rather than less, certain future. Forecasting is somewhat quantitative and precise. It aims at generating a "best estimate." As P.W. Beck, the Planning Director of Shell U.K., has pointed out, such an approach often tends "to provide the decision-maker with the equivalent of a straight line route through a minefield."[3]

Scenario-based analysis is another approach to the same problem: providing decision-makers with the information they need to make sound, practical decisions concerning important but complex problems. In the face of great ambiguities, scenario-based analysis is a much more useful technique than forecasting. As Andre Benard, then of Royal Dutch/Shell, has commented: "Experience has taught us that the scenario technique is much more conducive to forcing people to think about the future than the forecasting techniques we formerly used."[4]

Scenario-building provides a basis for conceptual understanding based on the use of a consistent group of key variables. Used properly, scenarios can assist the decision-maker by identifying these key variables, potential configurations of them, and the implications of these configurations for various interests involved in the decision situation.[5] A recognition of the prevalence of uncertainty lies at the core of such an exercise:

> There are always elements of the future that are predetermined. But there are seldom enough of them to permit a single-line forecast that encompasses residual uncertainties. Decision-makers facing uncertain situations have a right to know just how uncertain they are. Accordingly, it is essential to try to put as much light on critical uncertainties as on the predetermined elements. They should not be swept under the carpet.[6]

Because of this emphasis on uncertainty, a scenario-based approach can be of great use to those who would attempt to understand the future implications of the comprehensive claims question for natural resource development and management in British Columbia.

Scenarios may be used to project how certainty might arise out of uncertainty. For the purposes of this study, identifying the critical uncertainties in relation to the comprehensive claims question and natural resource development and management is the first task. These uncertainties are generally shared by all involved. They are the elements of the native claims question as it touches on the three natural resource sectors in the province—the fishery, forestry, and non-renewable resources—studied here. These elements or issues are also closely related to one another. They form part of a picture, and, if comprehensive settlements are reached, solutions and responses to them will form various pictures. From the present, we may look to the future and arrange some of these pictures as scenarios, as artfully constructed visions of the key elements of the land question as they might be affected by settlements.

In this book scenario-based analysis consists of four steps:

1. The identification, based upon a review of the concerns of the principal parties and the development of the comprehensive claims question to date, of the critical uncertainties that characterize the most crucial aspects of the problem.
2. The framing of three broad scenarios, each of which is self-contained in the sense that it logically depicts a feasible, if not predicted, future, and

each of which rests upon a vision of how some, if not all, of the critical uncertainties may be resolved.

3. The exploration of current and emerging initiatives involving native peoples in natural resource development and management in British Columbia and elsewhere, with a particular emphasis on those developments that are currently unfolding in the fishery, forestry, and non-renewable resource sectors, which may indicate the likelihood as well as the implications of particular scenarios if settlements were reached.

4. An analysis of the lessons to be learned about the comprehensive claims question and natural resources in light of the evidence and the scenarios that have been put forward.

In Chapters One and Two the first two steps in this approach are taken. In the succeeding chapters, step three, the exploration of current and emerging initiatives, is addressed. In the final chapter, the lessons to be learned are examined.

Contents

Foreword   v

Introduction   viii

The Authors   xx

1: COMPREHENSIVE CLAIMS AND NATURAL RESOURCES   1

  1.   Structure and Scope of the Study   1
  2.   A Persistent Question   5
  2.1   Unfinished Business   5
  2.2   The Federal Government Background   8
  2.3   The Provincial Government Backgound   12
  2.4   Native Governments Background   13
  3.   Current State of the Issue   15

2: SCENARIOS: FROM THE PRESENT TO THE FUTURE   20

  1.   Three Critical Uncertainties   20
  1.1   Economic Dimensions   21
  1.1.1 Costs   21
  1.1.2 Benefits   22
  1.1.3 Economic Relationships   23
  1.1.4 Pace and Direction of Natural Resource Development   24
  1.2   Political Dimensions   24
  1.2.1 Extent and Nature of Regulatory Activity   25
  1.2.2 Size and Complexity of Public Bureaucracies   25
  1.2.3 Political Relationships   26
  1.2.4 Jurisdictional Arrangements   26
  1.3   Environmental Dimensions   27
  1.3.1 Health of the Resource Base   27
  1.3.2 Enhancement of the Resource Base   28
  2.   Three Outlines of the Future   29
  2.1   Partners in Development   29
  2.2   Allies and Adversaries   31
  2.3   Homeland and Hinterland   33
  3.   The Next Step   35

3: THE FISHERY: A SPECIAL RESOURCE   36

  1.   The Fishery in British Columbia   36
  2.   Native Peoples and the Fishery   37
  3.   Roles and Concerns   39
  3.1   The Federal Government Perspective   39
  3.2   The Provincial Government Perspective   42
  3.3   Native Perspectives   45

3.4	Third Party Perspectives	47
4.	Current and Emerging Initiatives	49
4.1	Partners in Development	50
4.1.1	Special Native Licences	50
4.1.2	Native Fishing Corporations	51
4.1.3	Salmonid Enhancement and Community Economic Development	52
4.1.4	Special Harvesting Rights	53
4.1.5	The Tahltan Fishery Strategy	56
4.2	Allies and Adversaries	58
4.2.1	The Musgamagw Demonstration Project: The Fishery Component	58
4.2.2	The Haida Co-management Proposal	61
4.2.3	Inter-tribal Fisheries Coordination	63
4.2.4	Co-management in the U.S. Pacific Northwest	65
4.2.5	The James Bay Agreement	69
4.3	Homeland and Hinterland	71
4.3.1	The Nisga'a Approach	71
4.3.2	The Kwakiutl Fisheries Management Proposal	73
4.3.3	The Gitksan-Wet'suwet'en Approach	75
5.	...To the Future	79
5.1	Economic Dimensions	79
5.2	Political Dimensions	81
5.3	Environmental Dimensions	83

4: THE FORESTS: THE LEADING RESOURCE SECTOR — 86

1.	The Forests in British Columbia	86
2.	Native Peoples and the Forests	86
3.	Roles and Concerns	88
3.1	The Federal Government Perspective	88
3.2	The Provincial Government Perspective	89
3.3	Native Perspectives	91
3.4	Third Party Perspectives	96
4.	Current and Emerging Initiatives	100
4.1	Partners in Development	100
4.1.1	Cariboo Indian Enterprises	101
4.1.2	Hecate Logging	102
4.1.3	Other Native Ventures and Co-Ventures in British Columbia	103
4.1.4	Native Forestry in Southeast Alaska	104
4.2	Allies and Adversaries	107
4.2.1	Tanizul Timber	108
4.2.2	The Nuu-chah-nulth Tribal Council Forestry Program	110
4.2.3	The Musgamagw Demonstration Project: The Forest Component	113
4.2.4	The Washington State Timber/Fish/Wildlife Agreement	117
4.3	Homeland and Hinterland	118
4.3.1	The Nisga'a Forestry Approach	119
5.	...To the Future	122
5.1	Economic Dimensions	123
5.2	Political Dimensions	126
5.3	Environmental Dimensions	127

5: NON-RENEWABLE RESOURCES: OPPORTUNITIES AND CONSTRAINTS 129

1.	Non-renewable Resources in British Columbia	129
2.	Native Peoples and Non-renewable Resources	130
3.	Roles and Concerns	132
3.1	The Jurisdictional Situation	132
3.1.1	The Onshore Framework	132
3.1.2	The Offshore Framework	133
3.2	The Federal Government Perspective	135
3.3	The Provincial Government Perspective	136
3.4	Native Perspectives	138
3.5	Third Party Perspectives	140
4.	Current and Emerging Initiatives	142
4.1	Partners in Development	143
4.1.1	Revenue Sharing at Fort Nelson	144
4.1.2	The Chevron/Fort Good Hope Agreement	147
4.2	Allies and Adversaries	149
4.2.1	The Lax Kw'alaams Band and Dome Petroleum Limited	150
4.2.2	The Tahltan Tribal Council and Gulf Canada Resources Limited	153
4.2.3	The 1943 British Columbia Indian Reserves Mineral Resources Agreement Amending Discussions	157
4.3	Homeland and Hinterland	159
4.3.1	The Inuvialuit Final Agreement	160
4.3.2	Coastal Zone Planning in Alaska's North Slope Borough	163
5.	... To the Future	167
5.1	Economic Dimensions	168
5.2	Political Dimensions	169
5.3	Environmental Dimensions	172

6: AFTER NATIVE CLAIMS? 174

1.	Possible Implications of Settlements	174
2.	Resource Sector Analysis	175
2.1	The Fishery	175
2.2	The Forests	178
2.3	Non-renewable Resources	180
3.	Critical Uncertainties	183
3.1	Economic Dimensions	183
3.2	Political Dimensions	186
3.3	Environmental Dimensions	188
4.	A Future of Diversity	189

Footnotes 192

Bibliography 199

Appendices 210

I. Organizations and Agencies which
   Provided Information and Interviews 210
II. Summary of Contents of Comprehensive Claims in
   British Columbia as Prepared by the Native Affairs
   Secretariat of the Province 213

The Authors

Frank Cassidy is a member of the faculty of the School of Public Administration at the University of Victoria. He has worked and written extensively on issues such as native land claims and self-government. He has an A.M. and Ph.D. in political theory and public administration from Stanford University. **Norman Dale** taught at the University of British Columbia's School of Community and Regional Planning between 1983 and 1986. He is completing a doctoral dissertation at the Massachusetts Institute of Technology and is presently consulting in the field of fisheries co-management.

1

Comprehensive Claims and Natural Resources

1. Structure and Scope of the Study

A large proportion of the land mass as well as the inland and coastal waters of British Columbia is currently the subject of comprehensive claims by native peoples.* Natural resource development and management in the province often occur in areas subject to native claims. There are no agreements on current comprehensive claims, and a climate of uncertainty exists for corporations and small businesses, for persons employed in the natural resource industries, for governments, and for native peoples. This situation clouds not only the status of current resource ownership and access rights but extends to the possible scope of future settlements and their potential impact on natural resources.

Currently an impasse has been reached in relation to the native claims question, an impasse no one wants, yet no one is sure how to overcome. Problems appear to abound; solutions do not. A review of past developments concerning the issue provides little indication that the impasse will be broken easily. Present developments directly related to the comprehensive claims negotiation or resolution process do not appear to hold much promise. This being the case, perhaps it is advisable to look elsewhere, to explore actual current and emerging initiatives which involve native peoples in the management and development of various natural resource sectors, both within and outside of the province, and to attempt to picture through a scenario-based analysis what might happen if, in one way or another, the native claims question were resolved. Perhaps by projecting into the future it will be possible to glean insights which will help us to resolve our present dilemmas.

The negotiations and litigation that pertain to comprehensive claims are extensive and merit close scrutiny by policy analysts, scholars and others. This investigation is not a study of the process of comprehensive claims, however. Instead, the work addresses another question: *If* settlements confirming various native peoples'

---

* The original peoples of what is now British Columbia are referred to as "natives" or "native peoples" throughout this study. The phrase "Indian" is used only in the legal sense as established by the *Indian Act*.

1

ownership and control over significant portions of the resource base in the province occur, what would be the implications for patterns of resource development and management? The aim is to look beyond potential settlements and to consider how certain outcomes arising from the present dispute could, in turn, affect the availability and management of natural resources.

The natural resource sectors selected for examination are the fishery, forestry, and non-renewable resources. The fishery has long been the sector most valued by natives, arguably the very essence of Northwest Coast native culture. Forestry and non-renewable resources occupy a primary place in British Columbia's economy as evidenced by the high level of recent controversy that has surrounded forest operations and non-renewable resource developments in relation to comprehensive claims.

The fishery is fourth among British Columbia's resource sectors in terms of aggregate economic impact, but this rank fails to reflect the many other reasons for the significance of this special resource. Other sectors, notably tourism and recreation, benefit greatly from sportsfishing opportunities. As well, the fate of fish stocks is often at the core of debates over development in other resource sectors, whether these debates are about the effect of logging on stream habitat, the impact of hydroelectric dams on salmon migration, or the environmental consequence of offshore drilling. Most important in terms of the focus of this study is the pre-eminent role that fisheries continues to play in native lives and communities. Fish provide a significant food source, a way of making a living, and a means of cultural expression for British Columbia's native peoples. In the course of the research for this study it became clear that, while native groups varied in their interest and awareness of opportunities in other resource sectors, all have devoted significant effort to fisheries issues.

Forestry is British Columbia's leading economic sector in terms of aggregate economic impact. Almost 20 percent of the labour force depends directly upon logging and wood processing for a livelihood. Over half of the province's export revenue derives from this sector. The government of British Columbia receives a substantial proportion of public revenue from direct rents and indirect payments from it. Because of its scale and extent the forest industry affects the woodlands of most of the province, and its activities often come into conflict with alternative uses of the resource such as wilderness travel, tourism, and fisheries. Increasingly native peoples have been involved in logging controversies. They have taken a growing interest in reaping some of the economic benefits British

2

Columbia's forests offer. They see the timber resource as a major potential source of wealth, yet one for which they receive a minimal share at present. They are deeply troubled by what they perceive to be destructive forest practices which could leave lands potentially involved in comprehensive claims settlements at a much-reduced level of productivity.

Like forestry, the non-renewable resources sector has played a long-standing and important role in British Columbia's economy. It ranks second in aggregate economic impact behind forestry among the resource sectors. Like forestry, developments in this sector have been the focus of land use controversies, and native groups have become more prominent among the critics. This was most evident during the 1985 hearings into proposals for offshore petroleum exploration. While native peoples' perspectives on fish and forestry are relatively clear, greater uncertainty surrounds their intentions in the area of minerals and fuel since there is no native tradition in British Columbia of large scale extraction of non-renewable resources.

Due to the plethora of data generated by this research strategy and because of the unavailability of this data elsewhere in printed form, it was necessary to be selective in the survey of resource sectors to be reviewed in the final study. Three major resource sectors are considered in detail, rather than all major resource sectors in broad overview. The omission of major resource groupings other than the fishery, forest, and non-renewable sectors as subjects for sustained analysis does not imply that they are less important or that comprehensive claim settlements would not carry important implications for them.

One significant resource sector not examined here is the water resources sector. High quality and ample water resources are essential for all other resource activities. British Columbia depends extensively upon power generated by hydroelectric dams. These facilities have major impacts on the lands and villages of native peoples, a point brought home, for example, in recent public discussions of the Ingenika Band whose traditional areas were flooded by construction of the Bennett Dam in 1958.[1]

Another significant resource sector not examined is wildlife. British Columbia is world-renowned for large trophy and game animals. Non-native guiding and outfitting businesses, often based in remote areas where other economic opportunities are scarce, have increasingly become an important economic activity. As with the fishery, this development has taken place against a background of extensive and long-standing native activity. All native groups used

3

terrestrial animals, and a significant number of native communities still depend upon wildlife for food and commerce. In addition to trapping, the business of guiding hunters is one that offers considerable prospects and has been significant for natives elsewhere. There are many parallels with fisheries issues, and some of the more important litigation on aboriginal rights in British Columbia have been over native hunting in relation to provincial laws and regulations.

A third resource sector which is not considered is agriculture. British Columbia's land base for farming and ranching is limited compared to other western provinces. Where farming in fertile river valleys and ranching in the plateaus of the interior is feasible, the sector is remarkably productive. Natives did till the soil and work as ranchers to some extent in the early years of this century, but for many years thereafter they played a relatively marginal role in this resource sector. More recently ranching and farming have become very important to many native groups in British Columbia's interior. Native individuals and communities in regions such as the Chilcotin, the Fraser Valley, the Kootenays, and the Nicola Valley have developed profitable businesses. For their non-native neighbours, the advent of comprehensive claims has raised deep concerns.

There are no natural resources in the province that are not affected by native claims, yet little has been written about what might happen to fishery, forest, and non-renewable resources if comprehensive claims agreements were reached. This is the focus of the study. In this light, attention should be drawn to aspects of the native claims question that are *not* covered here. First, this book is concerned with comprehensive claims, not specific claims. Specific claims are "claims made by Indians against the federal government which relate to administration of land and other Indian assets and to the fulfillment of Indian treaties."[2] These claims deal with lawful obligations already recognized by the federal government. Although specific claims occur in British Columbia, including the so-called cut-off claims, these are not the concern of this study. Here the focus is upon comprehensive claims where the extent and even the existence of an obligation based on traditional use, occupancy, ownership, and control are at issue. Second, as noted above, the present study is not about the process of claims negotiation. Some of the negotiating positions taken on resource use and management are used here as data on how things might turn out if settlements were reached, but the reader will not find analysis of the strengths and weaknesses of particular positions or the overall process.

4

Before turning to the substance of the investigation, it is necessary to conclude this discussion with a brief examination of some relevant historical developments which would affect the likelihood and the shape of any comprehensive claims settlements in British Columbia if they were to come about, and to summarize related governmental policy development as well as current native approaches and responses to the matter. A few words about what have come to be known as third party interests are also in order.

2.   A Persistent Question

2.1 Unfinished Business

The native peoples of British Columbia are not a homogeneous whole. They speak many different languages, engage in different cultural processes, pursue economic well-being in diverse ways, and enjoy a variety of governing systems, yet they share and have historically shared many characteristics and conditions of existence. Before contact with Europeans, the natural resources of what would become British Columbia offered native peoples, especially those on the coast, material abundance. The waters and forests yielded their resources generously, and a complex as well as a rich culture evolved.

It is not surprising that most of the early European arrivals to the region were motivated by a search for profits from its varied resources. The main interest in the late eighteenth century was the pelts of the sea otter and later other furs. In the second half of the nineteenth century, the promise of gold, salmon, lumber, and agricultural products drew increasing numbers of non-native inhabitants to the province.

As the nineteenth century elapsed, three significant trends became evident. First, the native population of the province declined drastically, both relatively and absolutely, from an estimated several hundred thousand people at the time of contact to a low point of 22,605 people in 1929. This sharp decrease was due primarily to smallpox and other epidemics. Alcohol and the availability of firearms contributed further. The rate of decline in most parts of the province was effectively halted in the 1890s.[3] Second, those natives who survived, increasingly found employment in the resource-based sectors of the non-native economy. Native British Columbians were an important part of the wage labour force in the logging, packing, fishing, canning, and mining industries. They also ran many small, independent or family-owned businesses.⁴ Third, Indian reserves were increasingly set aside for the use of the native population. As is well known, with the exception of the Vancouver Island treaties negotiated by James Douglas between 1850 and 1854 and an 1899 treaty in the Peace River country, no other treaties were negotiated in the province. For the most part, reserves were created not to fulfill a treaty requirement, but rather to meet the terms of federal-provincial agreements, including Article 13 of the 1871 Terms of Union. It is also important to note that these reserves were markedly smaller than those elsewhere in the country.

These trends — population decline, increasing wage employment, and growth of the reserve system — were controverted by developments after World War One. Better health care and high fertility rates resulted in a young and rapidly growing native population. By 1985 there were approximately 62,000 status Indians in British Columbia, nearly 18 percent of the national total and about 2.2 percent of the province's population.

The Depression of the 1930s caused much distress to the local and small-scale enterprises that tended to hire native workers. This, combined with the more-developed skills increasingly necessary to work in the resource sectors, meant that employment in the resource sectors was and has continued to be more difficult for native peoples to find than it was when the province was first settled by non-natives.

The legitimacy of the reserve system was also questioned by provincial native groups. Almost from the moment that it became obvious to native people that the newcomers were no longer just trading for furs, wading back to the boat, and sailing away, there have been protests about the reserve system and continued assertions of aboriginal rights and title. From at least the early 1880s to 1909, these protests were localized, consisting mainly of reactive speeches and individual letters of petition and acts of civil disobedience. The various native peoples were too separated by language and ethnic divisions and by the lack of easy transportation and communications within the province to mount a concerted and unified campaign aimed at alleviating their common concerns.⁵

As the province filled with settlers and the concomitant infrastructure that accompanies development, the land claims question was raised with increasing urgency and frequency by natives. The formation of the Nishga Land Committee (1908), the organizing efforts of Joe Capilano (1909), and the creation of the Allied Tribes of British Columbia (1916), were just some of the more prominent efforts to confront the matter. In 1926 the federal government appointed a Special Joint Committee of the Senate and the House of

Commons to examine the Allied Tribes' demands. The report of the following year (1927) declared that the natives had not established any claim to the lands of British Columbia based on aboriginal or other title. That same year the *Indian Act* was amended to prohibit fundraising among natives for the prosecution of any claim.[6] This section of the *Act* was not removed until 1951.

For several years, the land claims movement ceased to be a vital force. Its proponents were discouraged by the lack of parliamentary success and the inability to raise funds legally. The question was not forgotten. It was only held in abeyance. During the 1950s the land claims question was raised once again, and the issue has been put forward more and more strongly as the ensuing thirty years have elapsed.

The formation of the Nisga'a Tribal Council in 1955 signalled the appearance of several new broadly-based tribal groups concerned with a wide range of issues.* The Nuu-chah-nulth formed the Allied Tribes of the West Coast in 1958. This step was followed by the formation of the Southern Vancouver Island Tribal Federation (1964) and the Sunshine Coast Tribal Council (1964). The "White Paper" (see below) put forth by the federal government in 1969 led directly to the formation of the Union of British Columbia Indian Chiefs, as it sought to oppose the government's avowed policy of ending special rights and status for native peoples. This province-wide group had as its main goal a comprehensive claims settlement. With growing inter-tribal dissension in the post-1977 period, the impetus returned once again to bands and tribal councils, in particular, and as a result many new tribal councils were founded.

The increasing importance of tribal councils in the discussion of and agitation about the land claims question complements another strong trend of this period, namely the greater willingness of status and non-status native people to work together for common goals. In general, the early years of the movement can be characterised as being dominated by status Indians, namely those who possessed a place on a band list and came under the jurisdiction of the *Indian Act*. The focus changed in 1969 when the province-wide British Columbia Association of Non-Status Indians was founded, signalling a tendency to emphasize more traditional tribal groupings rather than distinctions maintained by government regulation. In

---

* The spelling Nisga'a is the one now used by the Nisga'a Tribal Council. In this study an attempt is made to adopt the most recent spellings used by each native grouping. An exception is made where materials predating these recent usages (e.g., "The Nisgha Forest Proposal") are referred to.

1976 the organization changed its name to the United Native Nations and accepted both status and non-status members.

Concomitant with the rise of the tribal councils has been the growing vigour of band councils. Established primarily at the village level, by and large these councils work within the structure and core funding of Indian and Northern Affairs Canada (INAC). They have increasingly become the chief administrators of day-to-day life on the reserves. The chief councillor and the council oversee mundane but vitally important services such as roads, housing, and fire protection. They are also most often responsible for representing their communities' interests in relation to matters such as education, health, economic development, and many other fields of governmental activity.

During the last thirty years the intellectual environment within which the land claims question is discussed by native British Columbians has also changed significantly. Well-publicized settlements have been made elsewhere in Canada: the *James Bay and Northern Quebec Agreement* of 1975, the *Northeastern Quebec Agreement* of 1978 and the *Inuvialuit Final Agreement* of 1984. Alaska native claims legislation was passed in 1971. Analysis of these initiatives has been enlightening for the native leaders in the province, serving not only as an indication that settlements can be reached but also as a reminder of what can succeed or go awry when they have been negotiated and implemented. There has also been a tremendous revival of interest in traditional native ways, which has included significant work with native language projects, local histories, and a resurgence in the arts, coupled with more explicit attempts to honour the wisdom of the elders in public affairs. Recently, there has been a renewed emphasis on the traditional underpinnings of native governments, with much attention being drawn to institutions such as the feast or potlatch system.

As the federal and provincial policy responses to native claims are discussed below, it is necessary to bear in mind that the comprehensive claims issue is not likely to go away. It has not disappeared in over a century. The native peoples will not die out, as once was thought, nor will their commitment to their position.

2.2   The Federal Government Background

While the denial of aboriginal title in 1927 by a Special Joint Committee of the Senate and House of Commons sounded a temporary death knell to the land claims movement in the province, the denial of aboriginal rights forty-two years later by the govern-

8

ment with the "White Paper" policy of 1969 re-kindled the British Columbia native land claims movement. A brief description follows of the development of federal policies concerning the resolution of comprehensive claims in the years since the *Statement of the Government of Canada on Indian Policy* (the "White Paper").[7]

With the "White Paper" policy the federal government essentially called for the termination of the special status of aboriginal peoples within Canadian society. Native peoples, the Trudeau government suggested, should have the same rights and opportunities as other Canadians. They should receive provincial as well as federal services. As noted above, the publication of this paper resulted in widespread protest. The government subsequently withdrew the paper.

In 1969 the Nisga'a Tribal Council decided to pursue its claim independently through the court system (*Calder et al.* v. *Attorney-General of British Columbia*). Although a split occurred on the question of whether or not title had been extinguished for the Nisga'a, six of seven Supreme Court Justices found that aboriginal title existed in Canadian law. This meant that the "White Paper" policy had to be adjusted. As Prime Minister Pierre Trudeau said at that time: "Perhaps you had more legal rights than we thought you had when we did the White Paper."[8]

Federal policy on aboriginal title was reversed in August 1973.[9] The new policy established a basis on which the federal government could consider two broad categories of native claims — "comprehensive" and "specific." Comprehensive claims were identified as claims based upon the traditional native occupancy of lands not previously dealt with by treaty or other means. Specific claims were defined as those which occurred where an existing act (such as the *Indian Act*), agreement, or treaty was allegedly violated. These claims previously had been mandated to the Commission on Indian Claims. In 1974 the Office of Native Claims (ONC) was established as part of the Department of Indian and Northern Affairs Canada (INAC) to receive, analyze and administer the resolution of comprehensive and specific claims. Since then progress has been slow and costly. Between 1974 and 1985, $26 million was spent on the operation and management of the claims process, and about $94 million in loans were made to claimant groups for the development and negotiation of comprehensive claims.[10] On the basis of the federal government's policy, only six comprehensive claims could be negotiated at any one time.

The federal government's comprehensive claims policy was re-stated and clarified in the document entitled *In All Fairness* issued by INAC in 1981.[11] This was followed in 1982 with a clarification of the specific claims policy in the booklet *Outstanding Business*. The 1981 policy on comprehensive claims was founded on several broad positions. Among them were: the desire to protect the cultural identity of native people while allowing for their full participation in the development of the economy; the unwillingness of the federal government to consider the issues of native self-government and constitutional reform concurrently with the matter of land claims; and the insistence that all settlements be final and result in the extinguishment of aboriginal rights in exchange for specific benefits.

In 1985 the Minister of INAC, David Crombie, announced the creation of a new task force to conduct a fundamental review of the federal government's comprehensive claims policy. This review was needed because of political and legal developments in the 1980s. The *Constitution Act, 1982* entrenched aboriginal and treaty rights. The 1983 report of the Special Committee on *Indian Self-Government in Canada* (the Penner Report) called for the constitutional entrenchment of the principle of self-government.[12] Court cases such as *Guerin v. The Queen* (1984) re-affirmed the existence of aboriginal title.

The task force's report to Cabinet, *Living Treaties: Lasting Agreements*, was released in 1986. The task force, chaired by Murray Coolican of Halifax, produced a report based upon ninety meetings held across Canada with native groups, governments and other interested parties and upon a review of seventy-three written submissions, including fifty-two from native groups. As the report noted: "...in spite of more than a decade of negotiating, little progress has been made in the settlement of [comprehensive] claims. Settlements have been achieved only when the federal government was eager to facilitate an economic development project."[13] The report included a series of recommendations based upon fifteen principles, including:

1. Agreements should recognize and affirm aboriginal rights.
2. The policy should allow for the negotiation of aboriginal self-government.
3. Agreements should enable aboriginal peoples and the government to share both the responsibility for the management of land and resources and the benefits from their use.
4. The interests of third parties to the dispute (e.g., industry, the general public, etc.) should be treated fairly.[14]

Later in 1986 a new Comprehensive Land Claims Policy was unveiled by Bill McKnight, Minister of Indian and Northern Affairs.

In accordance with the Coolican report, the policy reaffirmed the basic commitment to the resolution of claims by direct negotiation rather than litigation and the need to have the Crown "secure clear title to required land, in the process of settling comprehensive claims."[15] It proposed to have agreements deal only with "those land based rights, encompassed in the term aboriginal title."[16]

As an alternative to the approach of explicitly extinguishing title in return for a grant-back of lands and land-related rights within agreed areas, McKnight's policy suggested abandoning "the requirement for the use of the terminology of extinguishment," although he indicated aboriginal title might still be conveyed to the Crown with a grant-back procedure.[17] As a second alternative, the new policy suggested the conveyance to the Crown of some specified parts of land claim areas, while "aboriginal title would remain undisturbed in other lands selected by the claimant group."[18]

INAC's new policy indicated that the focus of the settlement packages would change to allow for negotiation on a "broader range of self-government matters"; increased managerial participation in "environmental matters including water, land use and wildlife management"; and, an opportunity to receive a "percentage of the Crown's royalties derived from the extraction of resources in the entire settlement area."[19] Part of the thrust of the new policy initiative was an attempt to speed up the negotiating process and to resolve uncertainty over land and resource ownership in the affected areas.

Despite the intentions stated in the 1986 policy statement it is by no means certain that negotiations will be accelerated. Irrespective of McKnight's proposed "grant-back" procedure, any kind of relinquishment of aboriginal title is anathema to most native negotiators. Moreover, the federal government is experiencing a time of restraint. In 1985, for example, the Indians and Natives Study Team of the Nielson Task Force on Program Review suggested that the government "(d)efer the negotiation of comprehensive claims until the government policy on native self-government has been determined and implementation is well underway."[20] The cost of settlement of the outstanding claims, in the study team's opinion, was "likely to be several billions of dollars", even if "(s)ome part of the cost of settlement will, in the long term, be offset by reducing the cost of other government programs."[21] Given this perspective only the future will determine how the federal recognition of comprehensive claims as a legitimate issue will be balanced with its emphasis on reducing the costs of government.

2.3 The Provincial Government Background

The provincial position is very explicit. As the Secretariat for Indian Policy and Programs of the provincial Ministry of Attorney General argued in its paper on "Indian Land Claims in British Columbia" (December 1985):

By Article 1 of the Terms of Union, Canada assumed any outstanding liabilities of the Colony at the time of Confederation.... the Government of British Columbia believes that Canada is fully within its rights in making treaties and/or land claims settlements, and that Canada must bear the burden of the cost of such settlements. If Canada seeks the assistance of British Columbia through the contribution of lands and resources, it is the responsibility of Canada to propose to British Columbia how the Province and third parties would be compensated for any lands and resources that might be made available.[22]

Since Confederation the government of British Columbia has followed a policy of denying the existence of native title or special rights or it has asserted that comprehensive claims are a federal responsibility. This position, of course, affects the likelihood of comprehensive claims settlements. Since the Crown lands outside of designated reserves are held by the province, agreements concerning any native claim which might involve significant portions of the land base are difficult at best. At the outset of the Nisga'a negotiations in 1976, British Columbia attended several meetings. After the submission of the formal statement of claim by the Nisga'a Tribal Council, the province indicated a willingness to listen to and try to respond to native grievances but reiterated its position that aboriginal title had long been extinguished. On this basis the government of British Columbia refused to participate formally in the one set of comprehensive claims negotiations currently underway.

Given this stance by the provincial government, the impression could be left that the province and native groups exist as two solitudes, with minimal interaction. This has not been entirely the case and recent initiatives have, in fact, increased the degree of contact. In 1982, for example, the province passed enabling legislation to facilitate the resolution of the cut-off lands dispute. In 1986 and 1987 it participated in the Sechelt Indian Band self-government agreement with the band and the federal government. Other instances of native/provincial cooperation will be noted in subsequent chapters. These include the awarding of a Tree Farm Licence to Tanizul Timber, a company wholly owned and operated by Carrier-Sekani natives (Chapter Four), and the 1980 revenue-sharing agreement between the province and the Fort Nelson Band (Chapter Five).

Recently, administrative changes within the provincial government have raised native issues to a higher level of priority and prominence. A new cabinet-level committee on native affairs involving six ministries has been established. Exploratory meetings were held between the provincial government and several band and tribal councils throughout 1987. Administrative reorganization has also occurred with the Indian Policy and Programs agency moving from the Ministry of the Attorney-General to Intergovernmental Relations to Highways. The agency has been expanded and renamed the Native Affairs Secretariat. In 1986 the Premier requested that all provincial agencies analyse their programs to seek new areas and means of co-operation with bands. The Secretariat co-ordinated this review.

The thrust of provincial policy on native issues is quite clear. On the one hand, the province is willing to work on new arrangements for local self-government, the delivery of services to reserves, and the possibilities for co-management of resources. On the other hand, there has been no change in the basic stance that aboriginal title and rights, if ever they existed, were long ago extinguished. As a reflection of this view, at a First Ministers' Conference in 1987, the Premier of British Columbia took a particularly strong position against constitutional entrenchment of an inherent and independent right to self-government.

2.4 Native Governments' Background

The provincial government's steadfast position and the federal government's negotiation process are deeply troubling to many native groups. More and more, they are unwilling to face the potentially long years of waiting for their chance to be one of the six groups taking part in the federal negotiation process at any one time. They are looking for other ways of addressing their concerns. Part of the motivation for taking other routes has been movements by resource-extracting companies into areas under claim. As the federal government's 1986 *Comprehensive Land Claims Policy* put it, many native peoples " . . . have a legitimate concern that while they are negotiating, they will suddenly be confronted by the development and alienation of traditionally utilized lands."[23] Those native groups wishing to go around the current impasse have taken several approaches. Some have taken the matter to the courts. Others have tried indirect strategies involving control of self-government, particularly at the band level. Still others have resorted to direct action.

Although the route through the courts is not attractive to any of the parties involved in the dispute, the new government initiatives on the land claims question did commence in 1973 with the *Calder* decision, which was the outcome of a legal action initiated by the Nisga'a Tribal Council. In 1986 the Kwakiutl won a court injunction preventing a private contractor from logging Deer Island, near Port Hardy on northern Vancouver Island. In 1987 the Tsawout people on Saanichton Bay north of Victoria won a British Columbia Supreme Court decision enabling them to block a private 500-berth marina proposal in the bay. The Court supported the Tsawout claim that one of the pre-Confederation treaties negotiated by James Douglas gave them the rights to the bay's various fisheries. Most prominently, three groups in British Columbia have sought court rulings on issues relating to land claims: the Gitksan-Wet'suwet'en Tribal Council on their entire comprehensive claim territory; the Clayoquot and Ahousaht bands on Meares Island; and the Alliance of Tribal Nations on the twin tracking of the Canadian National Railways through their claimed territories.

The Gitksan-Wet'suwet'en case is the most comprehensive one to be placed before the courts to date. Initiated on October 23, 1984 by the hereditary chiefs of the Gitksan and Wet'suwet'en people, this action challenges the ownership and jurisdiction of the province of British Columbia over 57,000 square kilometres of land in the northwestern and north central parts of the province. The Gitksan-Wet'suwet'en claim had been accepted for negotiation by the federal government in 1977. Preparations for negotiations had been undertaken for several years before it was decided by the Gitksan-Wet'suwet'en that negotiations were not going to take place in the near future and that it was necessary to act aggressively in the courts to protect their land and its resources from developments by the Aluminum Company of Canada, Gulf Canada Resources Limited, logging operations, and others.

Other native groups have taken more indirect approaches to obtaining their basic objectives. One method has been to negotiate directly with INAC and other federal as well as provincial government agencies for increased powers and the administration of programs at the band level. Most bands and tribal councils now administer a variety of federal as well as provincial programs. In 1986 and 1987 the Sechelt Band's self-governing powers were recognized in separate pieces of federal and provincial legislation. INAC

14

is currently attempting to engage several other British Columbia bands in a process which may lead to similar special legislation or broad agreements concerning band administration of programs. This process and its projected outcomes promises to bring more control over local services to native peoples immediately. It is not intended to address the comprehensive claims question.

The *Sechelt Indian Band Self-Government Act* was negotiated to get the band and its reserve lands out of the jurisdiction of the *Indian Act*. It was specifically stated to be without prejudice to aboriginal or treaty rights and the band still maintains an aboriginal title claim against the federal government. Under the legislation the band is able to adopt its own constitution, provide for the application of provincial laws, pass a broader range of its own laws and dispose of its property as it sees fit without the intervention of the federal Crown. The legislation also provides for the establishment of the Sechelt Indian Government District, which affords the Sechelt Indians quasi-municipal authority over non-natives occupying Sechelt lands. The effectiveness of the district is dependent upon the implementation of complementary legislation which was passed by the provincial government in April 1987.

Native groups have also been using the *Indian Act* creatively to frame specific by-laws about everything from fishing to bingo. These by-laws are often an attempt to claim jurisdiction over specific activities. There is also an increasing number of native groups who have initiated resource planning and development as a conscious means of moving towards the re-assumption of responsibility for resources in claimed territories. Many of these will be discussed in subsequent chapters.

Where attempts to utilize the laws, institutions, and processes of the Canadian system of governance have proved inadequate or inappropriate, native groups in the province have in some cases turned to direct action. Demonstrations at such places as Deer Island and Lyell Island have been used to block development when other efforts have failed (see Chapter Four).

From the native perspective, the land claims movement will proceed in whatever ways it can, until settlements are reached.

3. Current State of the Issue

Where does the process of comprehensive claims stand in British Columbia? Most of the comprehensive claims which have been submitted by the Government of Canada but which have not yet

Figure 1-1
*Boundaries of Accepted Comprehensive Claims
in British Columbia*

reached active negotiation are in British Columbia.* Figure 1-1 indicates the boundaries of submitted comprehensive claims in British Columbia. These boundaries are presented on three maps because of overlaps between some of the claims. There are additional comprehensive claims which are under current review by the Minister. The point is often made that the extent of the accepted and under review claims comprises a land mass roughly equal to that of the entire province. Table 1-1 provides a breakdown of the approximate area of each claim. These figures include some coastal water areas and several claims which extend into the Yukon. Still, considering that there are seven of what INAC calls "anticipated claims" yet to be included, the cumulative claimed territory will ultimately include most, if not all, of British Columbia and adjacent waters.**

Before this data precipitates confusion or fear, two important qualifications must be noted. First, it is inherent in any bargaining process and a result of the federal comprehensive claims policy guidelines that native peoples will include as broad an area as possible in their initial claim statements. Precedents from comprehensive claims settlements elsewhere in Canada indicate the likelihood that final settlement territories will be smaller than those claimed. Second, and more important, is the fact that, for the most part, native groups state clearly that they neither plan to exclude other users nor to exercise unfettered sovereignty over all settlement lands. Time and again their leaders have pointed out that they seek a just settlement package based on general recognition that non-native use and occupancy of these broad territories have gone forward without treaties, extinguishment, or compensation.

In concluding, it is important to say a few words about what has come to be known as third party perspectives on the land claims question. The term "third party" is becoming the most common generic term for non-native, non-government interests in relation to land claims. This is unfortunate because it suggests that somehow these groups do not figure primarily in the deliberations. There is an increasing realization that the resolution of the native claims question has consequences for people who are neither directly involved in the negotiations process nor represented in the courts.

* For a detailed summary of the contents of comprehensive land claims in British Columbia, please consult Appendix II at the back of this book.

** The anticipated claims are ones from the Chilcotin Tribe, the Lillooet Tribal Council, the Okanagan Tribal Council, the Salish of Georgia Strait, the Shuswap Nation Tribal Council, the South Vancouver Island Tribal Council and the Sto:Lo Nation.

One consequence has been further uncertainty in the provincial resource sectors and further economic costs. This new understanding of the uncertainties relating to the native claims question and their costs was summarized by the Minister of INAC, Bill McKnight, in an interview with *The Financial Post* in January 1987: "I firmly believe that the lost opportunity cost, the lack of economic self-reliance, the lack of development, the inability to plan in Canada in the claimant areas, is much greater than the cost of settlement."[24]

Table 1-1
Approximate Area of British Columbia Comprehensive Claims Accepted and Under Review

NOTE: For comparison, that the total land mass of British Columbia is 948,600 sq.km. Percentage of this total represented by each claim shown in parentheses.

Claimant Group	Area in (sq.Km)	
1. Nisga'a Tribal Council	23,750	(2.5)
2. Kitwancool Band	8,200	(0.9)
3. Gitksan-Wet'suwet'en Tribal Council	51,720	(5.5)
4. Haisla Nation	10,904	(1.2)
5. Association of United Tahltans[1]	107,947	(11.4)
6. Nuu-chah-nulth Tribal Council[2]	14,690	(1.6)
7. Council of the Haida Nation	9,840	(1.0)
8. Heiltsuk Nation[2]	12,970	(1.4)
9. Nuxalk Nation	14,220	(1.5)
10. Nazko-Kluskus Bands	17,340	(1.8)
11. Kaska Dena Council[1]	84,840	(9.0)
12. Carrier-Sekani Tribal Council	175,780	(18.6)
13. Alkali Lake Band	4,530	(0.5)
14. Taku Tlingit (Atlin Band)[1]	26,720	(2.8)
15. Allied Tsimshian Tribes[2]	9,840	(1.0)
16. Council of Tsimshian Nation[2]	28,750	(3.0)
17. Nlaka'pamux Nation	18,590	(2.0)
18. Kootenay Indian Area Council	63,590	(6.7)
19. Kwakiutl First Nations[2]	45,620	(4.8)
20. Sechelt Band	3,910	(0.4)
21. Homalco Band[3]	—	—

[1] Areas include some claimed territory within the Yukon.
[2] Areas include coastal wasters.
[3] Data not available.

Source: Comprehensive Claims, INAC.

In the present study a special effort has been made to delineate in more detail the nature of many of these third party concerns, particularly those of industry. Indeed, one motivation for conducting this work lies largely in the hope that uncertainties and misunderstandings underlying all parties' fears may be dispelled to some extent by a clarification of the issues and by informed speculation on what resource use and management may be like if comprehensive claims settlements were reached. If this is to occur the issues must be clearly outlined, and possible ways in which they might be resolved pictured. This is the task undertaken in Chapter Two.

2

Scenarios: From the Present to the Future

1. Three Critical Uncertainties

This investigation focuses upon three critical areas of uncertainty with regard to comprehensive claims and natural resources in British Columbia. These areas of concern relate to the ways in which comprehensive claims settlements might affect:

- the capture and distribution of the direct economic benefits of natural resource use as well as the extent and responsibility for related costs — the *economic dimensions* of the question;
- the extent and nature of governance and regulatory systems as well as the planning and review processes surrounding resource management and development — the *political dimensions* of the question;
- the state of the resource base, its health, and the dangers it may face — the *environmental dimensions* of the question.

How might these uncertainties be resolved? What would be the implications for natural resource management and development? What would happen to natural resource management and development if comprehensive claims settlements were to take place in British Columbia? As the next three chapters will show, one way to answer these questions is to examine and analyze current and emerging developments and relationships among native peoples, governments, industry, and other third parties and to analyze how these various groups presently seek to use, regulate, protect, and profit from natural resource development. Such an effort is complex; it is limited by the fact that these developments and relationships reflect current conditions and are often based on activities intended to achieve much more specific objectives than those that comprehensive claims settlements might achieve. In order to use information concerning actual current and emerging developments as a basis for shedding light upon what might happen if settlements are reached in the future, it is necessary to distill and interpret this information. In this study, this task is primarily accomplished through the use of scenarios, through depictions of possible futures.

In the following chapters each scenario is construed in terms of the economic, political, and environmental dimensions of natural resource development and management. To understand the background behind the scenarios and the contours of the comprehensive claims issue in British Columbia it is necessary to explore these critical areas of uncertainty in some detail.

1.1 Economic Dimensions

Nowhere is there more uncertainty with regard to comprehensive claims and natural resource development and management than in the economic dimensions of the issue. The interested parties ask the same questions over and over. What would be the costs of agreements? Who would pay these costs? What benefits would be received in return? Would the same parties who receive benefits be the ones who have borne the costs? If not, who would pay so others can benefit? What kinds of business and financial relationships would exist between the concerned parties after agreements are reached? And, perhaps most significantly, how would the pace and direction of resource development be affected?

1.1.1   Costs

Any comprehensive claims agreement would contain provisions for compensation for past grievances, including what is identified for the sake of the agreement as improper prior uses of the land and resources and the profits arising from this use. In the Inuvialuit settlement in the western Arctic, approximately $45 million was involved.[1] In the James Bay settlement in Quebec, well over $200 million in compensation was paid. Since these agreements were signed, times have changed. Governments are now under much more fiscal constraint. This reality would undoubtedly affect the magnitude of the role monetary compensation would play in agreements. Nevertheless, compensation would play a role.

Native peoples are used to having their concerns treated as debated responsibilities by and between federal and provincial governments. The matter of potential compensation within the context of comprehensive claims is no exception. The federal and provincial governments, it would be fair to say, each want to pass the burden off to the other. Various business interests as well as other third parties and the general public are no less involved with this question than are the different levels of government. They are concerned about the possiblity of eventually having to pay, no matter which government is formally responsible. Since governments would have to generate revenue to provide compensation, the concern, particularly on the part of the business community, is that such a possibility might reduce the pool of available capital and create a climate not favourable to investment in natural resource development.

Economic uncertainty does not only exist in relation to the costs of compensation. There is a general unease about the potential costs of implementation, particularly with regard to the costs of the bureaucratic frameworks which might proliferate as resource management proceeds. Natives and non-natives alike are concerned about the possible negative economic effects as well as the costs of administration. Previous comprehensive claims agreements have created an enormous bureaucracy of boards and committees.[2] Often, these new agencies, have increased transaction costs and, to some extent, introduced duplication of effort.

There are other costs involved in comprehensive claims settlements and their implementation. These costs may not be as obvious as those relating to compensation and bureaucracy, but they are nevertheless real. Many native people worry about the further destruction of their traditional indigenous fishing, hunting, and trapping economies even if settlements are concluded. They worry about what they might have to concede if they are to obtain settlements. Many non-natives are concerned that they would have little, or even no, access to needed resources after settlements. They are uneasy with the thought that royalites, taxes and other forms of payment for access to and use of native-held or controlled land and resources may be so excessive as to inhibit resource development and consequent economic growth in the province.

1.1.2 Benefits

Although settlements are costly, they also bring tangible benefits. The problem is that it is difficult to estimate the exact nature of these benefits and who might receive them. After comprehensive claims settlements, native peoples, as prospective landlords of new and substantially larger areas than their current reserve land bases, would be concerned with finding optimal strategies for collecting economic rent in order to obtain adequate payments for providing portions of their lands and resources to those seeking to use them. More broadly, they would be concerned with capturing for their communities maximal social and economic benefits from land use and resource extraction. Given past experiences, native leaders are unsure about the success of such endeavours. Non-native interests as well as the federal and provincial governments are also concerned about their shares of the benefits of resource development. They fear that the costs might outweigh the benefits if settlements were concluded.

The issue of jobs is also an important economic dimension of the native claims question. Natives currently experience a relatively high rate of unemployment. As they look to claims settlements, they perceive increased employment opportunities as one possible benefit. In many instances they would like to see guarantees of jobs associated with any large development projects. Business interests tend to find such guarantees to be at best necessary "costs" which create further barriers to investment. Other third party interests worry about the effect on their employment possibilities. They ask: "Would guaranteed jobs for natives mean less employment for non-natives?"

There are also concerns that settlements would have varied effects on employment possibilities in different resource sectors. It is generally believed that agreements on claims would affect the development and management of natural resources, but there is a lack of consensus on how they would affect various resource sectors. Would some sectors benefit or suffer more than others? Native peoples, for example, do not have the same kind of historical attachment to developmental activities involving sub-surface resources as they do to fishing or hunting. Some non-renewable resource companies are concerned that this fact could translate into a negative attitude toward the use of native land for the development of minerals and energy resources.

1.1.3 Economic Relationships

Economic prosperity is usually accompanied by a high degree of positive relationships between the various interested parties. What kind of economic relationships would exist after comprehensive claims settlements? Virtually everyone is unclear about the answer to this question. There are frequent indications from the native side that they would prefer to establish, own, and operate their own natural resource development companies. This at least raises the potential of displacing existing non-native businesses. It also raises the issue of control. The question of who would guide and manage economic relationships is a matter of particular delicacy. Business interests ask: "How much control would rest with the natives?" The natives ask: "How much control would rest with business?" Other third parties ask: "Would we be actively involved?" Governments ask: "What would our roles be in joint venture arrangements?"

Some business people question the competence of native organizations to manage and develop successful, revenue-generating commercial ventures. Some natives question the businessmen's awareness of native cultural realities. The natives ask: "Do they understand?" Business interests ask: "Can they manage in a business-like way?" Other third parties ask: "Would anyone worry about working positively with us?" Governments ask: "Can the native peoples and third party interests work together — and can they work with government?"

1.1.4 Pace and Direction of Natural Resource Development

All of the economic concerns relating to the comprehensive claims issue ultimately focus on one topic: the pace and direction of natural resource development in the province. Would the pace of development slacken or increase if settlements are reached? How would the province develop? Would developments take place equally in relation to all resource sectors? Would large developments still take place? Or would "small is beautiful" be the order of the day?

Behind these questions lie radically divergent assumptions about the relationship between native peoples and natural resource development. Fears and hopes stem from a sense that native governments would seek a restoration of a close-to-pristine environmental state of affairs. A highly skeptical counter-argument runs that, behind the rhetoric, natives only want "the cash" and that their lands would become splattered with billboards or scarred by worse abuses. What is necessary is a greater understanding of the alternative philosophies affecting the pace and direction of resource development, if settlements are to be reached. In the absence of such an understanding, anxiety remains high.

1.2 Political Dimensions

The comprehensive claims question and its effect on natural resource management is a major political issue in the province. Everyone is worried about the new resource management structures and procedures which might be required after settlements are reached. Would there be many fragmented authorities controlling resource use? Would integrated resource management prevail? What would the roles of various governments be and how would they be accountable to the public.

The powers and relationships of the various levels of government — federal, provincial, and local — with regard to natural resource management and development are central issues. These issues may be examined in terms of the following factors: the extent and nature of regulatory activity; the size and complexity of public bureaucracies; overall political relationships; and jurisdictional arrangements in relation to resource management.

1.2.1 Extent and Nature of Regulatory Activity

At issue here are such matters as requirements for environmental and social impact assessments, rules governing the rate and timing of resource extraction, and standards for performance by all resource users. These matters touch upon practical, everyday activities on the part of those who work in the natural resource sectors of the province. They involve, for example, regulations about the kinds of gear which can be used to catch fish or the standards for reforestation.

These matters may be practical, but they are no less open to dispute. Business interests are concerned that regulatory provisions might be so stringent after comprehensive claims settlements that development would become economically impossible. On the other hand, natives are concerned regulatory provisions may not be much different from those that they now perceive as inadequate for the long-term conservation of resources or for the control of the "spill-over" effects caused by the mining or forest industries. The general public and various third parties are bothered about these matters also. They want to know what their role in regulatory activity would be or if they would have a role at all.

1.2.2 Size and Complexity of Public Bureaucracies

Comprehensive claims settlements in other jurisdictions have given rise to a range of new administrative structures such as project review boards and sectoral resource management agencies as well as coordinating mechanisms between affected governments. Both natives and non-natives worry that the governing apparatus would become so complicated and involved that little development or control over development would take place.

Of special concern is the issue of which interests would participate in and benefit from governance and which would not. Business interests are worried that native and environmental groups would join with eager public servants to create a Leviathan which would stifle initiative. Native peoples are discomforted by the thought they would be submerged within a series of consultative processes which would not be taken seriously by governments unless they were supportive of the developmental intentions of the business and government elites. The general public is uneasy that its viewpoint would not be taken into account as special interests accommodate one another. Governments are distressed because their specific authority may be eroded by a costly and conflict-provoking process.

These concerns are not new, but they are heightened by the comprehensive claims question, particularly for native peoples. Natives have long been dissatisfied by their relationships with the bureaucracies of the federal government. They are apprehensive about the continuation of such relationships even after possible comprehensive claims agreements. Members of native organizations are worried that they may have difficulties generating revenue for their own governments because of continued bureaucratic barriers to economic progress. They look to Quebec and see that the James Bay Cree had to use a good portion of their "agreement opportunity" to obtain basic community infrastructures such as sewage systems, and they wonder if they would have much revenue to finance meaningful involvement in post-settlement resource development arrangements.[3]

1.2.3 Political Relationships

The concerns here are much like those that exist in relation to the economic dimensions of the question. Business interests have doubts about the administrative competence of governments and native groups in relation to the tasks of resource management and development. Business groups also wonder if native organizations would substitute direct political action for adminstrative decision-making when conflicts arise. Everyone wonders if the incidence and intensity of conflict would increase or decrease.

Native groups wonder how well other parties understand their traditions of interacting with the land and the resources it contains. They doubt if other interested parties are perceptive enough to recognize that their customary methods of resource development involve skills and competencies which are intricate and sophisticated. A concern on the part of all parties is that no one party may speak the administrative language of any other.

1.2.4 Jurisdictional Arrangements

Jurisdiction is a significant matter because it determines who would have final authority to make decisions. All parties worry about the proliferation of a web of overlapping administrative agencies with unclear divisions of authority. They fear important matters would often "fall between the cracks."

The provincial government is concerned that its jurisdiction over natural resource sectors would be disrupted. The federal government is uneasy about challenges to its jurisdiction over the fishery, as well as matters affecting native peoples. It would prefer to share its jurisdiction over native affairs. Other parties are concerned the federal government wants to share financial costs more than authority. Most native governments also have jurisdictional concerns. They want more than delegated authorities which can be overruled by ministers of the Crown. They want a recognition of what they perceive as their inherent jurisdiction over all matters pertaining to them. They want self-government in the fullest sense and they want self-government to be directly or indirectly tied to a resolution of the comprehensive claims question.

1.3 Environmental Dimensions

The renewable resource base in British Columbia is itself the subject of general concern and uncertainty. People are increasingly concerned whether or not the forests can sustain current levels of harvesting. In the fishery there are perennial fears about the fate of particular stocks and species. Environmental concerns also surround the performance of non-renewable resource use. Proposals for new developments, such as coal at Mount Klappan in northwestern British Columbia or offshore petroleum exploration, have precipitated controversy.

The environmental dimensions of the comprehensive claims question revolve around two related issues. One concerns the health of the resource base if accommodations are reached. Would rates of use be sustainable? Would overall environmental quality change and how? The second and more specific issue concerns post-settlement levels of enhancement and restoration for troubled resources.

1.3.1 Health of the Resource Base

Having a sustainable resource base is a concern almost pre-emptive of all others, for there is little long-term benefit for anyone who wins a larger share of a "shrinking pie." Natives and others have argued that the forests and fishes of British Columbia are being harvested at rates in excess of what natural regeneration supports. Testimony before the landmark commissions on forestry in the mid-1970s and on the fishery in the mid-1980s revealed a broad concensus that diminished productivity is inevitable without a change in current practices. Part of this change may well have to be reduced harvest levels, in absolute terms. This possiblility exacerbates the concerns non-natives have about reallocation of the harvest to native communities. Non-natives have sometimes challenged the assumption that a more sustainable use of natural resources would be featured under native management. They allege, for example, that excess catches and wastage of fish by native peoples are already common and would increase.

Of course, the harvest of timber and fish is not the only factor affecting the ability of the resource base to sustain those dependent upon it. A major issue is whether post-settlement regimes would lead to a change in overall environmental quality. Under new management would stream quality improve, stay the same, or deteriorate? Would the care with which non- renewable resource projects are planned and developed be better or worse? Would reforestation slacken or be accelerated? These are critical questions with uncertain answers.

1.3.2 Enhancement of the Resource Base

For both the fishery and forestry the concern over the state of the resource base has led naturally to enhancement programs. The Salmonid Enhancement Program initiated in the mid-1970s and the more recent Forest Resources Development Agreement between Canada and British Columbia reveal the priority placed upon such efforts by governments. Industry has inevitably supported allocation of new funding to restore resources. Natives decry the lack of enhancement efforts in the past and often have argued that non-natives have over-exploited the environment without investing in renewal.

With the common priority placed by everyone upon environmental enhancement, the fate of restorative efforts under post-settlement resource management is an unquestionable concern. Some believe that native participation in management would mean greater emphasis in this area; others argue that native governments, faced with enormous new responsibilities and expectations after land claim accommodations, would be caught in a fiscal bind. Like present governments, the argument goes, they may have to divert funds from long-term environmental enhancement to pressing social needs.

2. Three Outlines of the Future

Given the range of issues outlined above, it may appear that there is almost an infinity of futures as far as the resolution of the comprehensive claims question is concerned. Indeed, there may be, but, based on past experiences in other jurisdictions, current tendencies in the management of natural resource development in British Columbia, and the articulated aspirations of those most involved in the native claims question, three broad scenarios can be posited: "Partners in Development," "Allies and Adversaries," and "Homeland and Hinterland." Each is discussed in detail here.

2.1 Partners in Development

The scenario "Partners in Development" presents one version of what might happen if comprehensive claims settlements are reached in British Columbia. Under this scenario settlements would emphasize provisions concerning the means to expand native peoples' share of economic rents and the secondary benefits of resource development, particularly jobs and infrastructural development. There would be a strong emphasis on forming profitable, consistent, and businesslike relationships and partnerships between native peoples and non-native commercial interests. Development, in the sense that it has been most generally pursued in the province over the past century, would be the order of the day. The difference from the pre-settlement situation would be that for the first time native peoples would become full partners in development; they would have the means, the money, and the access to resources which would enable them to pursue development in a substantial way. The pace and direction of development would be determined, to the greatest extent possible, by economic imperatives.

Such a scenario might arise after comprehensive claims settlements take place if there is a general consensus among interested parties that a strong priority should be placed on the development of natural resources in response to market demands and in search of monetary gain. The resulting settlements, as a consequence, would put to rest most outstanding questions for each of the key participants. Each would agree that a businesslike approach to natural resource management should prevail. For resource developers, in particular, this scenario would be close to optimal. For this group the expected benefits of settlements would outweigh their costs, as much greater certainty would characterize the economy. Valuable

29

forest, and non-renewable resources would be freed from
ıbrances such as court cases, develpoment freezes, and con-
g claims of ownership.

ǝ "Partners in Development" scenario would hold the promise
of benefitting government and native interests as well. While the
recognition of native proprietary rights might tend to erode some
aspects of provincial jurisdiction in practice, for the most part the
federal and provincial governments would maintain their jurisdictional powers.They could expect to balance costs with greater
revenues from increased natural resource development. For natives
there would be an expanded capital, revenue, resource, and land
base. These would be used as a means of achieving other social and
economic priorities. The benefits natives would receive would be
"purchased" with a change in self-perspective, as native communities
would alter their holistic view of themselves, the land, and the riches
it contains, replacing it with one that would separate, to a much
greater extent, economic, political, and environmental values, placing a higher priority on the economic values of resource development.

Self-government issues would be detached to a great degree from
land and resource ownership. Claims that the right to self-government is an inherent right resting upon sovereign nationhood would
be replaced by a focus on self-government as a vehicle for economic
development involving the exercise of municipal powers as well as
delegated federal and provincial powers. In general, concerns for
political power and environmental protection on the part of native
peoples would become secondary as they sought to accomplish their
economic and cultural goals through a focus on the business of
natural resource development. An emphasis on the use of natural
resources as the basis for generating economic prosperity rather
than an overarching concern for political or environmental matters
is what makes this scenario a distinct picture of the future when
compared with the other scenarios.

If markets allowed, the commercial fishery industry would likely
be rebuilt on a foundation of co-operative economic relationships
betwen natives and non-natives. The forests and non-renewable
resource sectors would likely experience similar conditions.Third
parties from the business community and native peoples would
likely seek to de-emphasize the role of governments as regulators
and arbitrators. The economies in settlement areas would be driven
by the machine of natural resource development. The expected
profits would deter anyone from attempting to throw this machine
off the track. There would be an emphasis on development rather

than political control. This would truly be a "made in British Columbia" solution to the native claims question.

2.2 Allies and Adversaries

The dynamics of the second scenario, "Allies and Adversaries," would be much more complicated than the first. It would be based on more complex sets of arrangements within which native resource management systems would be meshed with federal and provincial authorities and legislative frameworks. Bureaucracies and intergovernmental co-ordinating authorities would proliferate. Regulation and mediation as well as consultation would become the order of the day. The role of the federal and provincial governments in managing and reconciling differences between business, other third party interests, native peoples, and the various levels of government would be expanded to the point where political and administrative frameworks were the predominant factor in determing the pace and direction of development. Economic and environmental goals would be mediated by political and administrative means.

In this scenario explicit special resource use, self-government, and cultural rights for native peoples would be recognized or created within the existing constitutional framework. The jurisdiction of the federal and provincial governments would remain as it now is. A third order of native government would not be established, but considerable federal and provincial powers would be delegated to native governments in some instances, and delegated to intergovernmental co-ordinating authorities in others where conflict resolution or a high degree of co-ordination was required.

"Allies and Adversaries" settlement packages would result in an expanded land base under native ownership, considerable compensation, the creation of a large range of corporate entities to enhance everything from native cultural life to economic development and the recognition of special rights to develop or protect specific portions of the land and resources which had been under claim. These measures would not necessarily be taken because of any increased consensus concerning native title rights in the province. Rather they would be the outgrowth of concessions made by the federal and provincial governments as well as other involved interests to native groups in response to one or more sets of pressing circumstances. There might be a need, for example, to clear the way for one or several large developments in the non-renewable or water resource sectors. This is, in part, what happened in Quebec to spur the 1975 and 1978 settlements with the Cree, Inuit, and Naskaspi. Or there might be a general view articulated by a variety of interests that the native claims question must be resolved to some degree, if not entirely, so that a limited form of certainty could be established in the political and economic sectors of the province. In either case, native peoples as well as the federal and provincial governments would reach the conclusion that they should settle native claims even if they each could not obtain everything they wanted.

The compromises involved in a limited solution of this kind would not be greeted equally well by all parties. For example, business and other third party interests not involved in potential "mega-developments" as well as the taxpaying public might question the benefits they would receive. They might also question the general circumstances caused by continued conflict over natural resource development. Those who are especially concerned about the health and enhancement of the environment might feel that their concerns were submerged beneath the dynamics of an administrative process which was fundamentally development-oriented. Natives might accept settlements because they perceived themselves as "trapped," with no other alternative. The federal and provincial governments might see settlements as a politically viable, if otherwise ill-advised, cause of action.

The potential of the developments pictured in this scenario might be considered to be very bright. For whatever reasons, all parties might accept the differences which existed between themselves as the working basis for proceeding with resource development and conservation. They might conclude that contrasting views of the principles of natural resource development, the importance of responding to world markets, and the preservation of the natural resources could stand side by side in a peaceful or at least jointly-managed coexistence.

In such instances various groups would grasp the opportunities presented to engage in joint or co-management of natural resources and become "allies." In other instances some groups would continue to view others as "adversaries," and they would seek to use the regulatory and mediating mechanisms created by agreements to outflank these "adversaries." If this were the case, settlements might be accompanied by a high degree of continuing conflict between natives, governments, and third parties over the general nature, pace, and control of resource development.

What makes "Allies and Adversaries" a distinct scenario is the emphasis placed upon political means to accomplish economic and environmental goals. If in the "Partners in Development" scenario economic imperatives predominate in the determination of the pace and direction of resource development, in the "Allies and Adversaries" scenario political and administrative authorities would do so.

Settlements would bring prosperity if market forces or government intervention provided the basis for enhanced natural resource development. The fishery sector would likely prosper as long-standing problems were resolved through more coordination and communication. The forest sector could also benefit as the result of bringing many more native people into co-management activities. Non-renewable resource development would probably experience mixed blessings, as some efforts were enhanced and some disrupted by the presence of new regulatory and environmental agencies. In any case, the role of governance in the management and development of natural resources would be expanded.

2.3 Homeland and Hinterland

The third scenario used in this study is called "Homeland and Hinterland." It envisions a series of well-defined jurisdictions on an expanded land base in various parts of British Columbia within which native control and use of resources would predominate. Jurisdication over natural resource development and governance on the federal and provincial levels would be redefined to a significant extent by the recognition of wide powers on the part of native communities to preserve and enhance their "homelands" and to counter efforts to further transform them into "hinterlands" for the more metropolitan and international corporate interests in the economy of the province.

Among the three put forward in this book, "Homeland and Hinterland" would be the scenario that would come closest to maximizing the current wishes of many native peoples throughout the province regarding a resolution of the comprehensive claims question. Comprehensive claims settlements would be based upon a recognition of extensive aboriginal title and rights. In exchange for benefits such as compensation, guaranteed funding for economic development, increased revenues through royalties and licencing requirements, as well as the protection of traditional pursuits and the environment, natives would relinquish title and special rights within part of their claimed territorial area. They would also retain a large part of their claimed area. Rather substantial powers of native self-government within these areas would be recognized.

Conflict concerning resource development and management among all parties would remain high, as various interests would have diverse goals for natural resource development. This diversity would be accommodated by providing to natives clear and substantial land bases, resources, and rights and by providing to other concerned parties some degree of certainty concerning access to and the use of resources outside of native-retained land. Many resource development and management questions that could only be solved through measures applying to both homelands and the hinterland would require some kind of mediation or arbitration mechanisms such as those commonly used by governments whose jurisdictional powers are independent of one another.

As a result of the creation of many native "homelands" throughout the province, there would be a much greater degree of regional variation than is currently the case. In some regions good working relationships might be established between native peoples and those third party and local governing interests who would prefer and benefit from greater autonomy from the provincial and federal governments. In other regions such harmony might not exist because of perceived jurisdictional conflicts between natural resource development opportunities and native ownership. In still other regions a somewhat separate native economy and polity might stand side-by-side with the general economy and political system. In one part of the province environmental concerns might be seen as central to development. In others they might have a marginal role. Overall, the impact on the environment might be very sharp as a high degree of concern with environmental matters in some areas alternated with a lack of attention to the environmental effects of development in others.

The province would be at once a homeland and a hinterland. For native peoples, their vision of the land and resources as part of a homeland would be retained and enhanced. For other interested parties, a large part of the land base would remain open to development as a natural resource base for metropolitan markets in the Lower Mainland and throughout the world. Depending upon the allocation of resources and land, various resource industries would benefit or suffer. In any case, a fundamental accommodation between various parties would have taken place and there would be a lasting recognition that the province of British Columbia was both a storehouse of valuable resources waiting to be developed and a homeland for its original peoples.

Such a development would be accompanied by many questions and disputes about the application of provincial and federal laws within areas where the jurisdiction of native governments was confirmed. There would also be questions and disputes about the ways in which the actions of such governments affected natural resource development, management, and protection outside of their regions. For everyone the world would have changed greatly and, for better or worse, the economic and political fabric of British Columbia would become more regionalized. In many parts of the province community and cultural priorities would have replaced economic imperatives or governmental regulation as the leading factor in the development of natural resources. In this sense, "Homeland and Hinterland" could be viewed as a distinct alternative to the "Partners in Development" or "Adversaries and Allies" scenarios.

3. The Next Step

The three scenarios depicted in this chapter are not a series of forecasts, ranging from the most to least likely. Each is self-contained in the sense that it logically depicts a feasible future. Each rests upon a vision of how the critical uncertainties in the economic, political, and environmental realms might be resolved to some extent. Actual post-settlement resource development and management practices, if comprehensive claims settlements were to come about, would be likely to involve a mixture of approaches which would reflect aspects of each of these scenarios as well as others not described here. One set of arrangements imprecisely corresponding to one of these scenarios might predominate in one region of the province, while another would characterize a different region. One scenario might characterize arrangements relating to a specific resource sector while another may characterize a different sector in the same claims area. Taken together, all three of these scenarios provide an indication of some general outcomes which might be expected as the result of the settlement of comprehensive claims in British Columbia.

The following three chapters will examine recent developments in the fishery, forestry, and non-renewable resource sectors. These chapters will undertake the third stage of the scenario-based analysis used here: the exploration of current and emerging initiatives involving native peoples in natural resource development and management in British Columbia and elsewhere.

3

The Fishery: A Special Resource

1. The Fishery in British Columbia

Fishing and forestry are industries symbolic of the history of Canada's west coast. The commercial fishery stands fourth among British Columbia's resource-based sectors (after forestry, mining, and tourism-recreation) in terms of aggregate economic impact, but this ranking seriously understates the significance of the fishery for the livelihood and lifestyle of British Columbians. The fishery is a special resource. Great economic and aesthetic benefits are derived from sports and recreational fishing. Almost all native communities depend upon fish both for food and for inter-community trade and direct sales. The commercial fishing subsector provides a large proportion of the total employment for some tribal groups.

While native peoples in British Columbia are seeking community economic development in many economic sectors, it is probably fair to say that none has received such continuing attention as the fishery as a source of opportunity:

For many coastal Indian communities the basic policy choice is now fairly clear. It is between increasing subsidies ... in the form of welfare funds and personnel needed to cope with the growing problems of unemployment, dependency and demoralization, on the one hand, and subsidizing fisheries programs that will provide productive employment and contribute to individual and community morale on the other.[1]

Using the fishery as a prime force for native economic development is not without its problems, for few policy arenas are so beset with conflict. In 1982 Peter Pearse began his Royal Commission report on the west coast's fishing sector with the terse pronouncement: "Canada's Pacific fisheries are at a crisis point." Today the sense of crisis remains, and, in fact, may have heightened due to new forces at work within and upon the sector—notably the increased assertion of aboriginal rights to fish and to participate in fishery decision-making, as well as the regional and worldwide rapid growth of aquaculture.

The conflicts over the fishery are expressed in various and sometimes contradictory ways. Biologists have long despaired about the presence of numerous factors which depress stock levels far below the original productive capacities of the region's river systems. These factors include damage from other activities — hydroelectric dams, poor logging practices, aquatic pollution — and the problem of chronic overfishing. Economists tend to see the difficulty as one of "too many boats chasing too few fish." It is often pointed out that the present commercial fleet has the capacity to take the annual harvest in a matter of hours. Purposeful regulations to reduce the efficiency of the fleet must be enforced. Senior administrators focus on the political impossibility of taking almost any action without offending some significant interest group in the fishery. Finally, there is the part of the issue that motivates the present report: the assertion of special aboriginal rights to use and manage marine species.

2. Native Peoples and the Fishery

It is clear from the oral tradition of the Northwest Coast native peoples and from detailed investigations of several generations of anthropologists that fisheries resources have always been indispensable — economically, culturally and spiritually. Drucker (1963) summarizes a general conclusion:

That they (Northwest Coast natives) were able to attain their high level of civilization is due largely to the amazing wealth of the natural resources of their area. From the sea and rivers — (came) five species of Pacific salmon, halibut, cod, herring, smelt and the famous olachen or "candlefish"... and other species too numerous to mention.[2]

One of the impressions early visitors to the Pacific coast often held was that, because of the fabled abundance of salmon and other marine species, the natives of the area needed to do little more than scoop up the riches. Yet it has become clear from research conducted both by natives and anthropologists that native use and governance of the fishery was complex and adaptive. The existence of a resource management regime was unmistakable. Explicit responsibilities fell to the chiefs, and there were well-defined territories inter-tribally and intra-tribally.

Cove (1982), for example, has described the traditional concepts of land ownership among the Gitksan of the Skeena watershed and has argued that patterns in distribution and availability of salmon created the basis for territoriality within the community. Similarly, exclusive fishing rights underlay territorial divisions among the Kwakiutl:

The *nunayms* (extended families) of all the tribes also own the rivers. They do not allow the members of other *nunayms* to come and use their river to catch salmon. When a man disobeys and continues to catch salmon, they fight, and often both or sometimes one is dead.[3]

The Nuu-chah-nulth of western Vancouver Island provide yet another example of pre-contact resource governance. In testimony made at hearings on offshore oil exploration, one elder expressed his sense of how things had been:

... all the chiefs had privileges on rivers, oceans and the forest and it was the policy that each chief had his own hunters, his own fishermen ... we lived by policy, only by the laws and policies were we able to survive and be wealthy, wealthy because we practiced sharing all our resources.[4]

The pre-contact existence of a well-developed set of management and use rights underlies much of the modern claim that British Columbia's native peoples make for fisheries governance. They emphasize that their demand is not merely for a greater share of resources: it is also for the recognition and recovery of aboriginal authority over the fishery resource.

Native peoples played a changing but always important role in the development of the commercial fishery in British Columbia in the post-contact period. In the early days natives provided the fur traders with fish for immediate personal consumption and for salting for the long voyages to Asia and Europe. Although a small commercial trade existed for salted fish, the real impetus for the commercialization of fishing was the advent of the tin canning process by the 1870s. With the enormous increase in the demand for salmon, a sudden jump in the need for both fishermen and shore-workers arose. While Chinese and Japanese immigrants played an important role as cannery workers in southern British Columbia, natives predominated in the outlying areas. As the industry grew, a native labour force developed, one that was employed both in the canneries and the packing houses.

In the early 1900s more and more independent fishermen came to own their own boats and sell salmon to the canneries. Initially, natives were important participants in this trend. Ralston (1965) estimates that by 1900, some 555 independent native gillnetters were operating on the Fraser River alone. At least half of the 800 gillnetters working the Skeena and Nass Rivers were native vessels (Knight 1978). As the canning industry was consolidated in the first quarter of the twentieth century, the structure of the industry changed in ways that dramatically affected the ability of small independent owners and fish company employees to participate.

Because of geographic and occupational immobility and relatively greater difficulties in securing personal financing, native peoples tended to suffer disproportionately from the trends of centralization in the canning industry and increased capitalization in the fishing industry. With their status as being essentially wards of the federal government, native people could not readily get personal credit while fishing became increasingly capital-intensive as the shift from small boat gillnetting to seining and trolling occurred. Despite a wide array of policy interventions by the federal government, the decline of native participation in the commercial fishery has continued to the present.

3. Roles and Concerns

3.1 The Federal Government Perspective

Fisheries jurisdiction is sometimes thought to be relatively straightforward with the federal government unquestionably paramount. The situation is not that simple. Jurisdictional arrangements in relation to the fishery are much more complex than they are as far as forest resources are concerned, for example. Under head 12 of Section 91 of the *Constitution Act, 1867*, the federal government is given exclusive legislative jurisdiction over "sea coast and inland fisheries." It exercises this jurisdiction through the *Fisheries Act* administered by the Minister of Fisheries and Oceans and his department. Section 91 provides the basis for the federal government to regulate the fishery with closures, gear restrictions, and limits on catches. An important recent decision of the Federal Court of Appeal suggests that the federal government may impose closures not just for stock conservation purposes but also to allocate the available harvest among various sectors of the fishery for socio-economic purposes.[5]

In describing the framework for managing fisheries issues related to native peoples, it is necessary also to note the role of the Department of Indian and Northern Affairs Canada (INAC). INAC has regulatory and programmatic responsibilities which affect the native fishing issue in two broad ways. First, for many years it has conducted and/or financed programs in part or in whole to assist fisheries development. The second pivotal role played in native fisheries is a regulatory one. Under Section 81(1)(o) of the *Indian Act*, band councils can make by-laws for "the preservation, protection and management of fur-bearing animals, fish and other game on the reserve." The Minister of INAC alone has the authority to disallow such by-laws.

It is not appropriate here to outline the full variety of viewpoints which constitute the federal view of native rights in the use and management of the fishery. There are important differences between and within agencies. The broad direction of federal government concerns over the fisheries aspects of comprehensive claims can be drawn from several sources: the relevant provisions of the *Inuvialuit Final Agreement*; a briefing note on negotiations with the Nisga'a Tribal Council which came to light during a court case on fishing by-laws; a 1986 federal policy proposal on co-management and native fisheries; and the Department of Fisheries and Oceans' (DFO) submission to the Coolican Task Force to Review Comprehensive Claims Policy. The key issues reflected in these sources are: 1. allocation between natives and others; 2. the nature and breadth of user rights; and 3. the character of the management process.

The first issue, the matter of *allocation of the resource* between natives and non-natives, is a particularly controversial one. Under the *Inuvialuit Final Agreement* natives are granted preferential treatment, but of a limited kind. The conditions differ between marine mammal and fish harvests. For the former, the Inuvialuit have first priority not only for subsistence but in the development of commercial fisheries. For commercial fishing the Inuvialuit are guaranteed a quota; beyond this, however, their allocations are on the same footing as other users.

The proposed fisheries component in the Nisga'a negotiations reflects a different federal perspective. Based on information from senior federal negotiator Fred Walchli, the proposal involves a substantial increase in the Nisga'a catch for both the food and commercial industry. Unlike the Inuvialuit provisions, this implies a federal willingness to make a net increase of native fish catches part of an agreement.

A third source in delineating federal policies, the "Policy Proposal for a B.C. Columbia Indian Community Salmon Fishery," is not explicit on increased native allocations. It reiterates a long-professed federal policy that, next to conservation, the native food fishery is to have highest priority. But "(a)llocations for Indian community fisheries, in excess of those for traditional food fisheries must be determined when the TAC (total allowable catch) is allocated by the Department of Fisheries and Oceans in consultation with all user groups."[6]

This concern is most directly expressed in DFO's brief to the Task Force to Review Comprehensive Claims Policy, which conducted hearings during 1985. Here DFO pointed out that most fisheries stocks are fully utilized at present and that reallocation to natives as part of a comprehensive claims settlement would unavoidably diminish the shares of other fishermen. DFO recommended that any displacement be achieved through a gradual and voluntary purchase of existing interests at fair market value and that as far as possible enhancement and habitat restoration be used to increase native harvests.

The second policy issue which is important in defining the federal perspective is that of the envisioned *nature and scope of user rights.* This has been a most controversial matter because of sharply different views on whether natives should be at liberty to sell or trade fish caught as part of the "food fishery." Natives by and large hold that the distinction between food and commerce is neither valid nor any business of outsiders. The very fact that Ottawa has continued to use the phrase "food fishery" indicates the federal government's sustained intention of distinguishing fish that can be sold from those needed for community consumption.

In the *Inuvialuit Final Agreement* subsistence and commercial usage of marine mammals are treated identically, both are protected by special preferential rights. Limited knowledge of the proposed terms of a settlement with the Nisga'a makes it difficult to decipher the federal government's policy on this matter. Again, however, the use of the term "food fishery" does suggest that the distinction would be maintained. The "Policy Proposal for a B.C. Indian Community Salmon Fishery" seems to indicate that federal policy is hesitantly shifting towards permitting direct sales from community fisheries. Opposition to this from non-native user groups is vehement. More recently, the Minister of Fisheries and Oceans has been actively consulting with these interests to find a resolution to the issue of the sale of "food fish."

The third and final general policy issue and, in the long term, the one with potentially the greatest impact is that of *the structuring of the management process.* Here the key word is "co-management," which has come rapidly into usage in British Columbia and elsewhere since 1983. This phrase has very different connotations depending upon who is speaking. For some it means an improved advisory process, without demonstrable shifts in who has authority. In contrast to this use of the term, some native groups have used "co-management" to denote a radically different regime in which they would have final authority at least in some restricted geographical areas. The federal government's perspective on "co-management" is somewhere in between, but, certainly, the government has been

41

consistent in maintaining paramount jurisdiction and responsibility for the Minister of Fisheries and Oceans.

The Inuvialuit framework presents a clear view of co-management. A Fisheries Joint Management Committee was established with equal representation from the Inuvialuit and government sides. It has broad managerial responsibilities — reviewing fishing plans, determining harvest levels, licencing, enforcement policy, and the like. Nevertheless, the relationship to the Minister of Fisheries and Oceans is clearly subordinate. The Joint Management Committee is to operate by forwarding recommendations which the Minister has authority to vary or reject. The "Policy Proposal for a B.C. Indian Community Salmon Fishery" is also clear: "The responsibility for the overall management of the resource resides with the Minister of Fisheries and Oceans."[7]

The DFO submission to the Task Force to Review Comprehensive Claims Policy addresses a broader range of co-management issues than just who is to have final authority, although once again the need for ultimate ministerial authority is asserted.[8] The problems foreseen in extending true joint authority include interference with Canada's international policies and obligations; increased management costs through bureaucratic expansion and duplication of expertise and efforts; fragmentation of management authorities; disruption of current advisory approaches; and, potentially, further exclusion of non-natives from decision-making.

In sum, the federal government has clearly revealed an intention to expand the native share of both the fishery and decision-making about the fishery. In the case of the latter there is no indication that a partnership of equals is intended. Advice and limited direct decision-making, in the federal view, must be clearly subsidiary to the final authority of the Minister of Fisheries and Oceans.

3.2 The Provincial Government Perspective

The provincial government also has an important role in the regulation of the fishery, although the source of its power is somewhat more diffuse. First, and foremost, the provincial government, for the most part, owns the bed (solum) of non-tidal waters in the province. As a matter of common law, the owner of the solum has the exclusive right to the fishery on non-tidal and non-navigable waters. This right is, therefore, the property of the province and subject to provincial jurisdiction. The province can grant the exclusive right to fish in non-tidal waters and can also establish closed seasons for these waters. The owner of the solum underlying tidal and navigable waters does not have these rights, for there is said to be, as a matter of common law, a public right to fish in tidal waters.

Second, provincial ownership of areas of fisheries habitat and the surrounding uplands has consequences for the ability of the federal government to protect the environment of spawning fish. The Supreme Court of Canada, for example, has placed a limit on the use of federal power to protect fisheries habitat by striking down a section of the *Fisheries Act* that prohibited any deposit of logging debris into streams inhabited by fish; in the future, actual harm to the habitat would have to be established.[9]

A third source of provincial authority over the fishery lies in its general powers over property and civil rights and in matters of a local or private nature. These powers give the province the capacity to regulate processing and intra-provincial marketing of fish. The final source of provincial power is delegated from the federal government. Under the federal *Fisheries Act*, the Governor in Council is empowered to make fisheries regulations such as controls on gear and the timing of fishing. These are passed for each province but, in respect to non-tidal water fisheries, the province has the delegated authority to amend and expand upon the regulations.

Taken together, these four sources of provincial authority are significant. Despite the broad language of section 91 (12) of the *Constitution Act* quoted above, the federal legislative jurisdiction is significantly more limited than it might appear at first sight. Consequently, it becomes difficult to make the argument that in this sector the federal government is free to strike whatever deal it wishes with native peoples without the need for provincial involvement or consent.

Provincial leasing policy also has enormous effects on the disposition of nearshore resources, including those near Indian reserves and within the "sea claim" areas outlined by coastal tribal groups. This has particular significance for aquaculture operations. The province generally owns the foreshore (that area between low and high water) and, in any case, most if not all aquaculture operations will be land-based. Operators therefore need to purchase or lease upland areas, which typically are owned by the province and are subject to provincial jurisdiction. The province can grant a preliminary permit, referred to as a Section 10 licence, which allows aquaculture operators to carry out detailed site surveys and production planning.

In 1986 a new policy came into effect whereby Section 10 licences were automatically granted for a period of one year. The resulting "gold rush" of site applications alarmed some native and fisheries organizations. As of mid-1986, over 750 permit applications were before the provincial authorities responsible for aquaculture licencing. For some native groups this burgeoning industry has become an area of much concern, and several tribal councils have joined with commercial fishermen in demanding that the province place a moratorium on new licences. For a brief period in late 1986 a moratorium was in effect. Other native groups lobbied against such measures, illustrating once again that British Columbia's natives are not homogeneous in their perspectives on resource use.

The general perspective of the provincial government of British Columbia towards aboriginal rights has been considered earlier. Its position regarding the fishery is consistent with the continuing assertion that no special rights exist and that natives should have no more or no less opportunity than other citizens. This can be seen, for example, in response to native requests for special aquaculture zones around reserves where band members alone would be given leases. The province has not agreed to these requests. Instead it encourages native groups, whether individuals or bands, to make Section 10 applications for preliminary licences for aquaculture operations and thus to become business participants in fish farming. This stance is consistent with statements the province has made regarding its willingness to explore special community economic development strategies in recognition of the particular hardships native peoples face. There is a recognition of social disadvantage among natives, but provincial assistance is not seen as a way of meeting obligations created by aboriginal title.

A further indication of the provincial government's perspective on native fishing rights was the intervention by the Attorney General of British Columbia in two recent instances. As a response to the controversy over the Gitksan-Wet'suwet'en fisheries bylaws in 1986, the province sought and obtained an injunction preventing four of the Gitksan bands from implementing bylaws that were to have come into force in mid-June. The province, acting on behalf of the Pacific Fishermen's Defense Alliance and the British Columbia Wildlife Federation, based its argument on the idea that the resource belongs to everyone and that allowing special use and management rights is a derogation of federal responsibilities. In 1987 the province joined the Alliance as plaintiff in a legal action against the federal government on the fishing component of the Nisga'a comprehensive claim settlement.

3.3 Native Perspectives

In contrast with the province's authority over aspects of the fishery, native bands' involvement in governance, from the perspective of Canada jurisprudence, derives at present from federal legislation. The courts have generally only been prepared to recognize a native right (whether aboriginal or treaty) to fish on Indian reserves subject to the terms of the federal *Fisheries Act* and regulations. Inland bands particularly have been severely affected by these rulings with respect to the salmon fishery because of their upstream position and the difficulties of calculating and allowing for adequate escapements for conservation purposes.

Recently band councils have attempted to better their legal position through fishery bylaws. Under the *Indian Act* a band council may make bylaws for "the preservation, protection and management of fur-bearing animals, fish and other game on the reserve."[10] Both the courts and the federal Department of Justice have taken the position that where there is an inconsistency between band bylaws and the federal *Fisheries Act* the former will prevail.[11] Hence, it is possible for band councils to prescribe for themselves a less restrictive regime than that found in the *Fisheries Act* and regulations. There are two important restrictions on the utility of these band bylaws. The first is that band bylaws must be placed before the Minister of INAC for a forty-day period during which the Minister may disallow the bylaw. The second is that the bylaws apply only on the reserve.

The need for ministerial approval has proven to be an important impediment to the use of band bylaws on fisheries. Although some British Columbia bands do have valid fisheries bylaws, others have faced repeated disallowance. Once passed, however, the bylaws may provide a defence to charges of *Fisheries Act* violations and may also strengthen the negotiating position of bands in their demands for fisheries co-management and a larger share of the resource.

As noted, band bylaws regarding the fishery have been in effect for many years and on many reserves. Until quite recently these bylaws rarely constituted a challenge to federal authority. This changed as tensions grew between DFO and native groups in the late 1970s. A notable example of the new more assertive use of band bylaws is the Squamish Band's Bylaw 10, which was passed largely to provide a legal basis for band members to fish without DFO regulation. Bylaw 10 also differs from DFO's regulations in the kinds and numbers of fish which can be taken, the fishing methods used, the permissible times and the areas of fishing. A more controversial case of native fisheries regulations arose in 1986 after several Gitksan-Wet'suwet'en bands enacted bylaws. This circumstance is discussed later in this chapter. Implict in the new wave of band bylaws is a theme that has persisted for decades among native leaders: that the aboriginal right not only to use but to manage fish has never been extinguished.

Native peoples believe the fishery has been destabilized through poor management, particularly through the failure of the federal government to control overfishing. Despite the DFO's priority on the Indian food fishery, natives argue that their communities are usually last in line. Stocks, they contend, may be drastically reduced by ocean fisheries by the time they reach traditional native fishing sites. There is a strong feeling among native fishermen that they are more tightly regulated simply because the in-river fishing effort is more visible and more readily controlled. In recent years there has been an increasing number of arrests of natives for alleged fishing violations.

This state of affairs is deemed unacceptable by most native peoples. They assert original ownership of the resource and make the claim that proprietary and managerial rights have never been extinguished. Native peoples adopt two principal approaches for asserting these rights: pursuit of fisheries elements and/or "sea claims" within the comprehensive claims process and passage of fishing bylaws under the *Indian Act* that intentionally conflict with provisions of the *Fisheries Act*.

Despite the term "land claims," rights in the fishery have been a key element in the assertion of comprehensive claims and aboriginal title. After the federal government's major policy shift on claims in 1973, a formal statement was made by the Native Brotherhood of British Columbia, an organization primarily involved in fisheries matters:

The Native Brotherhood, on behalf of the Indian people of British Columbia, declare our position of ownership since time immemorial of our surrounding waters and resources...We the Indian people of British Columbia, are now prepared to negotiate to share our resources with our fellow Canadians.[12]

At a recent Native Brotherhood convention, demands were specified for making a 50 percent native share the "bottom line" in comprehensive claims agreements. Other resolutions called for a joint management regime and a moratorium on new licences for non-natives. Advocacy of fishing rights through the pursuit of comprehensive claims agreements now occurs both at the level of each claimant group and through a new intertribal organization, the B.C. Aboriginal Peoples' Fisheries Commission, established primarily to advance the cause of native jurisdiction over fisheries.

Before concluding this discussion, it is important to note a recent and important judicial decision on native fishing rights in relation to federal jurisdiction. In December 1986 the British Columbia Court of Appeal made a far-reaching determination on these matters in a case involving a native fisherman who had been charged with illegal fishing.[13] The decision has come to be known as the Sparrow case, named for the particular fisherman who had been convicted in an earlier trial. The court held the view that natives have an unextinguished right to the fish for food and also believed that the term "food fishery" should be given a broad interpretation. This was not so clearly established before this case. However, the court ruled that the natives had no absolute right of self-regulation when it came to the fishery. In effect, the court has ruled that natives have a constitutionally protected right which provides them with priority over other users subject to federal authority to ensure conservation of stocks.

3.4 Third Party Perspectives

There are a very large number of non-native people who participate in the business and avocation of fishing. One reflection of this is the great diversity of organizations that have existed for many years to advance these interests. There are at least ten interest groups exclusively representing commercial fishermen, not to mention the United Fishermen's and Allied Workers' Union, which has both fishermen and shoreworkers as members. There is also the Fisheries Council of British Columbia, which represents large fish processing firms as well as many individual smaller companies. Numerous local sportsmen's associations and province-wide bodies such as the Sports Fishing Institute, Pacific Marine Charter Boats and Fishing Guides, and the B.C. Wildlife Federation speak for the diverse interests of recreational fishermen.

Recently non-natives involved in the commercial and sport fisheries of British Columbia have expressed growing interest in native fishing issues. Groups concerned with the potential impact of comprehensive native claims and co-management initiatives coalesced in 1983 to form an organization which has come to be called the Pacific Fishermen's Defense Alliance. Most of the major fisheries user groups support this group with the significant exception of the United Fishermen's and Allied Workers' Union. The latter has taken a far more conciliatory approach, supporting fair comprehensive claims agreements in principle although still objecting to most specific policy changes.

The concerns most often raised by these various third party fisheries interests are fourfold:

1. loss or deterioration of the *resource base*;
2. administrative and jurisdictional *fragmentation*;
3. *fairness*, related to *displacement* of non-natives from the industry;
4. diminishment of *product quality with resulting loss of market reputation.*

The first of these concerns is based upon the premise that, if natives police themselves through bylaws and other means, over-fishing and waste will take place. Most of the major fishing organizations do support a version of co-management involving detailed joint planning between users and resource managers but with final authority residing with the DFO. Behind this is the idea that natives are really "just another user group" and that user groups cannot be entrusted with setting their own limits. Stories of wastage of fish by natives in the food fishery were often recounted to the researchers for this book. Many people allege that, far from being selective and sensitive, native methods of gaffing and netting salmon lead both to inadvertent losses and to intentional discarding of species not preferred in the native diet.

Perhaps the concern on which non-native user groups are most adamant is the problem of administrative and jurisdictional fragmentation. Their argument is that the resource, especially the highly migratory salmonids, ought to be managed in a unitary, comprehensive manner. If native authority at the tribal council or band level is affirmed, this would mean a very large number of separate management bodies. This is seen as untenable: "Multi-agency management, even with best will and intentions in the world, will not work. Such a system would be chaotic."[14] Critics often use the example of potential fragmentation on the Fraser River, citing the presence of ninety-two bands on seven hundred reserves as *a priori* illustration that native jurisdiction over the fishery is unworkable.

The concern about fairness and equality follows directly from the idea that natives are merely another user group:

We do not argue with native participation in the industry; indeed native Indians are as capable as any other group of developing and utilising the industrial skills required for success in the fishery. It would however, be inequitable to provide preferred access to the resource for one group of Canadian citizens.[15]

48

The idea that no preferential access to the resource ought to be granted has been basic to protests against allocating surplus fish to certain bands (see section 4.1.4 below). This position is now being advanced in lobbying and litigation against the comprehensive claims process. As non-native user groups see it, fish are being used as a currency in land claim negotiations, primarily because the resource is perceived to be the only one with paramount federal jurisdiction. A related issue is the lack of any substantial role for user groups in the comprehensive claims negotiation process.

A final concern, which applies primarily to a native commercial inland fishery, relates to the impact of poor quality fish on the long-term marketability of the Canadian product. There are really two aspects to the concern. The first is that native fish processing under self-regulation would not maintain the high standards of the industry. The second is that the quality of salmon deteriorates as fish move up river towards their spawning grounds. According to this view, products derived from a commerical inland fishery would be sub-standard. The result would be a low economic yield and considerable damage to Canada's international reputation as a producer of high quality salmon products.

It should be pointed out that relations between non-native user groups and natives are by no means completely adversarial. A great deal of cooperation has emerged on matters of habitat protection as, for example, in relation to hydroelectric dams and offshore petro-leum exploration.

4. Current and Emerging Initiatives

Throughout British Columbia today, there are major initiatives on the part of natives and non-natives to enhance the use and management of aquatic resources. Some of these efforts are examined here as indications of how fisheries use and management might look after comprehensive claims settlements have been reached.

When the nature of initiatives involving natives in the fishery is examined, the diversity is striking not only between but within tribal groups. This is not surprising, nor is it reflective of inconsistent goals or values vis-à-vis the fishery resource. Most groups have chosen to pursue a mixed strategy, seeking the short- to mid-term benefits of business ventures while pursuing a stronger role in fisheries policy-making through negotiations, litigation, and band legislation. What follows is a selective survey of these activities organized under headings which parallel the three scenarios discussed in Chapter Two. The inclusion of a particular initiative within one category does not suggest that the native group in question has committed itself to only that model for fisheries development. Almost every native leader interviewed spoke of the need for mixed strategies and suggested that, while one approach might be useful at the present, very different ones could be adopted as circumstances change.

4.1 Partners in Development

Many of the long-standing initiatives involving native peoples in the fishery have been intended primarily to improve native participation in the industry. These initiatives have involved attempts to change some problematic aspects of the current levels of participation and related social problems. As noted above, there is reason for concern over the decline of the native-owned fishing fleet. Moreover, the socio-economic conditions of many bands have been consistently substandard in comparison to provincial standards. Community economic development has been seen as the primary corrective means for these difficulties, and, for a majority of British Columbia native groups, the fishery is deemed the most promising and appropriate base for such development.

The experiences reviewed within these categories all involve, as a centerpiece, efforts to foster the involvement of native peoples in development that is primarily, if not fully, geared to economic purposes. As such, they may foreshadow post-settlement futures in which native people join with industrial interests and governmental authorities to forge "Partnerships in Development".

4.1.1 Special Native Licences

Recognition of the problem of having "too many boats chasing too few fish" had become quite widely accepted during the 1960s. After years of debate, the federal government introduced a limited licencing program to try to reduce overcapitalization in the fleet.

The so-called Davis Plan (named for the then Minister of Fisheries) provided for several categories of licences explicitly for natives. The most important was the "AI" salmon licence, created in 1971. Vessels licenced "AI" could be owned only by status Indians and were subject to an annual fee of only ten dollars, whereas the "A" licences available to other fishermen carried fees of two hundred dollars and up. The Department also created special native-only licencing for the roe-herring and halibut fisheries.

It may be the case that confidential discussions and negotiations between the federal government and some tribal groups have included consideration of extending the native licencing provisions as an indirect method for enhancing the native share of the resource. This is one of the policy instruments which could result in changes in the relative size of the native harvest with comprehensive claims settlements. An implication of such changes would be that non-native fisheries would clearly be reduced not only relatively but in absolute numbers. Fleet reduction, often euphemistically called fleet rationalization, has been repeatedly advocated by informed observers quite aside from the issue of enhancing native participation in the fishery industry.[16]

4.1.2 Native Fishing Corporations

Another approach for enhancing native economic participation in fisheries is the establishment of native-owned companies. This has been tried a number of times along the Pacific coast. At present the best-known and largest of these companies is the Northern Native Fishing Corporation (NNFC). The NNFC was incorporated in 1982 with one common share held by each of the Nisga'a, Gitksan-Wet'suwet'en and North Coast Tribal Councils. It was established primarily in response to a plan by B.C. Packers Limited to sell its large northern gillnet fleet. The purchase of the fleet was financed through an $11.7 million federal grant. The NNFC initially leased the fleet of some two hundred fifty boats and licences to native fishermen, but in 1983 it began to negotiate sales exclusively to members from the three tribal council areas. As the NNFC has sold its original fleet, it has continued to seek other vessels with the intention of playing a continuous role as something of a "boat-bank" for would-be native vessel owners.

In addition to its role in native boat acquisition, the NNFC has established a boat repair facility and a "floating repair shop," a vessel manned by marine mechanics. It has also conducted several kinds of training programs. In 1986 the NNFC financed the construction of ten new "bow picker" vessels (small, fast, and highly maneouverable gillnetters). Unlike some other native organizations, the NNFC has generally supported the advent of aquaculture—provided natives can acquire a fair proportion of the leases.

Relations between the NNFC and B.C. Packers, which purchases much of the NNFC fleet's catch, are reported to be excellent. The NNFC's financial position appears to be stable despite the wide fluctuations in recent years in landings along the north coast. The model of native-owned non-profit or for-profit corporations is one that non-natives seem to accept readily. Cash derived from comprehensive claims agreements could be used by other tribal councils, either singly or in cooperative ventures, to emulate the NNFC.

4.1.3 Salmonid Enhancement and Community Economic Development

The Salmonid Enhancement Project (SEP) deserves a special place in a survey of present native activities in the British Columbia fisheries sector. The program has the overall purpose of reversing historic declines in salmon and steelhead stocks and fostering economic development for the entire region. SEP includes an explicit and special goal of aiding native economic development. At the outset of SEP in early 1977, DFO commissioned a special study to explore the possible impacts on native peoples of the multi-million dollar program and how the positive impacts might be optimized (Cummins et al. 1978). During 1977-78 a Native Project Pilot Program was also initiated with the intent of exploring ways of involving native bands in SEP on a contract business.

In 1980 the approach became known as the Community Economic Development Program (CEDP). Although from its outset CEDP has included non-native projects, it deals primarily with native communities. The main objective of CEDP is enhancement of salmonid productivity, but there are four subsidiary objectives:

- satisfying employment for the under- or unemployed;
- training community and band members so that local people can provide all of the personnel needed for sustained fishery development;
- community development through fostering local leadership and reduction of out-migration;
- improvement of community/DFO relations.

Typical native projects under CEDP now include several technical elements such as constructing hatcheries and spawning channels, clearing streams of debris and barriers, doing biophysical inventories, and establishing monitoring and tagging programs. In line with its employment and community development objectives, the CEDP operates with a philosophy that is seen as a major break from earlier efforts:

As part of the realization of CEDP objectives related to training and community development, Band and community group contractors were made as responsible as possible for work done. They had authority for all aspects of day-to-day management, including hiring a project manager and crew, work supervision, equipment purchase and so forth. DFO on-site involvement was limited to supplying technical advisors who would be present nearly full-time to provide technical support but would not directly plan or oversee job activities. In this way the contractors, not DFO, were directly responsible for the success or failure of a project.[17]

In 1986 there were twenty-eight CEDP projects operating in British Columbia. Through these projects community leaders come to recognize the industry's importance and gain the experience required to take a more active role in decision-making and ultimately policy-making. Many of the native individuals who are now playing a pivotal role in the assertion of native fishing and fish management rights have been associated with the CEDP. In all likelihood, this progression will continue. It will constitute a potentially significant element of fisheries development if comprehensive claims are negotiated.

4.1.4 Special Harvesting Rights

SEP has had an unmistakable impact in increasing (or rather restoring) large salmon runs to a number of important streams. Because of the difficulties of estimating run size while the fish are still at sea, it has been fairly common for more fish to return to SEP hatcheries than were anticipated. These surpluses above the numbers needed for spawning must be harvested if fish are not simply to go to waste. Generally the federal government has sought bids from independent contractors to catch and market these surpluses. In a few cases the DFO has reached agreements directly with native groups allowing them to harvest the surplus fish and retain a substantial portion of the resulting economic benefits. This practice has been a controversial one with ocean fishermen. In light of the fact that many native groups, especially those inland, have indicated an interest in a terminal fishery as part of a claims settlement, it is important to review these early experiences.

Fort Babine Enterprises is a non-profit society operated by the village of Fort Babine at the outflow of Babine Lake.[18] In the early 1950s the important sockeye populations that spawn in Babine Lake were seriously reduced by a rock slide that blocked migrations. Among the measures ultimately taken to restore stocks was the construction of several spawning channels in the Babine system. Since these facilities were constructed, there has been a marked increase in the proportion of "jacks" among the migrating sockeye. "Jacks" are fish which return from the ocean before the usual age of maturity. They are not important as spawners and therefore are surplus to escapement needs.

Fort Babine Enterprises has operated a fishery on "jack" sockeye salmon for approximately ten years. In the words of the Director of Fort Babine Enterprises: "The jack fishery in the past has made us a little money some years while other years we only make wages."[19] Recently, Fort Babine Enterprises has been pressing DFO for permission to extend its harvest to the mature sockeye surpluses which have become common at the entrance to Babine Lake. A huge over-escapement in 1985 became something of a media event and led to questions about the efficacy of DFO's harvest management. Hundreds of thousands of sockeye were unable to the reach the lake for spawning, touching off strident debate over whether DFO had wasted millions of dollars of commercial fish because of the inaccuracy of their stock assessment.

The debate is worth noting because it is one that native groups, especially those living on rivers rather than the coast, have entered in advancing the case for commercial inland fisheries.[20] The accuracy of stock estimation dramatically increases as fish leave the ocean and return to freshwater spawning grounds. DFO in principle must err on the side of over escapement in controlling the harvest at sea but can assign surpluses with accuracy and confidence for in-river fisheries. Natives have repeatedly suggested that, given a chance, they could practice very selective fisheries inland, harvesting species and stocks that are in good shape while permitting the weaker runs to escape to the spawning beds.[21] This argument is at the core of the Gitksan-Wet'suwet'en management proposals considered below. It is also the basis for Fort Babine Enterprises' proposed harvest of mature sockeye.

In an interview for this study, Pat Michelle of Fort Babine Enterprises emphasized that the Fort Babine people want to coordinate their plans with all others who depend on Skeena River and Babine Lake stocks. To this end, he has represented the company at multilateral meetings with the Gitksan-Wet'suwet'en and the Skeena Watershed Sportsfishermen's Coalition (see below).

The Big Qualicum Project is situated on Vancouver Island north of Nanaimo. As at Fort Babine, the project predates the inception of SEP; indeed, the project was first considered in 1957 and has from the outset moved forward at the behest of the Qualicum Band. As Cummins et al. (1978) suggest, the project can hardly be seen as a typical one especially in light of distinctive features of the band:

The Qualicum Band differs from most Indian Bands in several respects...
levels of employment and personal income are much higher than in most
Indian Bands...the degree of interaction and assimilation with non-

Indian society is higher than many other bands. Band members interact regularly with their non-Indian neighbours... A final important consideration is the capability and aggressiveness of the Qualicum Band's leadership. The Band leadership has shown no disinclination to confront the appropriate Federal Government Departments when they feel the rights of Band members are infringed upon, and they widely publicize their complaints (e.g., within the Native Brotherhood).[22]

Physically, the Big Qualicum project includes a hatchery, counting fence, spawning channels and flow control facilities. It was constructed adjacent to the band's reserve land starting in the early 1960s. Events of more recent years have shifted attention towards the disposition of surplus stocks. Excess escapement among fish returning to the hatchery became noticeable by the mid-1970s. The Qualicum Band immediately requested that they be given exclusive rights to harvest this surplus not only for food but for commercial purposes. DFO took the position that surplus production benefits ought to accrue to all the people of Canada as they had financed the enterprise. Thus, harvest of surplus fish would be by the successful bidder in a standard tender. For several years this procedure was in place but, when the band's bid was unsuccessful, they threatened to prohibit and, if necessary, block transport of the fish from the reserve.

By 1983 DFO practice, if not policy, had changed significantly. In the interim the Pearse Commission had recommended natives be allowed not only to eat but to sell the fish provided by over-escapements. The Qualicum Band was able to negotiate a contract with the Minister of Fisheries permitting the harvest of surplus stocks for processing and sale. It has been reported that for an investment of $10,000, approximately $250,000 worth of fish has been taken annually and 20 people have been employed seasonally in processing. The precedent-setting nature of the agreement was recognized by non-native commercial fishermen who protested vehemently to then Fisheries Minister Pierre De Bane. The latter's response gives some indication of the development of federal policy on native surplus fishing which, it must be added, has not changed significantly since the Progressive Conservatives came to power in September 1984:

... my department identifies the Big Qualicum operation as an opportunity to test Dr. Pearse's concept. To that end, the Big Qualicum Indian fisheries project is a pilot study designed and implemented in a manner that would assess the feasibility of permitting sales by Indian bands in the future.... My officials will be evaluating the results of this project and perhaps one more, and will be discussing the results with the industry and Indian organizations. If these projects are found to be successful, *they will form a basis on which to shape future agreements on the commercialization of Indian fisheries and also on the co-management of the resource.*[23] (emphasis added)

In December 1986 yet another native group was permitted to harvest surplus salmon. The *Chehalis Band*, which has reserves on the Fraser River near Agassiz, harvested over eight thousand chum salmon and exported these to the United States. At the time of the harvest, non-natives in the fishing sector once again protested the preferential treatment given to natives. The estimated profit from the operation was approximately $15,000, with an additional grant from the federal government to aid in the establishment of a marketing system. In January 1987 the band issued a press release and displayed the diverse final products made from the chum. Apparently these have readily found markets in the United States and no concern has been raised with their quality. Chief Bill Williams was quoted as suggesting that: "(t)his is the beginning, an introduction to how we think we'll proceed in the future."[24] In the same article, the Director General of the Pacific Region of Fisheries and Oceans stated that a policy for allocating and using surplus fish would be developed within several months.[25]

4.1.5 The Tahltan Fishery Strategy

Recently the Tahltan of northwest British Columbia have initiated a strategy for fisheries development. This is part of a broader program that has been framed as "creating an industry from a way of life".[26] The emphasis of the program and of the fisheries strategy is primarily economic. What is interesting in the Tahltan strategy is that tribal members previously had not been deeply involved in the commercial fishery on the Stikine River. Their approach illustrates how native groups might choose to enter commercial fisheries if new, more extensive access to the resource was part of a comprehensive claims agreement.

The Tahltan people live in the high plateau country of the Stikine watershed in the extreme northwest of the province. The Tahltan Tribal Council represents three thousand members. In 1985 a Tahltan Nation Development Corporation was established. It is this agency which has prepared the comprehensive development strategy, including a fisheries strategy.

At first, the Tahltan fishing strategy was directed primarily towards establishing a commercial fishing enterprise on the Stikine River. To pursue this, the Tahltan followed some of the suggestions made in the federal government's "Policy Proposal for a B.C. Indian Community Salmon Fishery". The project involved the purchase and operation of three vessels. It was necessary to secure new licences from DFO — an action which precipitated angry and public criticism from some non-native fishermen. This seems particularly unfortunate because the economic development strategy adopted by the Tahltans contains one of the more explicit and detailed considerations of relations with third-party interests.

A section of the Tahltan fisheries sector analysis is titled "A Rationale for Working with Independent Fishermen on the Stikine River." It advises that "(i)n re-establishing the Tahltan presence in the Stikine commercial fishery, the Tahltan Tribal Council... work(s) to secure the participation of independent fishermen."[27] The reasons given include the political acceptability of having beneficiaries who are perceived to be broadly representative of the community; a reduction of harvest costs (since independent fishermen are responsible for their own vessels, insurance and so forth); the potential for the transfer of skills and technology from independents; and simply that "(c)ommunity harmony will be strengthened."[28] The disadvantages of non-Tahltan involvement are also listed but the general thrust is that any of these would be "... a small price to pay for the benefits generated."[29]

A companion document elaborates on the Tahltan fisheries strategy and emphasizes the benefits from the participation of non-Tahltans:

It is the intent of the Tahltan Tribal Council to ensure that the development of our renewable resource based economy will not be achieved through disruption and dislocation of non-Tahltan businesses. Indeed we forsee that a strengthening of the local non-Tahltan industrial base will follow as an outgrowth of the economic activity generated by our business ventures.[30]

The argument is made that the development of a broadly-based, native and non-native cooperative fishery on the Stikine would strengthen Canada's position in future negotiations with the United States for allocation of Stikine stocks. While it is far too early to assess the workability and the impact of the project in terms of non-Tahltan resource use, the Tahltan Tribal Council has expressed the hope that its fledgling commercial salmon fishery could become a pilot project for the development of new cooperative economic approaches.

4.2 Allies and Adversaries

The term "co-management" is used with some hesitation here, for, as was pointed out earlier, it has been used to refer to very distinctive initiatives. Nevertheless, it is a convenient phrase for interactions which truly involve shared or joint responsibilities in the governance of the fishery. The first two initiatives described in this section are the Musgamagw Tribal Council Demonostration Project and the Haida co-management proposal. These initiatives are quite different from each other in most respects, but they are both centred primarily on an effort to forge a cooperative approach between tribal groups, the federal government and third parties based on shared decision making. The next part of this section includes a description of several inter-tribal coordinating organizations in the province. The section concludes with an examination of the implementation of the fisheries provisions of the *James Bay Agreement* and the experiences in the American Pacific Northwest in the wake of the Boldt decisions.

In each of the instances reviewed the accent is on the generation of coordinating and regulatory mechanisms as part of strategies emphasizing mediation between different and somewhat contending interests. This emphasis on the use of administrative forms and shared authorities arises in circumstances where interests need to be continually adjusted because they cannot be ultimately reconciled. As a result, co-management is used as an approach for integrating native interests with those of other governments, industry and other third parties. The intended outcome is one in which potential adversaries will become allies in resource management and development. As such, current and proposed co-management regimes hold the promise of providing a glimpse into the manner in which the scenario "Allies and Adversaries" may unfold, if comprehensive claims settlements were concluded in British Columbia.

4.2.1 The Musgamagw Demonstration Project: The Fishery Component

The Integrated Resource Management and Development Demonstration Project of the Musgamagw Tribal Council (MTC) in some ways resembles those considered previously under the rubric of "Partners in Development." Indeed, the project draws upon some of the programs already described. It is included in this section for two reasons. The first reason is that it has entailed a largely unprecedented degree of inter-governmental cooperation in design and preliminary field work. The second reason for thinking of the project as a precursor of "Allies and Adversaries" type arrangements derives from its emphasis upon building a more effective, harmonious relationship with government agencies as well as the private sector. Policy development — and the capacity to participate in the policy process — is one of the principal elements articulated for the project. The project is based on:

Explicit recognition that the MTC and its member bands will undertake, through the course of the demonstration project, an important policy development process... An example in the marine area is the work required to evolve a joint management policy and strategy for fishery resources in the region.[31]

The approach and the problems the project has faced in its formative stages underscore some of the factors which will continue to be on the agenda of any post-settlement regime in the region.

The Musgamagw Tribal Council comprises five bands of Kwakiutl-speaking peoples situated on northern Vancouver Island, the adjacent mainland and smaller nearby islands. The demonstration project has been under development since mid-1984 although its official inception was in January 1986. The goal has been an integrated project in which forestry and marine resource planning proceed in a closely coordinated manner. This should be kept in mind as the marine resource components are focused on as another indicator of native aspirations vis-à-vis the future of fisheries. The forestry component of the project will be discussed in Chapter Four.

The approach of the MTC demonstration project is based on an explicit awareness of current constraints that have plagued a multitude of individual marine resource initiatives. These include the financial uncertainty of short-term budget allocations. Projects such as the SEP-funded project of the Nimpkish Band, one of the Musgamagw members, have faced uncertainties concerning levels of funding that do not permit the longer-term perspective needed for any significant fisheries development project. This has led to a second perceived constraint: the widespread attitude among the work force that any given project is just another make-work endeavour to which little or no personal commitment should be made. Insufficient training programs and a severe lack of knowledge about the features of the biophysical environment are also seen as important constraints, ones which the demonstration project is intended to remedy.

The approach in the marine sector has been to concentrate initially on an improved information base, assessing both the overall potential of nearshore areas and specific opportunities. This is seen as essential not just for planning particular community fisheries development projects but as the basis for MTC's informed participation in policy dialogue. The initial results have played this kind of support role in the expression of MTC's concerns about aquaculture to the province. During 1986 the first phase of a cooperative marine data collection and mapping program was completed. Plans have been made for more detailed surveys targeted on clam beaches, herring spawn areas, abalone beds and identification of aquaculture sites. One of the main thrusts of the MTC project is in the area of training. The MTC biologist has used the resource inventory as a setting for technical teaching. The rationale is to create the capacity for MTC to become a co-manager of fisheries resources by developing skilled technical staff.

Special mention should be made of the issues surrounding aquaculture development as these interact and, to an extent, conflict with the MTC project. The coastal zone of north Vancouver Island has been one of the most attractive in the past several years for entrepreneurs interested in aquaculture. The "gold rush" of non-tribal members staking the Section 10 aquaculture leases granted by the provincial government has been of particular concern to the MTC. The tribal council feels a special urgency in identifying locations of high potential before they are alienated. Provincial officials interviewed for this study suggested that MTC and other native groups are at no disadvantage in applying for aquaculture leases and would be best advised to join in the applications rush. Conceivably, the MTC resource inventory could be re-directed towards providing the research and logistical support needed for individuals and bands to gain provincial final approval of aquaculture projects.

The aquaculture issue is complex for the MTC. First, there is some concern about the implications of the MTC following provincial regulations (i.e., recognizing jurisdiction over the foreshore and inland waters) for future land claims negotiation or litigation. In addition, there are several perceived resource conflicts with more long-standing marine activities. Alert Bay, the largest community in the MTC area, has been an historic center for natives in the commercial fleet. Commercial fishermen have generally opposed rapid aquaculture development for reasons such as the potential transfer of diseases from cultured to wild stocks. Another area of potential conflict is in the competition for sites between aquaculture and the traditional intertidal harvesting of shellfish. MTC project personnel have expressed concern that the orderly planning envisioned for the demonstration project may be jeopardized by what they see as the unplanned allocation of sites by the province.

Nevertheless, the tribal council intends to apply for a number of sites on the basis of the reconnaissance in progress under the demonstration project as well as protesting Section 10 leases.

What can be concluded about future post-claims directions from the demonstration project? Its emphasis on integrating the planning of marine and forest resources is likely to remain under any future regime. This means in essence the development of mechanisms for conflict resolution as the needs of marine and forest resources clash. A second major feature of the project has been on-the-job training aimed at creating long-term capabilities within the Musgamagw peoples for resource management and development.

Member bands and the council itself have demonstrated the intention to work closely with government agencies and the private sector. Local DFO staff have played a significant and cooperative role in the marine resource inventory and have become aware of the high quality of information the MTC staff and trainees are able to acquire. One of the most positive effects of increased native involvement in marine resource management may well be a better assessment of the quality and opportunities of British Columbia's enormous coastal zone. The MTC demonstration project is not only an experiment in local capacity-building but has provided an impetus for efforts on the part of federal agencies to coordinate better their multifarious programs and authorities.

The progress of the MTC demonstration project has slowed, in large part due to funding uncertainties. The work nonetheless represents an important attempt that bears retelling. If problems continue or worsen, the MTC project will still furnish lessons about the attempt to establish cooperative fisheries management without formal recognition of aboriginal rights.

4.2.2 The Haida Co-management Proposal

The Haida of the Queen Charlotte Islands first developed a strategy for fisheries development in 1984-85 and submitted these ideas to DFO as a "... proposal for a fisheries co-management agreement."[32] Although the strategy was seen by the Haida as a short-term one that needed to be closely linked to the need for comprehensive claims agreements, it reveals a clear set of principles which could very well guide fisheries management in a post-settlement regime.

The approach is an evolutionary one. It forsees a Haida Fisheries Commission that would take on a gradually increasing set of responsibilities. The commission would initially become involved in management for unutilized or underutilized marine species. This has two important advantages. First, it provides a low-risk training ground for building Haida scientific, technical and managerial skills. More importantly, it places emphasis upon creating "new wealth" through fuller use of species that are of little or no commercial value currently, rather than seeking a reallocation from other groups.

DFO was unwilling to move immediately on the Haida proposal, responding instead that it needed to develop its own policy regarding co-management. This response appeared in the form of the draft policy of 1986. The philosophy and key elements of this policy have been described in section 3.1 of this chapter. A look at the Haida reaction provides some further indication of what is seen as a minimally acceptable future for co-management.

The 1986 federal policy was deemed "completely inadequate" by the Haida for several reasons. First, the policy envisioned a process of reaching agreement through consultation with all user groups. The Haida raised an objection to the implication that native people were "just another user group."[33] Their second objection was to continued bargaining for shares of the fishery within the Minister's Advisory Council: "Consultation with native groups through unrepresentative, undefined, unfair or inadequate mechanisms does not constitute co-management".[34]

Dismayed at what they perceived to be the conservatism of the federal co-management proposal, the Haida developed a "new thrust." Its key elements are:

- seeking specific percentage allocations of each stock;
- undertaking independent research on stock levels and dynamics;
- development of 5-year plans by the Council of the Haida Nation for species wholly under current native harvest;
- creation of a Queen Charlotte Islands Fisheries Management Board for co-managed stocks with 50 percent Haida representation.

The "new thrust" is more assertive yet still retains the concept of joint decision-making. The Haida, like most other coastal native peoples in British Columbia, appear to recognize the mixed stock problem that makes joint management essential. The evolutionary approach, at least prior to the "new thrust", is based on an appreciation of the political difficulties that would be faced if non-native user groups were summarily excluded from important current fisheries. The Haida leaders say that they do not intend to reduce or eliminate non-Haida commercial fishing in the vicinity of the Queen Charlotte Islands. This is consonant with the Haida philosophy of evolutionary change for native percentage allocations to be increased through a phasing-in period and through overall stock enhancement.

4.2.3 Inter-tribal Fisheries Coordination

The interface that is usually in focus in discussions of co-management is that between native groups and a non-native government. In light of the complexity of the fisheries resource — the multiplicity of stocks and species, the long migration routes through several jurisdictions — inter-tribal coordination also becomes a requisite of native/non-native co-management. The concern so often expressed by various user groups about the balkanization of management and jurisdiction is a serious one. At present there are several inter-tribal organizations whose purpose is policy coordination. Two in particular are concerned explicitly with fisheries.

The *B. C. Aboriginal Peoples Fisheries Commission* (BCAPFC) was established in 1984 "... to be the major consultative body between Indian people involved in the British Columbia fisheries and the federal government."[35] It was a direct outgrowth of a province-wide Native Fisheries Conference in 1983 at which a working group had been established for negotiations with DFO. At a subsequent meeting with the then Minister of Fisheries and Oceans, Pierre De Bane, the group was advised of the federal government's commitment to seek input from native people in the design of a new fisheries management system. The BCAPFC was set up to become the prime coordinative force in a much revised approach to consultation, but the Commission's role had yet to be affirmed in any tangible changes in the consultative process. The 1986 policy paper on consultation released by DFO refers to the Commission but is discouraging about its potential to fulfill the role for which it was established:

The BCAFPC is not representative of all Native fisheries, and, therefore, it would likely have difficulty in effectively dealing with allocations between Native groups and with coastwide allocations between all user groups.[36]

BCAFPC is currently open to representation from any band or tribal group in the province. A unique feature of the commission is its attempt to represent both coastal and interior tribes while building the organization. Since early 1985 it has operated under a dual chairmanship with interior and coastal co-chairmen. In addition to frequent meetings with the Minister, BCAFPC's activities have included presentations at a variety of hearings such as the parliamentary Standing Committee on Fisheries and Forestry and the British Columbia government's aquaculture inquiry; coordination and liaison with consultants on a project to identify native aquaculture opportunities; and preparation of inter-tribal reactions to federal decisions and policies.

A separate inter-tribal coordination mechanism for fisheries has been established among certain tribes of the interior. The *Interior Indian Fishing Commission* (IIFC) was set up in early 1984, drawing membership from the entire Fraser River watershed as well as from groups living in the Columbia drainage system. Indeed, the capacity of this organization to mediate inter-tribal and inter-governmental fisheries issues will be a major test of the oft-repeated contention that the numbers of bands and reserves on the Fraser River present an insurmountable obstacle for policy coordination. The IIFC has emphasized the problem of interior peoples being last in line as salmon move from the ocean towards spawning grounds. The IIFC has, on this basis, referred to the professed priority DFO places on the native food fishery as "logically imperfect . . . as the salmon are fished well before they reach our respective tribal areas."[37]

Following this line of argument, the IIFC pushes for a very active role in pre-season planning and in-season management. In this view, tribes must be confident restrictions they face are for conservation purposes and not an allocation to downriver or ocean fishermen. Events of the late summer of 1986, when Sto:Lo fishermen physically clashed with DFO officers underscore the difficulty and importance of the issues the IIFC has taken on. DFO ordered restrictions on food fisheries in the lower Fraser River on the basis of stock assessments and in consideration of food needs farther up river. Sto:Lo members proceeded with a fishery in spite of the regulations. Nets were seized and eighteen Sto:Lo were charged with fisheries violations as well as criminal assault.

Two other native organizations involved in fisheries issues must be mentioned. The *Native Brotherhood of British Columbia* is without question the most powerful and well-organized provincial native group concerned with the fishery. Although it has spoken often on broad policy issues, including land and sea claims, the Native Brotherhood is generally perceived as an organization run primarily for and by native commercial fishermen. It plays an important role in annual negotiations with fish processors on wages and prices and in the design and inception of assistance programs for native fishermen. The Native Brotherhood is an inevitable participant in any hearings on matters affecting fisheries policy despite keeping a relatively low profile for the past several years on sea claims advocacy.

Finally, the *Alliance of Tribal Councils* is an organization formed to provide a united front to oppose the Canadian National Railways' plans to add a second rail line along the Thompson and Fraser River valleys. The Alliance draws its membership from the Lytton, Nlaka'pamux and Sto:Lo peoples. The Alliance was instrumental in the successful request for an injunction halting further development of the railway expansion. As will be seen next in the case of Washington State, such inter-group coalitions for resource management and habitat protection seem to be a quite probable development when native fishing rights become more clearly defined.

4.2.4 Co-management in the U.S. Pacific Northwest

In February 1974 Judge George Boldt of the U.S. 9th District Court made an historic ruling affirming the rights of several tribes to use and manage fish. British Columbians with a stake in native fisheries issues are keenly aware of the landmark Boldt decision (*U.S.* v. *Washington* 384 F. Supp. 312 (D. 1974)). The Boldt decision came about within an ecological and sociocultural system very similar to that in British Columbia, one that is quite familiar to all of the key parties in the Canadian Pacific fishery. Washington State native fisheries managers are frequently invited north to explain and update the situation for British Columbia native groups. In May 1987 the B.C. Aboriginal Peoples Fisheries Commission co-sponsored a conference with two American inter-tribal fisheries organizations formed in response to the Boldt and related decisions to share experiences on the evolution of cooperative fisheries management. The Kwakiutl District Council and, separately, the Nimpkish Band have looked to the Washington approach when preparing analyses of fishing rights and management.

Non-native fishing interests tend to see the allocation and resulting co-management system that grew out of the Boldt decision as a nightmare. They also invite residents of Washington to Canada to lecture on what is to be avoided. Government officials are keenly aware of the Boldt and post-Boldt developments. In fact, INAC commissioned a study of the approach (Harper 1982) and DFO had the same consultant prepare an economic analysis of its consequences (Harper 1984).

There are, of course, substantial differences between the history and context of fisheries conflicts in the American Pacific Northwest and British Columbia. In the former, native fishing rights have been litigated on the basis of treaty obligations, virtually non-existent throughout much of British Columbia. In addition, the implementation of the Boldt decision took place within the very different and jurisdictionally more complex setting of American fisheries management. For these and other reasons, the British Columbia Court of Appeal in the recent Sparrow case (see Section 3.3 above) ruled that American case law could not be used as a basis in adjudication of Canadian fishing conflicts. Judicially admissible or not, the Boldt decision exercises a powerful influence on the fears and expectations of all British Columbian groups in the fishery.

In treaties signed in the 1850s certain tribes of the Pacific Northwest of the United States ceded most of their traditional lands. In exchange they were to retain their traditional fishing rights, but, over the next century, state resource managers and the treaty tribes vigourously disputed the ambit of these rights. When, the issue reached the courts, Judge Boldt ruled that the treaty should be interpreted as guaranteeing the native tribes a 50 percent share of fish stocks. The decision met with a hostile reaction from state resource managers and non-native fishing interests. Judge Boldt in response to the recalcitrance of state officials to enforce regulations took the unusual step of placing fisheries under his court's jurisdiction.

What have been the consequences of the Boldt Decision? The impact can be assessed by examining the changed distribution of benefits, the new management relationships and the condition of the fish stocks. Harper (1984) has examined the changes in the native share of revenues from the five salmon species over the period 1968 through 1982. In all cases there have been dramatic increases. For example, in 1972, just prior to the Boldt decision, the native share of sockeye was less than one percent of the dollar value for that fishery; by the early 1980s the figure was over 40 percent. For chinook salmon, the pre-Boldt range was 13 to 14 percent of landed value; the estimates for 1982 were in the vicinity of 50 percent. Obviously the non-native catch percentage decreased during the same period. Harper suggests that the effect of the Boldt decision upon non-native fishermen is unclear because of other influential factors, including a rapid increase in total numbers of licences just before Boldt and a sharp increase in the sports fishery, especially in the numbers of ocean-going charter boats. Some observers also note that the great expansion in Alaska fisheries during the 1970s drew many Washington-based fishermen northward. In all this, cause and effect become hard to separate. Those who moved to Alaska may have made their decision driven by the knowledge that non-native shares would be reduced over the last half of the 1970s.

Harper (1984) also presents and analyses data concerning the distribution of benefits within and between the tribes themselves. There are certainly grounds for concern when one compares the Lummi who live near the mouth of Puget Sound with tribes such as the Puyallup at the southern reaches. The potential for the latter losing out as stocks from their territory migrate through the "gauntlet" of the northern Sound is unmistakable. A rough verification of this expectation can be calculated from Harper's data. In terms of the total number of salmon caught, the Lummi landed 5.7 times the Puyallup catch in 1975; by 1982 the ratio was 17:1. Equity issues can also emerge within tribes:

... hierarchies develop within the Tribes because individuals are licensed to fish and are taxed by the tribe at a very low rate. ... The gap is widening between the elite and the rest of the tribe.[38]

It is no exaggeration to say that the Boldt decision has caused an almost revolutionary change in the governance structures and processes for the fishery. It could not have been otherwise, for, as soon as the natives had a fixed allocation, disputes began to arise about different interpretations of stock, escapement and harvest data. In the sour atmosphere which prevailed at first between state agencies and the new native resource managers, conflict over conservation issues was chronic. During fishing seasons, the two sides were in court on literally a weekly basis.

For natives, the new managerial responsibility demanded the creation of much better scientific and managerial capabilities. Within several years of the Boldt decision all of the Puget Sound and Columbia River tribes had hired their own staff biologists. To augment these capabilities and to provide other economies of scale, inter-tribal coordination was established. In 1974, the Washington tribes who had been party to the Boldt case set up the Northwest Indian Fisheries Commission. The Northwest Indian Fisheries Commission now has a staff of approximately thirty professional and support personnel. It is the principal mechanism through which fishing plans are negotiated with the Washington State resource agencies and it also serves as a policy coordinator among the tribes.

The relationship between the native and government managers has been conflict ridden until quite recently. As noted, litigation abounded as did the use of the technical advisory committees that conducted fact-finding for the courts. One effect of this contentiousness was that both sets of managers felt obligated to duplicate rather than complement each other's analysis. This and other redundancies led to a definite rise in management costs (Harper 1984, Russell Barsh pers. comm.).

By 1984 both parties were concerned with the costs and wasted time of managing fish by litigation. An independent mediative body, the Northwest Renewable Resources Center, coordinated a joint management project to develop new collaborative procedures. In the first year of the project, the state tribal management agencies were able to reach a mutually acceptable pre-season plan. The number of court cases involving natives and state managers during the fishing season dropped from over seventy in 1983 to zero. The adversaries, to some extent, had become allies.

A fundamental consideration of any change in fisheries management is what impact this has on the health of the stocks. Unfortunately, this is also the most difficult to determine. In addition to the impact of the Boldt decision other changes have taken place that also could have had important effects on the resource base: fleet expansion in the mid-1970s; habitat restoration projects; large fluctuations in natural factors affecting fish mortality; and the zealous harvesting of Puget Sound and Columbia River stocks by Alaskan and Canadian fishermen prior to the Canada-United States salmon treaty of 1986.

Despite all this, it is clear that early fears the new regime would lead to gross mismanagement, overly permissive harvesting and rapidly-declining stocks have not been sustained. Harper (1984) reports marginal improvement in most stocks. Some, although far from all, non-native fishermen believe that improvements in steelhead stocks are directly attributable to changes in the management regime. One of the leading national sportsfishermen's organizations, Trout Unlimited, has reversed its long-standing opposition to the post-Boldt regime:

It has been a rocky road for Trout Unlimited in Washington State. There were times in past years when fighting the Boldt decision was the glue that bonded us. However, during that period, management of the salmon and steelhead resource suffered; too much time was spent managing the battle.... After the Boldt decision things changed. State agencies were required to more closely monitor all aspects of fishery management. The requirement for increased data and a better management of individual stocks has benefited everyone especially the fish.... In the 1984-85 winter steelhead season sportsfishermen caught 115,000 fish while the tribes caught 103,000. The total is the highest on record and wild life escapement was good to excellent.[39]

A final point should be mentioned in regard to the positive impact of the new regime on fish stocks. In the original Boldt litigation, the tribes sought a ruling that they had a right to protect fish habitat. If they were entitled only to a percentage of stocks drastically reduced by habitat destruction, it would be an empty victory. Judge Boldt deferred litigation, asserting that treaty fish rights ought to mean the tribes could force a halt to environmentally destructive actions. Later "Boldt II," as it was called, affirmed these additional rights and, although that decision has been somewhat diluted by a further ruling, its impact has been considerable. According to Gaffney (1986) several major projects have been arrested by the "threat of invoking Boldt II."[40] Several of the larger timber, mining and hydroelectric developers have begun to negotiate with tribes on project proposals. In the long run, the added leverage that the affirmation of native fighing rights provides in controlling habitat destruction may be the most important of all consequences.

4.2.5 The James Bay Agreement

The Canadian federal government has concluded three comprehensive claim agreements, all with arctic and sub-arctic peoples whose dependence on fishing and hunting is, if anything, greater than most aboriginal groups in British Columbia. The kinds of arrangements included in these agreements for resource use and allocation are indicative of what has been at least minimally acceptable to federal negotiators and their counterparts in terms of native participation in resource management. This section will focus on the fisheries co-management provisions and performance under the James Bay agreement. Elements of the more recent Inuvialuit agreement were highlighted in the discussion of the federal government perspective in Section 2 of this chapter.

The *James Bay and Northern Quebec Agreement* was signed on November 11, 1975. It had been negotiated in the shadow of a mega-project proposal, the James Bay Hydroelectric Development Project. The underlying motivation for native peoples was clearly to do as much as possible to preserve traditional lifestyles in the face of such a development. The Cree and Inuit of Northern Quebec had previously maintained relatively undisturbed hunter-gatherer lifestyles and, not surprisingly, their negotiators pushed hard for provisions to protect subsistence resources. The agreement contained a wide range of instruments to achieve this:

- reservation of lands for exclusive native harvest;
- designation of certain species of fish for exclusive native use;
- guaranteed levels of native harvest, as well as the principle of priority for native harvesting;

- an income security program to supplement the cash income of hunters;
- an advisory group representing both natives and various federal and provincial agencies — the Coordinating Committee on Hunting, Fishing and Trapping.

Feit (1984) emphasizes the importance of another element of the agreement: that natives are to be given preferential treatment in resource-related economic development opportunties, notably first refusal at guiding and outfitting possibilities.

In a comprehensive analysis of these and other mechanisms Berkes (1986) finds reason for cautious optimism. Some important problems have been encountered nevertheless. Perhaps the most serious is the failure of the Coordinating Committee on Hunting, Fishing and Trapping to come to an agreement on appropriate guaranteed harvest levels. During the first seven years of the agreement's implementation, a joint study was conducted to provide a baseline for defining precisely how much of the resource the Cree and Inuit needed for subsistence. By May 1986 the "guaranteed levels" had still not been officially fixed. Yet, as Berkes reports, the Coordinating Committee has had to deal creatively with other issues of resource allocation:

An example of the kind of effective action by the Committee was the allocation of fishing areas to non-native workers. . . . When a request was received from hydro workers for additional winter fishing opportunities, the Committee invited a Chisasibi band councillor familiar with the area. The Councillor, . . . chose a number of lakes, taking care to avoid conflict with Cree subsistence fisheries . . .[41]

The Coordinating Committee has been criticized by both Berkes (1986) and Power (1979). Taken together, their comments imply that the body is not highly valued by either natives or government agencies. Power (1979) speaks of the limited commitment governments have made to improving the scanty data base upon which so many crucial decisions depend. Berkes (1986), having noted the disinterest and mistrust among the Cree towards science, concludes:

The Coordinating Committee, as the main co-management institution, has the disadvantage of being a white man's institution run by white man's rules. This effectively prevents the traditional fishermen-hunters from participating, and limits representation to articulate, southern educated persons who are comfortable in committee settings.[42]

What distinguishes the context of the James Bay agreement (and the same can be said of the Inuvialuit agreement) from that prevailing in British Columbia is the relatively much less significant role of non-native fishermen in northern Quebec. In the traditional territories of the Cree there have been only periodic incursions of competing non-native user groups (Feit 1984). In a sense the James Bay Hydroelectric Development Project had the unintended benefit for natives of bringing the issue of aboriginal harvest rights to a head before any substantial non-native competition became established. In British Columbia exclusion of non-natives from fisheries planning is unthinkable. In fact, non-native user groups are now pursuing litigation with the intent of attaining at least a consultative role in the actual claims agreements.

4.3 Homeland and Hinterland

The initiatives described in this section have sometimes been labeled "co-management" by their proponents. However, an important distinction exists between them and those just outlined. Each of the experiences described here are not just about cooperation but entail demands for autonomy for native governments. They represent a shift to decentralized decision-making within a claimed territory, a "homeland." This does not mean doing away with a broader managerial perspective and/or all federal fisheries authority. It does mean that for resources wholly within (or produced within) a recognized aboriginal territory natives seek relatively autonomous powers.

The Nisga'a, Kwakiutl and the Gitksan-Wet'suwet'en have each indicated they want certain economic benefits from agreements concerning comprehensive claims. They have also recognized that there will be mutual accommodations of varying political interests in post-agreement resource regimes. Beyond this, however, they assert significant authority in managing fisheries within traditional territories. While acknowledging that their lands and resources are currently a hinterland for those seeking profits from resource development, these native groups have pressed for greater autonomy in order to preserve them as "homelands."

4.3.1 The Nisga'a Approach

A foretaste of the kind of fisheries regimes which could exist once comprehensive claims agreements have been reached may well be the system under negotiation between the Nisga'a and federal claims negotiators. The Nisga'a are the only claimant group in British Columbia involved in active negotiation of land claims.

71

The Nisga'a Tribal Council represents approximately 5,000 members whose traditional homeland is in the Nass River Valley touching the coast close to the border between Alaska and British Columbia. The tribal council has been negotiating its comprehensive claim since 1976. It appears that the most progress has occurred in discussions of allocation and management regimes for salmon and other anadromous and marine fish species. Even in this area final agreement has not been reached but reports indicate some concensus on important elements of the draft agreement.

Of greatest immediate concern to the Nisga'a and others is the issue of fish stock allocations. The draft agreement, reached in 1987, provides for a substantial guaranteed percentage for the total food and commercial Nisga'a fishery. A federal negotiator has been quoted as indicating that this would be approximately 25 to 30 percent of all Nass River stocks.[43] In a break with past DFO constraints, fish caught in the community or food fishery could be sold or bartered. A scheme to retire non-native fishing boats and licences, with compensation, and transfer these to Nisga'a fishermen is also reported to be part of the draft agreement. A "buy-back" to reduce the capacity of the fishing fleet has often been proposed and discussed often before as a general measure rather than as part of any comprehensive claims negotiations. These are indications that the draft agreement between Canada and the Nisga'a also provides for a new $5 million enhancement program for the Nass River stocks.

The management system for the Nass River fisheries is likely to entail both a Joint Management Board involving equal numbers of representatives from all three governments—federal, provincial and Nisga'a—and a separate Nisga'a Management Board. The former would be responsible for devising annual fishing plans and monitoring and enforcing them. The Joint Management Board would also be in charge of habitat protection and control of interception of Nass River stocks. The province is included because of its jurisdiction over freshwater fish species. The Joint Management Board would administer aquacultural development by non-Nisga'a proponents.

The parallel Nisga'a Management Board would take charge of fisheries management within the watersheds of the agreement area. This would include the matter of allocation among Nisga'a fishermen and the conduct and control of Nisga'a marine farming and enhancement projects. It is envisioned that the Nisga'a Management Board would develop a research capacity to provide it with independent estimates of key parameters of fisheries management such as estimates of stock size, escapement requirements and harvest rates.

The philosophy underlying the proposed management regime, at least from the Nisga'a perspective, differs from the idea of maintaining paramount federal management authority with stronger native participation (which has sometimes been called co-management).[44] This difference has been clearly enunciated by one of the major Nisga'a fisheries consultants:

The Nisga'a are not seeking a system of "co-operative" management, where everyone gets together and argues about what should be done. The Nisga'a are seeking their own well-defined fishery and well-defined responsibilities and jurisdiction. The "co" in the Nisga'a co-management proposals refers to the need to coordinate independently developed and implemented fishing plans and policies.[45]

This perspective is not shared by other concerned groups. The federal government has always insisted that the Minister of Fisheries and Oceans must retain final authority in any co-management system. In terms of the language used here the Nisga'a and the federal government appear to be far apart on whether the post-settlement fisheries regime will be of the "Homeland and Hinterland" or "Allies and Adversaries" variety.

4.3.2 The Kwakiutl Fisheries Management Proposal

The Kwakiutl of northern Vancouver Island and the adjacent mainland inlets, like all coastal tribes, identify the fishery as a major element for any comprehensive claims agreement. In fact, they have been most explicit in framing their rights as a sea claim. Materials have been prepared by the Kwakiutl which lay out in a clear manner what they consider to be the basis of their right to manage the fishery, the problems with the existing management regime and the model they would prefer to see adopted.

The Kwakiutl District Council (KDC) represents eleven bands of Kwakiutl-speaking peoples. The Musgamagw Tribal Council, whose demonstration project was discussed above, is also represented by the KDC in comprehensive claims matters. There are more Kwakiutl within the commercial fishery than from any other tribal group. Their fishery, unlike that of many other native groups, depends extensively on fish which do not originate in their claims area. It has been estimated that Kwakiutl fishermen catch 3.5 times as many sockeye as are produced in the area under KDC claim.[46] This, according to the KDC, is by no means a recent phenomenon; use of transient stocks has been part of the life of the Kwakiutl since before contact. As a result, the sea claim includes some negotiable proportion of stocks destined for other areas.

The KDC sea claim addresses three issues which are important for our purposes: stock allocation between Kwakiutl and non-Kwakiutl; distribution of benefits within the Kwakiutl nation; and the structure of the management system, including the responsibilities of the Kwakiutl and others. With regard to the stock allocation between Kwakiutl and others, the KDC has indicated both a willingness to discuss options and a resolve to attain some clearly defined sharing formula. The initial negotiating position is that the Kwakiutl have primary rights to 100 percent of the fish originating in the claim area and some substantial portion of transient stocks, but Kwakiutl representatives interviewed for this study indicated that they are well aware that stocks from their claimed territory are subject to other fisheries, including ones pursued by other native groups. The 100 percent figure is seen primarily as a starting point for negotiations.

The KDC has reviewed some of the options for internal allocation for whatever share Kwakiutl people derive in claims negotiations. There is a significant commercial sector among the Kwakiutl in addition to a substantial food fishery. Native peoples in general argue that the distinction is not tenable, yet potential conflict exists in dividing the proportion of fish used locally with that which is processed and sold.

The assertion of aboriginal rights to manage the fishery are based on legends and long-standing conceptualizations of the Kwakiutl's responsibilities in relation to nature. Of special significance is the idea of *Oweetna-Kula*, meaning "at one with the land and sea we own". This principle and Kwakiutl legends portray humans as close kin of all animals used for food. Thus fish and animals are more than just resources. These ideas are the basis that the Kwakiutl advance in discussions of co-management, much as the governments of Canada and British Columbia evoke, for example, the *Constitution Act* and parliamentary tradition. Unless the Kwakiutl totally abandon these arguments, settlements may ultimately reflect a fusion of two very culturally distinctive sources of authority.

The KDC has made detailed proposals for a management regime for stocks originating and passing through their sea claim area.[47] These proposals broadly resemble those advanced by the Nisga'a in their comprehensive claims negotiations. The KDC envisions a two-tiered structure. They propose the establishment of a co-management board consisting of representatives not only from the Kwakiutl but also from any native claimant group whose resident fish stocks move through the Kwakiutl claim area. An equal number of DFO appointees would be on the board. The second tier would be the Kwakiutl Territorial Fisheries Commission (KTFC) comprising representatives of the eleven KDC member bands as well as the bands within the Musgamagw Tribal Council.

The KTFC is already established. The commission's constitution deals explicitly with the welfare of non-native fishermen. Included in its statement of organizational purpose and function is:

...to ensure through our jurisdiction over the salmon and other marine resources, that the principle of co-existence and sharing provides benefits to non-aboriginal users of the resource now and in the future.[48]

The commission derives its authority exclusively from the member bands and *nunayms* (families) within the bands. This structure and the reliance on traditional sources of authority creates a potential for internal controversy about fisheries issues and, from the perspective of some outsiders, delay and fragmentation. Although by no means unique in this, the Kwakiutl must find ways of living with the potentially contradictory goals of participating in an increasingly technological commercial fishery and yet meeting the social and spiritual needs of traditional food fisheries.

Although it is difficult to project from the KDC's submissions and proposals a clear image of the future beyond claims agreements, there does exist a keen appreciation for distributional consequences that can arise among Kwakiutl, between Kwakiutl and other native groups and between natives and non-natives. This is reflected in the Kwakiutl's preliminary thinking about resource allocation and in the mechanisms of resource governance they are considering.

4.3.3 The Gitksan-Wet'suwet'en Approach

Because of events during the summer of 1986 the components of the Gitksan-Wet'suwet'en approach to the use and management of fisheries stocks are probably more familiar in British Columbia than those of any other native claimant group. Four of the bands with membership in the Gitksan-Wet'suwet'en Tribal Council (GWTC) passed fisheries by-laws early in 1986. Unlike those previously proposed, the by-laws were not disallowed by the Minister of INAC. Earlier the GWTC had carried out a major study of fisheries in the region (Morrell 1985). They had already pursued several different avenues in advancing their claim of aboriginal fishing rights (see Morrell 1986). The study, the by-laws and recent discussions with Skeena sportsfishermen reveal an unusually clear model of how fisheries might be developed and managed under a regime emerging from the affirmation of native fishing rights.

The GWTC represents eight bands along the upper Skeena watershed and tributary systems in north central British Columbia. Until 1977 native challenges to DFO's authority arose most often in the form of individual violations of fishery regulations — fishing out of season, without a licence or with illegal gear. With time, the GWTC as well as other native organizations (notably the Union of British Columbia Indian Chiefs) began to provide financial and legal aid to native peoples charged under the *Fisheries Act*. As a result it soon became obvious to all parties that some negotiated agreement on the issue of native fishing rights was appropriate:

Negotiations began in 1979 and have taken place in one form or another in each year since then. From the outset it was clear that the two sides had different priorities.... The DFO negotiators' primary concern was to obtain Indian agreements to annual fishing plans and regulations in order to reduce the tension and eliminate the confrontational situation between fishers and fishery officers on the river. The Tribal Council's top priority was to secure DFO recognition of the management authority of the House Chiefs under Indian law.[49]

The last sentence underlies the fundamental position maintained by the Gitksan-Wet'suwet'en over the past decade: ultimate authority for fisheries management, including the allocation of resources, in the traditional tribal territory is the responsibility of the hereditary chiefs. This position remains unacceptable to DFO and to most of the non-native user groups of the region.

As noted, the GWTC prepared a detailed analysis of the fishery which included a plan for future use and management. The overall goal of the Gitksan-Wet'suwet'en plan is "that the salmon and steelhead resources of the area should be managed so as to yield maximum continuing long-term benefits to the Gitksan and Wet'suwet'en people."[50] To achieve this the plan lays out four broad objectives: conservation, harvest management, habitat management and enhancement. While the basic ideas for conservation are ones most fisheries biologists have advocated, the Gitksan-Wet'suwet'en are unusually definitive in advancing principles and practices for stock-by-stock management. In the plan and in discussions with Gitksan-Wet'suwet'en their representatives repeatedly emphasized two concepts during the course of the research for this study: first, that all wild stocks have both resource and spiritual value and thus, none can be seen as expendable; and, second, that in-river harvesting using highly discriminatory native techniques would make stock-by-stock management feasible. This last approach may be contrasted with the limitations of ocean fishing, where stocks are mixed and more difficult to fish selectively.

The Gitksan-Wet'suwet'en plan does not advance a particular percentage share of the fish produced in the territory although the overall goal of "maximum continuing long-term benefits to the Gitksan and Wet'suwet'en people" mentioned above would indicate the intent of favouring tribal members. Despite this objective of reallocation, representatives of the Gitksan-Wet'suwet'en have repeated that they do not wish to displace other users. They point out that their ancestors traditionally shared salmon with those visitors who did not challenge the authority of the chiefs.[51] A fair, undiminished living for all users is seen by them as feasible if fish populations and habitat are enhanced.

Gitksan-Wet'suwet'en fishermen have good reasons to develop cooperative allocations. First, a substantial number of tribal members are commercial fishermen in fisheries well outside the claimed area. Second, many of the fish taken even in the food fishery are not produced in the Gitksan-Wet'suwet'en territory. The most productive sockeye runs in the Skeena system are from Babine Lake which is situated primarily within the Carrier-Sekani claim area. The recognition of the needs and rights of others dependent on the resource is expressed in the proposed approach: "The actual mix of marine, river mouth and in-river harvesting for Skeena stocks is a matter for negotiation among the various management agencies and harvesting groups involved."[52]

The Gitksan-Wet'suwet'en plan calls for the establishment of a management agency with paramount authority for stocks from Gitksan and Wet'suwet'en territory. It would speak for the tribal council and hereditary chiefs in negotiations with other agencies and user groups. Unlike the Kwakiutl and Nisga'a proposals, this plan does not explicitly call for the establishment of an intergovernmental co-management body. One reason is that the Gitksan-Wet'suwet'en hold very strongly to the assertion that their hereditary chiefs are the ultimate authorities for matters within the territory. Neil Sterritt, President of the Gitksan-Wet'suwet'en Tribal Council, has provided a clear statement of their version of co-management:

In general: co-operative management based on shared authority. For the Gitksan-Wet'suwet'en ... (f)inal Authority for Management within the Gitksan and Wet'suwet'en territories lies with the Hereditary Chiefs. Gitksan and Wet'suwet'en management will be coordinated with other management plans affecting fish passing through Gitksan and Wet'suwet'en jurisdiction by negotiations with the other organizations exercising jurisdiction over other areas used by the same fish.[53]

While these earlier studies and plans may be useful for providing a longer-term vision of the tribal council's attitudes to fisheries management, it is also necessary to examine some of the actual developments in Gitksan-Wet'suwet'en policy. The band by-laws passed early in 1986 merit particular attention. As mentioned above, several bands of the Gitksan-Wet'suwet'en developed by-laws in accordance with the *Indian Act*. From 1983 to 1986 the Minister of INAC had repeatedly disallowed the by-laws, on the grounds of uncertainties in defining the boundaries of reserves along rivers. Undoubtedly the anticipated negative reaction of commercial fisheries groups and opposition from the federal Minister of Fisheries and Oceans also played an important role in the disallowances. Unlike all previous by-laws, those passed by the four bands in February 1986 were allowed to stand. When news of this came to light in April 1986, it unleashed intense conflict among fisheries users and managers.

Several features of the by-laws add to an understanding of what community-based fisheries management would involve. The band by-laws are seen primarily as an interim measure, based upon rights asserted in the GWTC comprehensive claim, made necessary because of the lack of progress on the claim. The by-laws give blanket permission for tribal members to fish when, where and how they wish, subject only to restrictions of the by-laws themselves. For non-members, fishing is prohibited unless in accordance with by-law provisions.

One of the most controversial elements is addressed in section 6: "Gitksan-Wet'suwet'en people are permitted to use, buy, sell, trade, or barter fish caught within waters of the Band in accordance with their traditional laws and customs." This measure is in direct contravention of federal fisheries regulations which restrict the "food fishery" to subsistence and ceremonial use. Another unusual and controversial provision is for licencing and regulation of non-native sportsfishermen. Clauses are also included to assert the primacy of the by-law vis-à-vis any other statute or regulation.

In May 1986 the Ministers of INAC and Fisheries and Oceans attempted unsuccessfully to foster province-wide negotiations on issues raised by the by-laws and by the discussion paper on Indian community fisheries. The Attorney-General of British Columbia was able to obtain a temporary injunction against enforcement of

the by-laws. In late June the Minister of INAC announced suspension of the bylaws until the end of December 1986. Yet, through th
summer of 1986, the Gitksan-Wet'suwet'en acted as if the bylaw
were in effect, operating fishing camps on the Skeena system as well
as small community fish processing facilities.

In autumn of 1986 representatives of the Gitksan-Wet'suwet'en
met on several occasions with the Skeena Watershed Sportsfishermens' Coalition, a group that initially vehemently opposed the
assertion of native managerial authority. These parties were able to
agree on some important matters — mutual dissatisfaction with the
existing consultative mechanism for the Skeena and the desirability
for new and more active planning involving all user groups and
managers. In November they agreed in principle on a pilot project
for fisheries co-management for the Skeena watershed calling on the
relevant Ministers to establish a task force representing natives,
sportsfishermen and the commercial sector. No government support
for this approach has been forthcoming.

5. ... To the Future

What sense can be made of these varied plans and experiences in
terms of common themes and the futures they portend? As outlined
in Chapter Two, there are three major categories of uncertainty in
relation to comprehensive claims settlements which beset those who
use and govern natural resources at this time. Economic, political
and environmental concerns abound. There are several issues to
which these cases speak in important ways.

5.1 Economic Dimensions

From both the statements of native organizations and governments
and the reports on federal government/Nisga'a negotiations it is
evident that a specific native allocation of the fishery may well be a
condition for comprehensive claims settlements to be reached in
British Columbia. There are several reasons to anticipate a much
increased native share in the fishery, if claims agreements are
obtained. During a period when most fishermen have faced financial
hardship and the prospect of having to leave the industry, the federal
government has supported programs and measures intended to keep
native peoples in it. The recently-initiated Native Fisheries Association, the grants for acquisition of the B.C. Packers gillnet fleet by the
Northern Native Fishing Corporation and the special licencing

measures described earlier all have been aimed at this. Such efforts would probably increase if settlements are concluded.

The food fishery share is also likely to be augmented in claims settlements if the Nisga'a negotiations and the 1986 "Policy Paper on a British Columbia Indian Community Salmon Fishery" are taken as indicators. The question then becomes what the impact of these increased benefits might be on non-native participation and what the likely distributional consequences would be among and within native groups.

The case most often referred to in discussions of this impact is that of the American Pacific Northwest fishery after the Boldt decision. Attention was drawn in the discussion above to other complicating factors which may have influenced a steep decline in the non-native catch, so the polemics which have been prepared about the post-Boldt years in the Washington State fishery may oversimplify and overstate. Nevertheless it would be naive or worse to say that it is impossible to trace a portion of this decline in non-native catch back to the reallocation to natives. It is common sense that in a non-expanding fishery the benefit one group gains must be lost by another.

Displacement from the fishery is a possibility which British Columbian vessel owners, crew and shoreworkers have just cause to fear. Except in the case of currently under-exploited stocks, there simply are not surpluses that could suffice to augment native catches. New allocations will be reallocations in the foreseeable future. It is in the longer term that the settlement of comprehensive claims could provide the basis and the impetus for expanding the supply of fish. This possibility is discussed later in this section.

It is difficult to translate increased percentage reallocations to natives as a result of claims settlements into the numbers of non-native jobs or boats which could be lost. The fleet is acknowledged to be in a state of excessive capacity. A much smaller number of vessels (and presumably workers) could readily catch the existing non-native precentage, let alone a reduced share. Commissions of inquiry, academics and the affected groups themselves have acknowledged repeatedly fleet overcapacity and the need to "rationalize," that is, to reduce capital investments. Pearse (1982) was firm on this, and subsequently, successive Ministers of Fisheries have aired the possibility of "buy-back" programs. Under the current federal deficit, the economic and political feasibility of supporting the "buy-back" has been in doubt; the same problems afflict potential comprehensive claims settlements.

It is possible that reallocations to native peoples and improvements in the structure of the industry could be rolled together: fleet rationalization could be advanced as being not only for the betterment of the fishing industry but as a logical co-requisite of claims agreements. If this were to occur, one implication of comprehensive claims settlements would be the adoption of rationalization in the industry in accord with policies rooted in "good economic fisheries management" rather than just comprehensive claims per se.

5.2 Political Dimensions

One of the principal concerns of everyone in today's fishery is the form and the procedures for the management regime which might take shape after comprehensive claims settlements. As noted above, the federal government and many non-native users are concerned that management would be overly fragmented. The fear is that, instead of one minister with ultimate authority, dozens of management entities would have responsibilities within limited home territories. Native peoples see this issue in a totally different way: not balkanization but the reconstitution of traditional regimes.

In terms of the scenarios used in this study, the first, "Partners in Development", by definition entails no change in the sorts of institutions and powers used in current fisheries management. The province in particular sees the augmentation of community economic opportunities, as in aquaculture for example, as the best route for developing the economic potential of native peoples.

Many — although not all — native groups press for changes which would move the system toward the "Homeland and Hinterland" scenario, at least for some fraction of the lands and resources in eventual settlement areas. The authority asserted particularly by groups such as the Gitksan-Wet'suwet'en and the Kwakiutl is one that, at least on the surface, seems to require this degree of independence. Sources of authority for these peoples reside in hereditary chiefs or ultimately in such principles as the Kwakiutl's *Oweetna-Kula*, native oneness with the land and sea. If these views are based on more than emotional outbursts or first negotiating positions, if they represent the way that some native groups and leaders actually look at the issues of jurisdiction — and the research recounted in this chapter indicates they do — comprehensive claims settlements might create fisheries management in some areas of British Columbia totally unlike the present regime.

81

A new type of fisheries management might be the outcome of comprehensive claims settlements. Negotiations are more likely to produce the "50/50 solution" which in this case could mean a form of co-management. If the federal and provincial governments were to make major concessions on this matter — in return possibly for major concessions by native governments on other matters — a resolution might be devised whereby in practice both sides could officially exercise the full authority they claim without necessarily requiring the other's formal recognition. For example, a co-management board could be devised and seen as a delegated body by the federal government and as a form of inter-tribal council by native governments. It might matter little in the day-to-day operations how each side defined the agency's nature.

Given the current relationships between concerned groups such an outcome might not be too likely. In any case, the best judgement must be that some system of joint management might be put in place if comprehensive claims settlements are reached. If so, something less comprehensive than one single pan-aboriginal voice for native governments would be possible, but the system would not likely be based on tribe-by-tribe representation of interests. Non-natives might find it very difficult to work in the context of such a regime. It seems more likely that several inter-tribal organizations would evolve, perhaps on a basis of major watersheds such as the Fraser and the Skeena and for other reasonably well-defined geographic areas such as the mid-coast and the Strait of Georgia. These might resemble the Northwest Indian Fisheries Commission of Washington State.

Could joint management organized along lines such as these work or is the Pacific Fishermen's Defence Alliance correct in its conclusion that multiple-agency management is a losing proposition in any case? There is no question that the task of making inter-governmental agencies function is an enormous one. There are several reasons to believe that they could function. A most pertinent example of the possibilities for concurrent management is, of course, the Pacific Salmon Treaty ratified in 1985 between Canada and the United States. More broadly, there are an increasing number of problems that clearly escape the jurisdictional boundaries of single agencies. In such cases a premium is placed on the collective ability of all parties to design a working, problem-solving relationship at the inter-organizational level. This may well be the case if comprehensive claims settlements are reached in British Columbia.

A reasonable possibility is that people in the British Columbia fishery would have no choice but to use mediation mechanisms such

as those viewed in the "Allies and Adversaries" scenario in tl
aftermath of comprehensive claims settlements unless those settl
ments very clearly extinguish or confirm an aboriginal right to
exercise governing authority over the fishery resource. As these
mediation mechanisms arise, experimental forms of cooperative
management may be tried and the price of learning may inevitably
be substantial conflict and higher management costs, at least in the
short-term.

5.3 Environmental Dimensions

In the final analysis everyone in the British Columbia fishery shares
a strong interest in the health and sustainability of the living
resources of coastal and inland waters. The implications of comprehensive claims settlements for the condition of the fisheries resource
base can best be discussed in terms of factors which have negative
versus positive effects on the health and enhancement of stocks.

In the category of negative effects on fish stocks the points raised
by groups such as the Pacific Fishermen's Defense Alliance should
be considered. Their basic fear is that native governments would be
unable or unwilling to enforce harvest management comprehensively.
They suggest that intra-tribal politics and inter-tribal competition
would re-create a new "tragedy of the commons" involving native
peoples. At the intra-tribal level, they also contend that fisheries
managers would be under heavy pressure from the many new native
entrants to allow over-fishing. They fear that spawning escapement
needs would not be met and stocks would decline. This internal
pressure could be exacerbated by inter-tribal competition. They
argue that each tribal group might expect others to overfish and
would, therefore, have no incentive to curtail their harvest.

Unquestionably important concerns underlie contentions such as
these. Much of the data recounted in this chapter indicates these
fears may not be confirmed by the direction of current and emerging
initiatives. The apparent success of inter-tribal fisheries coordination has been referred to above. One case in British Columbia
provides a strong counter-example to this concern. Pinkerton (1984)
describes how the Nimpkish Band through lobbying and control of
its own fishermen was able to persuade DFO to make a substantial
area closure. This was in response to the band's convictions that key
local salmon stocks were in deep trouble. This incident indicates
that, at least under some conditions, native communities will recognize the importance of conserving endangered stocks and muster the

organizational and inter-organizational resources to redress the situation.

Other positive factors that could foreshadow an expansion of fish stocks if comprehensive claims settlements were reached include the current efforts of native peoples to prevent further habitat loss and the wide range of measures that have constituted the existing Salmonid Enhancement Program. All of the native organizations and governments interviewed for this study subscribe to a set of priorities for future fisheries management that shares much with the philosophy and approach many conservation-minded fisheries biologists have long advocated. These priorities rest on principles which include stock-by-stock management, "fishing to the weakest stock" where mixed stock fishing is unavoidable, and enhancement of wild stocks rather than merely increasing fish numbers by artificial enhancement.

The stock-by-stock and watershed-by-watershed approach advocated by some native organizations and governments (and supported independently by many interest groups and associations) could benefit salmon productivity overall if settlements were obtained. Habitat protection rules may also be augmented. Scuh an outcome is foreshadowed most clearly by the aftermath of the Boldt decision. In that instance the courts recognized that the 50 percent relative share of fish affirmed for natives was meaningless unless it carried with it a right to protect the absolute numbers of fish.

Whether natives adopt or are forced by circumstances to accept an approach of strictly being "Partners in Development" in the fishing sector or come to share or even have certain exclusive powers in management, a stronger basis for environmental protection would be expected if comprehensive claims settlements are concluded. If the fisheries management priorities stated by groups such as the Gitksan-Wet'suwet'en, Haida or Kwakiutl or the fervent testimony questioning offshore oil exploration on the part of all coastal native groups is taken seriously, then the advent of an expanded decision-making role for native peoples in post-settlement regimes would imply a very different and more stringent era of fish habitat protection.

The results of the Salmonid Enhancement Program confirm these possibilities. It is not surprising that all native groups as well as non-native fishing interests have unequivocally supported salmonid enhancement. In addition to the direct fish production benefits, the present SEP has had important and positive effects on employment, training and on less measurable but still significant community parameters. Again, if we turn to what has been said and done by native governments in their fisheries plans and in the plethora of enhancement projects within the SEP, indications are that settlements would set the stage for more of the same.

There are additional reasons for expecting more fisheries enhancement efforts might be possible after comprehensive claims settlements. If, as may well be the case, non-natives were threatened by displacement, an enlargement of the fisheries pie would offer the one sure way to lessen the blow. The political—not to mention social and economic—benefits of merging claims settlements with fisheries enhancement projects may be very attractive. Settlement of comprehensive claims could become the impetus as well as the basis for redoubled efforts to protect today's fish stocks and vastly expand tomorrow's. A new stronger and clearer basis of native rights in the fishery, however it arose or was defined, could "push and pull" the system into a new era of management where the health and enhancement of the resource was a much higher priority.

4

The Forests: The Leading Resource Sector

1. The Forests in British Columbia

After more than a century of extensive logging British Columbia remains the province which comes to mind when a person thinks of Canada's rich forest endowment. Truly the resource base seems impressive. More than half of British Columbia is forested and 93 percent of this land is capable of growing commercial timber (Ainscough 1979). The forests of British Columbia have long been recognized as the basis for much of the economic life of the province.

Although the impact of forestry is impressive on its own, the contribution this sector makes to particular communities in the province is even more dramatic. Many towns along the coast and in the interior are almost completely dependent upon logging and/or sawmilling for their survival. When the sector is troubled — as it was in the early 1980s — unemployment in regional forest centres like Port Alberni and Prince George and in the many smaller one-industry communities can soar far above national and provincial averages.

The forests are not only used for timber harvesting. British Columbia has an extensive provincial parks system which, together with many other forested areas, attracts an increasing number of tourists and sportsmen. Wildlife and fisheries are directly dependent upon forested habitat. Because the timber harvest raises potential problems for some uses of the forest, and inescapable ones for others, such as enjoyment of the wilderness, conflicts are inevitable.

2. Native Peoples and the Forests

Before contact, the splendid architecture and artifacts of the native peoples who inhabited what was to become British Columbia were, in one sense, made possible by the livelihood provided by aquatic resources. It was the forest, however, which provided the raw materials for the cultural expression of this plenitude. Traditionally native peoples created a wide array of utilitarian and ceremonial wood objects. Their totem poles, canoes, masks, long houses, bowls and boxes are all known worldwide. Drucker (1963) describes the broad utility even of bark, a material which could be harvested without actually felling trees:

One could very nearly describe the life of the individual Indian in terms of cedar bark; as an infant he was swaddled in the bark. . . . woven robes and rain capes of shredded bark protected him from rain and cold throughout his life; checkerwork mats of red cedar bark were his principal household furnishings. . . . he made sails of heavily woven bark mats. . . . On ceremonial and festive occasions he wore turbans and arm and leg bands twisted and woven of shredded bark. . . . And when he died, the chances were that unless he was a chief and entitled to special treatment, his body would be wrapped in a cedar bark mat for burial.[1]

Because of the many traditional uses for trees, it is not surprising that they figured importantly in the spiritual life of native peoples. A common belief was that trees possessed vitality and thoughts as well as special powers. The construction of massive long houses, large dugout whaling canoes and the great totem poles all required the felling of trees. When a tree was felled or burned, its life force perished for it could not leave its body and become a ghost as people do. Because a tree would not live again, it was cruel to deprive it unnecessarily of its one short life. Prayers of forgiveness were said when a tree had to be felled.

As in the fishery sector, native peoples worked both as labourers and independent contractors in the early development of British Columbia's forest industry. In the 1880s and 1890s logging and sawmill operations spread over much of the coast. By the end of the century even remote areas such as the Homathko Valley and the Queen Charlotte Islands were being staked for timber. As this occurred natives provided an important part of the wage labour force. They also ran many of the small, family-owned businesses. Codere (1950) provides numerous examples of Kwakiutl involvement in mills and logging camps along the north coast of Vancouver Island and the adjacent mainland. She notes that three bands were obtaining the largest source of their cash income from logging by 1907. In some cases successful operations were initiated and run by natives using their own reserve lands; for example, the Cape Mudge Band obtained loans for horses and equipment and repaid this through log sales within one year (Knight 1978).

During the 1920s the industry changed in ways detrimental to small operators, including natives. Despite considerable awareness and avowed concern among the public and the government at the time, an inexorable process of corporate concentration was at work. Changes in technology, marketing and Crown land leasing all favoured larger firms. The ideal of sustained yield forestry gained broad acceptance and with it the perceived need to entrust larger tracts of public land to firms big enough to assume substantial and long-term responsibilities.

The Depression of the 1930s hastened the demise of small native firms. The Depression lasted for the resource sector until the Second World War when suddenly:

Indian men and women flooded back to their traditional work in the resource industries and also into a host of novel jobs.... Indian employment during the Second World War should have reminded observers just how rapidly and broadly Indian people could adapt... when given the chance and incentive to do so.[2]

The boom that the forest and other resource sectors experienced in the 1950s did not provide significant increases in opportunities for native peoples. In fact employment did not increase substantially for any workers in the forestry sector: capital was substituted for labour during this period.

It is difficult if not impossible to estimate the present levels of native employment in the forest sector. Looking at just one area, the Nass Valley, Marchak (1983) points out wide discrepancies between industry and Nisga'a estimates of the native contribution to the work force. Undoubtedly some native peoples, especially those living in the less-populated rural areas of British Columbia, have continued to benefit substantially from wages earned in the forest industry. Shebbeare (1985) describes several companies with high native worker participation rates. At Westar Sawmills in Hazelton, for example, between 60 and 65 percent of the work force is native.

3. Roles and Concerns

3.1 The Federal Government Perspective

Although the authority of the province, as discussed below, is paramount in forest resource management, the federal government has explicit and implicit responsibilities which make it an important party in the forestry elements of the comprehensive claims question. The federal government owns a very substantial proportion of the Canadian land mass, although most of this falls within the Yukon and Northwest Territories. In British Columbia some 450,000 hectares of forest land is federally owned; this is less than 1 percent of the total forests of the province.

The role of the federal government in managing Indian reserve forest lands is predominant although recent changes have transfered some authority to *Indian Act* bands. The Crown in right of Canada holds title to reserves for the use and benefit of bands. The federal government's "trust" responsibility is carried out under the Indian Timber Regulations made pursuant to the *Indian Act*. The regulations establish very clearly the dominant authority of Indian and Northern Affairs Canada (INAC) in the disposition of timber. Indians even require permits to cut reserve timber for their own use. INAC can also issue permits to non-natives, although consultation with a band is required if logs valued over $2,500 are to be harvested on its reserve.

Many native peoples' organizations have questioned INAC's management of reserve forests. A detailed assessment of reserve forest conditions conducted for the Nuu-chah-nulth of western Vancouver Island, for example, suggested that tribal members had been neglected in employment opportunities in the logging of their reserve lands. INAC has responded to such views. In addition to a gradual shift of forest management to bands, the federal government has also established new sources of funding and logistic support for Indian forestry on reserves. An Indian Forest Lands Program has been established and many bands in British Columbia have applied to conduct inventory and forest management planning projects. INAC has shown a willingness to devolve its authority over the forests but, until bands officially achieve self-government in resources through legislation as in the Sechelt agreement or as part of a comprehensive claims settlement, INAC is legally bound to maintain the responsibilities assigned to it by the *Indian Act* and because reserve land is federal Crown land.

Beyond INAC's mandate, the federal government has other responsibilities that involve it with forest resources. In the last decade federal funding of forest renewal has increased. In 1985 the Canada-British Columbia Forest Development Agreement was signed providing $300 million for forest improvement.[3] The Indian Forest Lands Program, mentioned above, is a component of this development agreement. In addition, native peoples are encouraged to benefit from improvements on non-reserve lands if they can organize small businesses to provide services for silviculture and reforestation. As will be seen below, there is considerable interest among native peoples in doing just this.

3.2 The Provincial Government Perspective

By virtue of the *Constitution Act, 1982* the province of British Columbia has paramount responsibility for land-based resources.

Section 4 of the British Columbia *Ministry of Forests Act* outlines the major goals of provincial forest management. These include: maximizing forest productivity; ensuring the highest possible social and economic benefits from forestry; coordinating multiple forest and forest-dependent uses; encouraging the processing sector; and collecting fair rents from industry for use of the forests.

Given the province's broad and comprehensive powers and responsibilities over forestry matters, it can be readily appreciated how equally broad its concerns would be if major tracts of forest land were transferred from provincial jurisdiction under comprehensive claims settlements. Corresponding to the broad forest management goals mentioned above, there are concerns surrounding the implications of possible comprehensive claims settlements. The provincial government is concerned that:

- under native control forest resources would be less efficiently and completely utilised;
- the net economic and social benefits to British Columbia would be diminished;
- multiple-use management and the coordination of forest activities with other government responsibilities would become complicated and ineffective;
- native-controlled forest enterprises would not be able to cope with the increasingly difficult world timber market;
- both a loss of provincial revenues and inequitable levels of rent collection might result.

Concerns are also raised that the services provided by the province to protect woodlands would be more difficult to administer. Pest and fire problems, for example, do not respect boundaries. This leads some to ask what would be the result for non-native lands if native governments adopted different policies and practices in areas placed under native jurisdiction.

Despite the vast size of the Crown forest land base, there are essentially no significant tracts which remain uncommited to some form of tenure. Of extreme importance to the provincial government are its potential liabilities with regard to the present lessees of any Crown lands that might be transferred as part of comprehensive claims agreements. Under its different tenure forms British Columbia has entered into a large number of contractual arrangements with third party interests. These contractual arrangements vary greatly as to whether and in what circumstances the province may cancel its obligations. Fundamental to the province's long-standing refusal to recognize aboriginal title is its concern about the moral and financial obligations for which it might have to provide compensation.

Recently the province has become more specific in what it sees as the alternative to comprehensive claims negotiations and settlements. While not recognizing aboriginal title, the province has provided some indications it acknowledges that natives have been victims of discrimination and impoverishment and that they need specially targeted programs of assistance. In the realm of forestry, this stance translates into encouraging native groups to apply for tenure through Tree Farm Licences, Forest Licences, Woodlot Licences and other permit and licencing instruments.[4]

A Tree Farm Licence gives the lessee up to 25 years of exclusive harvesting rights, is renewable every ten years and is intended to cover large parcels of Crown as well as privately-held land. A Forest Licence is a 25-year agreement for cutting on the Crown's public sustained yield units, tied to the lessee's obligation to have or build a timber processing facility. A Woodlot Licence is a shorter-term lease for exclusive cutting on four hundred hectares or less. In actual fact, there is but a slim chance that the most sizeable forms of tenure (Tree Farm and Forest Licences) will become available to most native groups because of prior commitments to non-native forest companies. The most probable form of tenure that the province could offer to most native groups is the Woodlot Licence.

3.3 Native Perspectives

It would be understandable if many readers were to perceive native attitudes towards timber harvesting and processing as one of hostility and opposition. In recent years the most salient images conveyed by the media are of native groups blockading logging roads and seeking injunctions against forest operations in such areas as Meares Island, the Stein Valley, South Moresby and Deer Island. These activities have been premised partially on the goal of preserving special places from any timber harvesting. Native opposition to logging has also been based on their assertion of aboriginal title and rights, their desire to be recognized as both an economic and a political factor in forestry, and their fear that forest lands are being developed at such a rapid rate that the resource will be exhausted before settlements are reached.

No blanket opposition to forest operations on the part of native peoples was encountered in the course of the research for this study. Instead, it was found that many native governments are generating plans for community development in which timber harvesting and processing are factors. This dimension of the native perspective on forestry will become clear when current and emerging initiatives are reviewed later in this chapter. Before doing so, it is necessary to discuss the most conspicuous of recent confrontations involving logging interests and native peoples. In these disputes there has been growing emphasis on the issue of aboriginal rights, but it is also important to note that criticism of logging operations by native peoples is increasingly coupled with arguments as to how these operations would be improved if natives had a stronger role in decision-making regarding them.

From the outset of the forest industry in British Columbia, native leaders have expressed opposition to the exploitation of the forests in the absence of treaties. The Port Simpson Tsimshian petitioned the provincial government in the 1880s for timber rights for the lands near their reserves. Groups such as the Nisga'a and Nuu-chah-nulth have linked the questions of aboriginal title and forestry management for years. Recently, conflicts have surfaced in which native people have taken a firm stand and, in some cases, direct action. The four most prominent conflicts centre around South Moresby, Meares Island, the Stein Valley and Deer Island.

Perhaps the most long-standing struggle in British Columbia between loggers and native people has been in the *South Moresby* area of the Queen Charlotte Islands, particularly over logging plans on Lyell Island. Controversy lasted through the 1970s and focused on the renewal of Rayonier Canada Limited's Tree Farm Licence #24. The Haida and the Islands Protection Society joined in political lobbying and later in several unsuccessful petitions to the British Columbia Supreme Court to prevent renewal of Rayonier's licence. During this time international attention focused on South Moresby. Proposals were launched for ecological reserves and one area, Anthony Island, was nominated as a World Heritage Site. Parks Canada undertook inventories and preliminary studies for the creation of a substantial national park. Meanwhile, as Pinkerton (1983) documents, the arousal of public interest in South Moresby as an environmental issue contributed to a renewal of Haida assertions of aboriginal title to all of the Queen Charlotte Islands. Since the early 1980s the conflict has been recast increasingly in terms of a comprehensive claim as well as an environmental dispute.

In 1985 matters came to a head as Rayonier's successor, Western Forest Products, directed its logging contractor, Frank Beban Enterprises, to proceed with logging on Lyell Island which included one of the proposed ecological reserves. The Haida blocked access roads to the intended cut area. Confrontations occurred, arrests were made and some logging went ahead. In October 1985 the province established a Wilderness Advisory Committee to examine a wide range of controversies in the province over parks, wilderness and extractive uses. The Committee's final recommendations were for some continued logging on Lyell but also for the establishment of ecological reserves in the area and a larger park, preferably a national one. In 1987 negotiations were concluded between the Governments of Canada and British Columbia to create an extensive new national park. While the Haida celebrated the resulting end to logging on Lyell Island, they were quick to state that the comprehensive claim remains the outstanding issue. A national park is seen by the Haida as another intrusive if not so disruptive a use of lands which they claim are theirs.

Meares Island near Tofino on the west coast of Vancouver Island is under claim by the Nuu-chah-nulth. The controversy over logging this island bears similarities to the South Moresby case. MacMillan Bloedel sought approval for plans for timber harvesting in an area for which it had long held cutting rights. Controversy ensued and the province established a study team to develop recommendations. A special planning team representing industry and environmental concerns was created to review the situation but MacMillan Bloedel withdrew after a year as it was unwilling to accept the inclusion of certain recommendations in the final report. In the company's view the planning team had exceeded its mandate by calling for measures such as cutting in smaller blocks and harvesting over a longer time period. It also objected to the committee's initiating a study of the negative economic effects of logging on tourism in the area. The company won provincial approval for its plans and began to establish a logging camp on the island. At this point, the Nuu-chah-nulth supported by a wide array of environmental organizations pursued strategies of both litigation and social protest.

In November 1984 protesters, both native and non-native, occupied strategic landing areas on Meares Island making it difficult for the staging of logging equipment and crews. By January 1985 the British Columbia Supreme Court had upheld MacMillan Bloedel's rights and ordered protesters to cease interference with forestry operations. In his ruling Justice Gibbs argued that to grant an injunction on behalf of the Nuu-chah-nulth would lead to a proliferation of similar applications throughout the province. The judge also ruled that the province had authority to extinguish native land claims through the Terms of Confederation. Separate appeals were launched by environmental groups and by the Clayoquot and

Ahousat Bands. In March 1985 the British Columbia Court of Appeal granted an injunction on behalf of the Nuu-chah-nulth pending trial on the issue of aboriginal title. Since then, with logging stopped, the Nuu-chah-nulth and the province have been involved in a major court case.

Discussions of the relative merit of logging versus the aesthetic and recreational values of the *Stein River Valley* west of Lytton have gone on for over a decade. Environmental organizations have been advocating complete preservation of the Stein Valley since 1974 when the government, during the regime of the New Democratic Party, imposed a two-year moratorium. Their argument is that the Stein Valley is the last remaining pristine watershed in the southern mainland of British Columbia and ought to be designated as British Columbia's first "wild river" (Jones 1983). The subsequent Social Credit government re-examined the moratorium primarily in terms of the economic value of harvestable timber and decided to lift it.

The forest firm with timber rights within the Stein Valley is B.C. Forest Products which also operates a mill at nearby Boston Bar. The company was asked by the provincial government to commence operations in the Stein Valley, necessitating construction of a logging road through hitherto virgin forest lands. In September 1985 a coalition of environmentalists and some native groups was formed which, according to spokespeople, was willing to adopt the same strategy as had been used on Meares Island—physically blocking attempts to move crews and equipment into the area.

Shortly thereafter, then Minister of Forests, Tom Waterland, affirmed the province's intent to have the logging road constructed and timber harvested. In making the statement the Minister first raised and then rejected the problem of native land claims, stating that he was not concerned because the "B.C. Government has never recognized aboriginal land title claims."[5] Immediately, the Lytton Band broke what had been a long-standing silence on the Stein controversy and announced official opposition to the road and logging. Previously the Lillooet Tribal Council had voiced their opposition. Now, with both of the major aboriginal claimant groups in the controversy, the issue of aboriginal title was added to the long-standing preservation-versus-development clash.

As noted in the discussion of the South Moresby case, a Wilderness Advisory Committee (WAC) was appointed in 1985 to make recommendations about 23 natural areas in the province. The Stein Valley was one of the natural areas. The WAC chairman asked for a three month moratorium on development in the Stein River watershed but the Minister of Forests rejected the request. In the interim, a tender for proposals went out to road contractors and one was selected. In response to this, landowners near the Stein River went to court and won an injunction.

Testifying before the WAC, the Lillooet Tribal Council raised the land claims issue, asking that the Stein Valley be declared wilderness, "(a)s a statement of faith to the aboriginal peoples that we are not going to strip the landscape bare before we will settle the question of aboriginal title, returning finally the empty husk..."[6] The WAC considered the issue of aboriginal title to be outside its mandate but its recommendations on the Stein Valley case reflected an implicit recognition of the importance of this question. It recommended that no logging road be constructed without "a formal agreement between the Lytton Indian Band and the provincial government." The Cabinet accepted the WAC's recommendations in principle but in October 1987 reaffirmed the decision to proceed with logging the Stein Valley.

Controversy involving native peoples and logging has also taken place on northern Vancouver Island. In this case the land in question was privately rather than provincially owned. A private contractor, Archie Haleta of Halcan Log Services Ltd., purchased *Deer Island* near Port Hardy in December 1986 from MacMillan Bloedel. The island falls within the claimed territory of the Kwakiutl who believe it has special cultural and spiritual significance. It is also subject to a specific claim by the Kwakiutl band of Fort Rupert, one of the few native groups in British Columbia who completed a treaty prior to the province joining Canada. In this case, no environmental groups played a prominent role in support of the natives.

When Haleta commenced operations in November 1986 forty Kwakiutl occupied the island and prevented further logging. A ceremony was held affirming aboriginal title. Haleta sought an injunction against the occupation in the British Columbia Supreme Court but this was denied. The court concluded that any further harvesting of trees on Deer Island would be pre-emptive of the Kwakiutl land claims and that the injunction should be against logging rather than the occupation of the island.

The case did have some positive features with regard to potential native/non-native cooperation. Prior to the commencement of operations, the Kwakiutl and the contractor had come close to reaching an agreement in which rights to log reserve lands on nearby Malcolm Island would be traded for Deer Island. Negotiations between the Kwakiutl and Haleta were held again in early December pending the trial. Once more these were unsuccessful. At the conclusion of the court case, the Kwakiutl announced that they would be looking for ways to raise funds to compensate and assist Haleta. This was not required of them.

These and other disputes concerning British Columbia's forests have riveted public attention — and they are enormously important. What is perhaps most interesting for the purposes of this study is the gradual re-framing of such controversies and the possibilities thereby created. Seen as an opposition of nature versus logging, the issue seems close to intractable. Cast in terms of aboriginal title, the central question changes: How can forestry be reconciled with native priorities and needs? As will be seen later in the chapter, native groups have already begun to formulate answers to this question and these answers are ones which do not exclude logging and wood processing.

3.4 Third Party Perspectives

As noted in the introduction to this chapter there are a very large number of individuals and corporations who would in some ways be affected by major changes in forest tenure and management. Foremost of these, in an economic sense, are the forest companies and organized labour. In addition there are also the recreational users and environmentalists.

The *forest industry* has two broad sets of concerns regarding the implications of comprehensive land claims. First, forestry firms have pointed to the problems and uncertainties created by not reaching claims agreements. They are concerned with the potential discouragement of investment in forestry and silviculture.[7] Conflicts such as those on South Moresby, Meares Island, Deer Island and in the Stein Valley have unquestionably interfered with logging operations. The present state of uncertainty poses distinctly different problems for British Columbia's forest companies than those which may exist in a post-settlement environment. This was emphasized by a Westar Timber executive who said in an interview that his firm was willing to work with whomever ultimately has jurisdiction; it is not knowing who this may be that creates deep problems for the industry. The second set of concerns involves the features of resource allocation, use and management after settlements may be reached. These concerns are the ones upon which this study focuses. In discussions with several forest companies, five inter-related themes emerged These were:

1. fairness and consistency in regulation and administration;
2. native peoples' capacities to participate in dependable partnerships;

3. native worker skills and habits;
4. a possible preservationist bias among native groups;
5. the potential loss of access to forest lands.

Forest companies are troubled about the fairness of obligations native governments may insist upon attaching to firms' activities if comprehensive claims are settled. These could include provisions related to taxes or rent collecton by tribal groupings, participation agreements and preferred employment arrangements. Companies are also worried that the number of claimant groups might lead to a confusing array of regimes across the province. This concern about *fairness and consistency* extends to the full range of administrative issues.

Similarly, with regard to provisions requiring participation in logging and processing, the industry has questions about native groups' *capacity to participate*. The worry is that, for at least some considerable time after settlements, native groups would not be sufficiently well-organized to provide consistent, dependable partnerships in commercial enterprises. The capacity to participate, the industry fears, might also be hindered by native groups not having sufficient access to capital, financial experience and marketing skills. Several industry officials noted that forestry is already beset by severe problems and challenges including competition from Third World soft woods, unstable world prices, uncertainty regarding future exports to the United States, a diminishing supply of accessible high grade timber and the need to modernize mills. Because even the survival of experienced medium-to-large firms is in doubt in the province, a somewhat rhetorical question is often asked: how would new native-operated enterprises fare in this environment?

Preferential employment requirements, seen as probable elements of future ventures involving native landlords, are a matter of concern. Further questions are raised by industry. Is the native work force adequately skilled? Is it willing to adapt to the schedules and work styles of modern logging and wood processing industries? Those who were interviewed for this study were careful to suggest that *capabilities for working* in the industry presently vary enormously among native groups in British Columbia. They noted that in some areas natives have been a dependable and essential part of the industry for a considerable period of time. In others this has not been the case.

In the minds of some British Columbians—and this includes many representatives of the forest industry—native claims have become closely associated with a *preservationist bias*. The coalition of native peoples and environmentalists has been a very real one in the leading cases of Lyell Island, Meares Island and the Stein Valley. The implication is sometimes drawn that a large proportion of the forests coming under post-settlement native management would be set aside as sacred, inviolable wilderness. Forest companies believe that the proportion of what is called alienated forest land is already a problem for the industry. Such a development would only compound the problem. There is also some concern that native regimes would demand more extensive and costly environmental regulations. These might include controls over the use of herbicides and insecticides, road construction, stream setbacks and the like. A proposal for forest management made a few years ago by the Nisga'a, for example, is seen as an ominous model of how tightly regulated the practice of logging could become (see Section 4.3).

Loss of access is the industry's most tangible fear. A substantial proportion of lands are presently under some form of Crown tenure. The industry concern is that after comprehensive claims settlements, native landlords could decide to "go it alone." They might withdraw major tracts of land from all logging. They could possibly exact regulations which would make forestry on native-controlled lands uneconomical.

Organized labour and other workers also are worried about the present impasse on the native claims issue. The International Woodworkers of America (IWA) is the major voice for unionized workers in British Columbia's forest sector. As the forest companies have but in a more sustained and consistent manner, the IWA has adopted the position that land claims ought to be resolved promptly so that uncertainties will not contribute further to problems in the forest sector. The IWA has also expressed considerable concern about the possible alienation of lands from the timber harvest and the consequent loss of employment opportunities if claims were to be resolved. Regarding the Meares Island controversy, for example, the IWA leadership was unequivocal: logging should proceed notwithstanding native claims. The controversy over South Moresby and Lyell Island has also been seen as a threat to the jobs of loggers and mill workers. In Sandspit, a community of 900 whose work force is primarily engaged in logging, there was strong hostility to the Haida roadblocks which prevented loggers from working. Similar concerns have been raised by non-natives in connection with the Gitksan-Wet'suwet'en claim and court case.

British Columbia's wilderness attracts a diverse group of *recreational and environmental interests* devoted to protecting the natural environment. Surveys conducted across Canada reveal that residents of the province are the most environmentally concerned in the nation. The list of organizations representing such interests in British Columbia is a long one. Some, like the Federation of Mountain Clubs, the Outdoor Recreation Council of British Columbia and the Western Canada Wilderness Federation have taken a particular interest in province-wide forest policy as well as site-specific disputes. In almost every instance where timber harvesting has been controversial, a new coalition group has emerged to advance the wilderness cause such as the Friends of Clayoquot Sound, the Valhalla Society and the Stein Action Committee.

In the most well-known logging conflicts of the past several years, a wide range of these environmental groups have allied with native groups in direct action against the timber harvest. These alliances and protests have led to a common assumption that the interests of environmentalists and natives directly coincide. To a some extent this is the case. Both parties espouse a reverence for nature, in particular for virgin forests. There is also a pragmatic side to this alliance. The environmental organizations realize that the native peoples often have a more substantial standing in resource conflicts than they do. They see native claims as providing essential leverage in court and for political lobbying. Native groups have benefitted from the expertise, organizational and fund-raising abilities of the environmentalists who have worked with them. Nevertheless, there are some *a priori* reasons to expect that tensions could arise in the future and that some of the outcomes of comprehensive claims settlements might be unwelcome by those with a strong preservationist leaning.

Comprehensive claims are, above all, an assertion of authority and ownership rather than a statement of the preferred state of the environment. This means that any native post-settlement resource agency would be free to choose strategies for development including practices such as clear-cutting. As will be shown below, bands and tribal councils have made it clear through plans and actions that logging, or more broadly modern forestry, has an important place in community economic development. The Lytton Band, for instance, which joined in the coalition against the Stein logging road is itself developing plans for forest operations.

Despite these trends, a close examination of both native and environmentalist strategies does not support the idea that natives and environmentalists will be at odds if comprehensive claims settlements are reached. In the case of the Lytton Band, Chief Ruby Dunstan distinguishes the band's small scale of operations and their planned intensive forest management practices from logging the Stein Valley which is seen to have sacred cultural values. The arguments raised by environmentalists have usually been for a shift in forest policy emphasizing smaller-scale operations, adequate investment in intensive silviculture, stronger recognition of multiple uses (especially non-extractive uses), and a greater local community role in forest use and management. Since these same elements appear in the forestry critiques and plans of groups such as the Nuu-chah-nulth and the Nisga'a, there does not appear to be any strong reason to anticipate the diminution of environmentalist support for native governments after claims settlements, providing the latter follow their own espoused principles.

4. Current and Emerging Initiatives

This section considers several cases where native peoples are becoming actively and positively involved in forest use and management. These cases are organized as in the preceding chapter in terms of the scenarios laid out in Chapter Two. As in the chapter on the fishery, the same qualification applies: native groups often pursue a mixed strategy as they approach forest resources. Sometimes they seek jobs and profits. Sometimes they strive for participation in management and conservation. At other times they seek to have what they perceive as their own independent authority recognized and respected. Occasionally they attempt to accomplish two or more of these goals.

The present involvements of native peoples in the forest sector may foreshadow developments after possible claims settlements, but they should not mislead observers. None of the native groups contacted during this study see business or co-management initiatives as a substitute for recognition of aboriginal title and rights and none see the recognition of aboriginal title and rights as sufficient in the absence of economic or political benefits. Partnerships in economic enterprise, participation in administrative coordination and regulation and assertions of autonomous authority are each, to varying degrees in varying situations, part of a complex and developing response on the part of native peoples and others to the comprehensive claims question.

4.1 Partners in Development

In the early days of the British Columbia forest industry native families and individuals were active participants as business people.

Capitalization and concentration in the sector from approximately the 1920s on reduced the native role to labouring primarily for wages. Wages earned in the forest sector continue to contribute significantly to native community income. Recently native businesses have re-emerged as sole proprietorships or as partnerships with non-natives.

This section examines examples of such approaches as well as some of the support programs which have been developed for them. The operations of Cariboo Indian Enterprises, Hecate Logging on western Vancouver Island and other native commercial logging concerns in the province are highlighted. This section concludes with a relevant example from outside of British Columbia, the experience with native corporate forestry in southeast Alaska. In each instance, native peoples and their commercial enterprises may be seen as being "Partners in Development."

4.1.1 Cariboo Indian Enterprises

Cariboo Indian Enterprises (CIE) is a corporation jointly owned by 15 bands in the Cariboo region in central British Columbia. CIE was formed to utilise some of the facilities of a former INAC forest training centre. The corporation obtained a Timber Sale Harvesting Licence (later changed to a Forest Licence) from the Ministry of Forests. CIE removed timber from federal military lands at Riske Creek, an area covering about 50,000 hectares with an annual allowable cut of 32,000 cubic metres. Initially this allowed CIE to operate self-sufficiently, selling its logs to sawmills in the Williams Lake area.

From 1979 through 1985 the company expanded rapidly. The annual allowable cut limitation in the area was waived by the province because of a beetle infestation that necessitated early harvesting of affected stands. CIE purchased the equipment needed to upscale its operations and hired additional contractors to meet the demands of the accelerated harvest schedule. These actions created some severe difficulties with the major recession of the early 1980s and the resulting reduction in the demand for lumber. In addition, the beetle-infested stands were completely harvested by 1985 causing a sudden shortage of readily-accessible timber stands. CIE laid off most of the field crew and sold their equipment. CIE managed to survive and sought to reorganize itself into a smaller enterprise with more well-defined long-term goals.

CIE's operations continue on both the military lands and on a timber licence it holds at Cariboo Lake. The former is harvested by a private native contractor, while the latter is logged by a non-native company that pays CIE a royalty for logging within its permit area. Recently, the Nazko and Kluskus bands have joined forces with CIE. These bands have held a timber license in an area designated as a "special native block" since 1974. At first the bands did not appear to be interested in or willing to form a business but the onset of a beetle attack prompted both bands and the British Columbia Ministry of Forests to a timber sale. The Nazko Logging Company was formed and is drawing on CIE for expertise and equipment. The Nazko-Kluskus bands provide the tenure and the labour force for what remains a very remote and inaccessible area. The main purpose of both CIE and the Nazko company has been the creation of employment opportunities. Liaison with the Ministry of Forests is frequent as CIE's directors search for new ways of meeting this objective at mills and in logging operations throughout the Cariboo region.

Spokesmen for CIE have been critical of the provincial Ministry of Forests for inadequate attention to reforestation. Despite having to pay stumpage to the province, CIE sees very little funding for forest renewal returning to the area. The solution they perceive — and this is one that many native groups include in their forestry objectives — is to secure a larger, longer-term forest tenure. The settlement of comprehensive land claims is seen as the longer-term solution not only because it may provide larger, secure forest tracts but also because it may allow and necessitate the development of forest management skills among the native peoples seeking to be "Partners in Development" in the region.

4.1.2 Hecate Logging

Hecate Logging is a good example of a co-venture between a native band holding a Forest Licence and a non-native company that required access to timber. In 1972 the Ehattesaht Band, a member of the Nuu-chah-nulth Tribal Council of western Vancouver Island, was granted a Timber Sale Harvesting Licence (now a Forest Licence) in the vicinity of its reserve. With some federal financial assistance it established a logging operation. Since then financial problems have been serious. Twice on the verge of bankruptcy, Hecate has survived through judicious use of public assistance programs and by entering into co-ventures with private firms:

The band found out quickly about the economic hazards (of logging). Its logging show in the Zeballos area, financed with $2.3 million in federal economic development grants and loans, and another $3.1 million through a bank debenture and unsecured loans, found it couldn't make enough to pay the bills. It finally discharged its operations to the bankruptcy trustee last year and the unsecured creditors got only 38 cents on the dollar.[8]

On this basis a small Vancouver Island firm, Coulsen-Prescott, bought a 50 percent interest in Hecate Logging from the Ehattesaht Band, although the band rather than the company remains the Forest Licence holder. Like many smaller firms in British Columbia, Coulsen-Prescott had faced difficulties in getting access to reasonably large tracts of timber. The Forest Licence of the Ehattesaht Band has a sufficient allowable annual cut to keep Coulsen-Prescott viable. The arrangement is described enthusiastically by Chief Earl Smith, President of Hecate Logging:

Private investors can be viewed as possible Joint Venture Partners. The private investor can bring a wealth of management expertise as well as financial assets into a business deal. The success of this approach is exemplified by Hecate Logging Limited, which operates a forest license in joint venture between the Ehattesaht Band and the Coulsen family on Vancouver Island.[9]

The Forest Licence allots an annual cut of 80,000 cubic metres, yielding a gross income of approximately $5 million. Much of this income is from log exports. The band will not receive any revenues until previous debts of have been liquidated. Hecate Logging Limited has had a troubled history. It has survived and has evolved into a new arrangement that offers a native band and a small forest company the opportunity to pool the strengths and needs of each.

4.1.3 Other Native Ventures and Co-ventures in British Columbia

There are a large number of other existing native endeavours in the forest industry. One long-standing arrangement which has provided benefits to a band and a major wood industries firm is the 1958 agreement between the Matsqui Band of the Fraser Valley and Scott Paper. Scott pays rent and stumpage for the use of a 250 hectare stand of cottonwood. In addition to revenues the band is guaranteed preferential hiring and subcontracting for harvesting and replanting activities. The band has indicated that it would like to receive a substantially larger revenue share.[10] The present 40-year lease will expire in 1998 at which time re-negotiations can provide an opportunity for such an increase.

Most native groups interviewed for this study had some form of forestry project in the early stages of development or planning.

Many groups were interested in acquiring a provincial Woodlot Licence. The Chehalis Band for example, has applied for this form of tenure for an area of approximately 450 hectares on and near its reserves in the lower Fraser River Valley. The Neskainlith Band of the Shuswap area is considering the purchase of a sawmill in partnership with an American firm. The Kingcome Band of the mid-coast has been developing working arrangements with Scott Paper for silviculture contracts on Scott's Tree Farm Licence. Five Carrier-Sekani bands participate in the Burns Lake Native Development Corporation which has an 8 percent interest in Babine Forest Products which operates a sawmill operation.

Discussions have been held between the Lytton Band and Lytton Lumber about a possible co-venture although no agreement has been reached because of their differing views on the sharing of authority. The Lytton Band has sought a 50/50 sharing of control but the company has wanted a 51/49 split in its favour. This raises an issue that is unlikely to dissipate even in the aftermath of comprehensive claims settlements. Private enterprises, responsible to their shareholders in the case of larger firms, may be leery about entering co-ventures with groups that they feel are inexperienced in business decision-making. One concern is that partners who work internally by consensus may not be able to cope with the rapid day-to-day decisions needed in the business world. If, however, substantial timber falls within native control, there may be no choice other than to accommodate culturally distinctive styles of management when they emerge.

4.1.4 Native Forestry in Southeast Alaska

The case of native forestry practices in the southeast "panhandle" of Alaska is an important one because it shows native peoples as "Partners in Development" from a different vantage point than the one prevalent in British Columbia to date. Native involvements in forestry in British Columbia have often upset industry and impressed environmentalists whether in the role played in opposing certain logging operations or in the approach to forestry in plans such as those of the Nisga'a or Nuu-chah-nulth (see Sections 4.2 and 4.3). In southeast Alaska, the tables have been turned to some extent and there is a worry among many environmental groups about an overemphasis by native corporations on short-term profits. Conversely, other forest business interests have welcomed the approach adopted by the natives of southeast Alaska.

The present regime for forest use and management in southeastern Alaska is largely a result of the *Alaska Native Claims Settlement Act* (ANCSA) of 1971. Through this legislation changes occurred in the ownership of land, the organizational structures for native involvement in resource use and the capital available for native business participation. The statewide approach and some of its consequences have been reviewed by Berger (1985); here focus is restricted to the "panhandle" and particularly to ANCSA's consequences in the forest sector.

In southeastern Alaska a regional corporation (Sealaska), 10 village corporations and 2 urban corporations were created to represent the native population. Under ANCSA the Sealaska Corporation was entitled to 137,600 hectares of land in the Tongass National Forest. The village and urban corporations were allocated 117,000 hectares in total. A substantial cash payment provided the necessary cash flow for corporate mobilization. Between 1971 and 1978 efforts were devoted to corporate structuring, planning and development by the native corporations. Major emphasis was put on land selection in an effort to acquire lands of highest timber quality. The final conveyance of most lands occurred from 1979 to 1981, almost ten years following the passage of ANSCA. Native corporations were keenly interested in moving into the forests where, until then, two companies had dominated timber harvest and processing within the region.

It is important to understand the forest sector in southeast Alaska before the entry of native corportions. The critical factor had been a long-standing prohibition of unprocessed log exports. This and the existence of large "overmature" forested areas in the southeast led to establishment of a forest sector dominated by the pulp industry. Over time the existing industry structure began to face increasing resistance from independent loggers who claimed that long-term sales to the two major companies prevented a competitive market for timber purchase. The early 1980s brought the recession and a sudden decrease in international demand for wood products. Plant production capacities at Alaskan pulp mills were severely underutilized by 1984. The integrated sawmills of both major pulp companies were shut down. Pulp, chip and sawlog production declined to record lows and, as a result, log consumption and harvest utilization fell sharply.

Meanwhile, native corporation timber entered the marketplace in 1980, creating a new industry in southeast Alaska based on round log exports. Although round logs could not be exported from the Tongass National Forest, which includes almost all commercial timber lands in the region, native-held lands were exempt from this prohibition. The value of native log exports quickly exceeded the value of wood pulp. Because of Japanese customers' preference for round logs over semi-processed logs and chips, the creation of the new round log export component of the industry by the native corporations significantly reduced the demand for the output of the region's sawmills. By 1985 the native timber harvest reached 50 percent of the total harvest in southeast Alaska and log export constituted 41 percent of the value of Alaskan forest product exports.

As a result of these developments, southeast Alaska's logging industry employment numbers reflect an increase in the influence of the native corporations during the general industry-wide decline during the period 1980-1985. The employment effects of native corporate involvement in forestry are not restricted to native communities. Galea (1987) has argued that without the surge of activity associated with Sealaska's logging, many small operators would have gone out of business in the early 1980s.

Important resource management issues have arisen as the influence of the native corporations has increased. Timber management and provisions for regulation were addressed in section 22-k(2) of ANCSA: "such lands are managed under the principle of sustained yield management practices for protection and enhancement of environmental quality no less stringent than such management practices on adjacent national forest lands . . ." Since passage of ANCSA in 1971, statewide controversy and litigation have arisen about the fidelity of native forestry to section 22-k(2).

In contrast to the patterns so far in British Columbia, native peoples have not been seen as part of the environmentalist coalition in Alaska. They have often pursued strategies and practices of logging and log exporting which have drawn criticism from environmental advocacy groups. Two broad areas of concern have emerged over the impact of native corporate forestry on the resource base: the fullness and extent of timber utilization and reforestation, and the implications for other forest-dependent resource activities. Native trading in the Japanese round log market has been driven by the availability of high grade Sitka spruce and Western hemlock sawlogs. As mentioned previously, world-wide slumps in the pulp market have lessened demand for pulp and utility grade logs. Relaxed timber utilization standards on native lands have resulted in significant volumes of lower grade wood being left on site. Concerns have also arisen over the perceived high-grading of the export

106

component within harvested stands and a lack of investment in reforestation in native-operated areas.

Maximizing timber harvest for short-term returns on Alaskan native land has created controversy over impacts on the fish and wildlife resources of the region. As in adjacent areas in British Columbia, the native (and non-native) fishery remains culturally and economically significant. Protection of subsistence activities from native corporate forest policies has become a troublesome issue. Rapid timber liquidation has been the principal driving force of native ownership within the southeast Alaska region, perhaps limiting alternatives for the long-term diversification of resource uses.

The continuation and even exacerbation of disputes over "forestry versus environment" in Alaska adds a new dimension to what was said earlier about the mixed and complex motives of native communities in this sector. In Alaska pressures created by ANCSA and the world lumber market have led to the kind of forest use strategy which is not environmentally sensitive. The results are applauded by those who would otherwise have been unemployed or out-of business; they are criticized by those who value old growth forests for uses other than logging. Indeed, the concerns over Sealaska's activities are much like those that the Nisga'a have raised over forestry in the Nass Valley, not far from the Alaskan border (see Section 4.3).

4.2 Allies and Adversaries

The word "co-management" is heard less often in the forestry than in the fishery sector. One reason for this may be that something quite like co-management has existed for a number of years. For the most part it is the private sector, particularly the largest forest firms, whose involvement with forest management has had this character.

In the cases discussed below native groups have begun to assume something of the role of co-manager in arrangements which, to a degree, are similar to those envisioned in the scenario "Allies and Adversaries". In the first case — perhaps the best known of current native initiatives in forestry in British Columbia — the Stuart-Trembleur Band obtained the most comprehensive form of tenure available under British Columbia's *Forest Act*: a Tree Farm Licence. This form of tenure creates opportunities and responsibilities which make the licensee very much a co-manager of a substantial forested area. The second case does not involve a significant new grant of tenure; instead the Nuu-chah-nulth Tribal Council conducted a comprehensive forestry analysis within its entire claim area and developed a mixed strategy for achieving change. The third case, involving the Musgamagw Tribal Council, features a complex, multi-faceted set of inter-governmental arrangements which could presage the sort of co-management regime which might come out of comprehensive claims settlements. Finally, a recent experience from outside Canada is considered. In the state of Washington formal negotiations with strong native involvement have led to a unique "alliance" on forest management.

4.2.1 Tanizul Timber (Stuart-Trembleur Band)

In many respects Tanizul Timber Company Limited resembles the operations included in the previous section—initiatives primarily devoted to enhancing native economic participation. What makes the Tanizul experience distinctive is the tenure form under which it operates. In 1981-82 Tanizul competed successfully with well-established companies for a Tree Farm Licence covering approximately 49,000 hectares in the north central region of the province and, as such, it has major resource management responsibilities.

The Tree Farm Licence (TFL) provides the longest term of tenure available under the *Forest Act*: 25 years, subject to renewal every 10 years. This provides some flexibility for the government and a long planning horizon for the licensee. Unlike a Forest Licence, the other major long-term tenure form in British Columbia, the TFL can and usually does include both Crown land and lands held by the licensee. All TFL's are designated as provincial forests. Five-year management and working plans are prepared by the licensee and submitted to the Chief Forester for review and approval. Such plans lay out a description of proposed harvests and forest management measures including identification of other resource values and how they will be accommodated. Approved plans specify an allowable annual cut to which the licensee has exclusive rights.

A TFL grants more than just cutting privileges; it entrusts the licensee with resource management responsibilities once seen to fall more properly to the public sector. Final authority rests with the Minister and in this sense the resulting arrangements are much like the vision of co-management held by the Department of Fisheries and Oceans for the fishery sector as described in Chapter Three. Still, by virtue of the licensee's responsibility for planning and the melding of private and Crown land to form a more manageable whole, the TFL represents a unique private/public arrangement. When the "private" party is actually an Indian band, the TFL becomes a testing ground for future approaches to shared resource management.

The TFL granted to Tanizul Timber was the first in British Columbia in 16 years. The Stuart-Trembleur Band at that time was desperately searching for some way to enhance employment and social well-being:

We explored the usual possibilities such as trailer parks or marina developments, and decided to focus on the forest resource. The logic of the choice flowed from the fact that we had abundant forest resources right on our doorstep. Non-Indian companies were logging in our backyard and yet provided little or no employment for our people. We wanted to change this.[11]

Tanizul Timber Company Limited was established because the *Indian Act* precluded the band from directly holding off-reserve tenure. The firm is wholly-owned by the Stuart-Trembleur Band operating through six shareholders who take direction from the band council.

In order to obtain the TFL, the band had to be prepared to contribute reserve lands to be managed as an integral part of the TFL. To this end the band procured the passage of a federal order-in-council which authorized the grant of a timber licence to Tanizul Timber for reserve lands of the band. Under the terms of the licence, the governmental supervision of operations is by provincial rather than federal officials. The document itself bears notable similarities to the TFL developed by the Ministry of Forests, but the most significant jurisdictional provision in the licence and regulations is the following:

The British Columbia *Forest Act, Ministry of Forests Act* and *Range Act*, as amended from time to time and regulations made from time to time thereunder, apply to reserve lands in respect of which any licence is granted as though the reserve lands were private lands within the meaning of the British Columbia *Forest Act*.[12]

This represents a significant concession of jurisdiction on the part of the band and the federal government. Presumably these provincial statutes would not ordinarily apply to reserve lands, either because on their own terms they did not apply or because they constitute legislation in relation to "lands reserved for the Indians."

The award of TFL #42 to Tanizul Timber was the result of nearly a decade of forestry research and planning, followed by the submission of a detailed application. Tanizul Timber has responsibility for an annual allowable cut of 120,000 cubic metres in the TFL which is near Tachie, the band's main village. Operations include logging, hauling, log marketing and reforestation. Most of the logs are sold to a sawmill operated by West Fraser Timber Limited at Fraser Lake. Ten percent of production is reserved for independent marketing. Tanizul Timber President Ed John estimates that his company contributed about $9.5 million to the economy of the region in its first two years of operation.[13]

Tanizul Timber employs anywhere from 12 to 60 people depending on the season. Much of the work is performed by small contractors, many of whose employees are Stuart-Trembleur Band members. In addition to logging work, employment arises from the reforestation required under the terms of the TFL. Band council representatives point out that the income and training opportunities have made a vital contribution to the morale of the band. Indeed, Tanizul Timber's case when competing for the TFL was strongly based upon social and community development objectives. In its initial working plan, Tanizul Timber repeated its rationale: "Opportunities for employment in the immediate area are severely limited. The Band's independence and self-sufficiency had, of late, sunk to a low level. An economic base, such as this TFL, close to the Band's villages will supply a vital element in a formula for recovery."[14] This document also reported that "...a marked improvement in the morale of the Band has already occurred with the award of the TFL and the resulting increase in employment".[15]

The Stuart-Trembleur Band is a member of the Carrier-Sekani Tribal Council whose comprehensive claim was accepted by the federal government in 1983. It is the largest claim to a land area in the province and has aroused a great deal of concern in the Prince George area among forest officials and municipal leaders. While the statement of claim does not indicate how forest management would proceed after an agreement is reached, the Tanizul story provides an indication that the Carrier-Sekani peoples will strive to form co-operative commercial and administrative relationships when they have the chance to do so.

4.2.2 The Nuu-chah-nulth Tribal Council Forestry Program

The Nuu-chah-nulth forestry program which began in 1978 is one of the most comprehensive forestry initiatives yet undertaken by a native group in the province. Under this program, the Nuu-chah-nulth Tribal Council commissioned a detailed inquiry into past practices on and off-reserve and outlined prescriptions for change. The analysis fostered a wide range of new understandings and projects. It also set the stage for the assertion of aboriginal rights in forested lands that led to the Meares Island legal battle.

The Nuu-chah-nulth Tribal Council (NTC) represents 15 bands with a combined population of about 4,200. The bands occupy a large part of western Vancouver Island, from Port Renfrew in the south to Kyuquot Sound in the north. They hold a total of 168 reserves covering approximately 4,900 hectares. Preliminary forest inventories suggest that about 1,500 hectares contain mature harvestable timber while another 1,100 have been logged and require rehabilitation.

Misgivings over the condition of reserve and off-reserve lands in the traditional area of the Nuu-chah-nulth were the prime reason a forestry program was initiated. In 1978 the Ahousaht Band asked the NTC for help in organizing opposition to local logging. The NTC held a community meeting and decided a comprehensive analysis of forestry was needed. INAC was approached for funding and agreed to a test study. There were four study components:

1. determination of past and present involvement of the Nuu-chah-nulth bands in the British Columbia forest industry;
2. determination of the on-reserve, and relevant off-reserve forestry resource base;
3. community consultation;
4. development of a long-range Nuu-chah-nulth forestry program.

In 1980 the study was completed. It reviewed the existing tenure in the whole area of what would later become the Nuu-chah-nulth comprehensive claim territory and concluded:

The present political economy associated with the forest resource within the study area is characterized by large companies controlling 90 percent of the cut and virtually all significant manufacturing within a context of legislation and regulation which enforces this status quo.[16]

The Nuu-chah-nulth holdings were but 0.43 percent of the area, of which almost 800 hectares were within Pacific Rim National Park and therefore alienated from timber harvesting. Many of the reserve lands had been logged in the 1960s and required substantial reforestation. The study was especially critical of INAC's trust role in reserve timber management. It concluded that a strong case existed for INAC being "obligated to fund the rehabilitation of the west coast reserve lands."[17] There were five main recommendations to the tribal council. The tribal council was advised to hire a forestry manager, undertake a detailed forest inventory, initiate a site rehabilitation program, develop a training program for Nuu-chah-nulth members and negotiate a takeover of INAC's trusteeship for native forest lands.

The tribal council followed up on the first recommendation immediately, hiring a forestry manager in 1980. Over the next several years a wide array of other activities were initiated. Funding has been a constant obstacle, but progress has been made in several aspects of silviculture. By 1984, 148 hectares had been subject to site rehabilitation, while 340 hectares had undergone stand-tending work. Only a small amount of actual harvesting has taken place (approximately 12 hectares).

Business development in forestry in the short-term has been forced to reorganize due to the downturn in the industry. From 1980 to 1984 four silvicultural contracting companies were established, employing altogether about 40 band members. Four portable saw-mills were acquired. Two Christmas tree farms were planted. Five small cedar shakes and bolt companies were set up and, prior to the American duties on shakes in mid-1986, were reported to be doing moderately well. In 1984 the NTC tree nursery became operational and now employs three people on a full-time basis. Ten more are periodically employed when major sales are made to large firms operating in the area. Present customers include MacMillan Bloedel and Canadian International Paper. Negotiations are underway to sell seedlings to Western Forest Products and British Columbia Forest Products.

According to the NTC, relations with the forestry firms of the area are excellent. The NTC almost always is awarded the contracts on which it bids. These may include work on tree planting, spacing, brush removal and weeding. Most of the time, conflicts over multiple use issues, such as debris left in streams by non-native operations, are handled by negotiation. Quite often, the necessary remedial work is contracted out to the Nuu-chah-nulth. The NTC forestry operations appear to have a positive impact on surrounding non-native busi-nesses. In addition to the spending of its employees, the NTC buys fuel, power and supplies, rents equipment and vehicles and has repairs done in the Port Alberni area. These expenditures are great enough in some of the smaller centres that local businessmen have said they could not have survived without the NTC.

Training in forestry has been a priority since 1980. Areas covered include: nursery operations and management, fire-fighting, timber cruising, forest surveying, intensive silviculture, forest first aid and horticulture management and training. The NTC has been successful in gaining support for training through Canada Employment and Immigration job creation funding.

The problem of enhancing the size of the resource base was an especially difficult one according to the Nuu-chah-nulth study. This has meant having to seek tenure on off-reserve forest lands, most of which are under leases and licences to major non-native firms. A recent objective of the NTC has been to obtain Woodlot Licences for five or six bands of the tribal council. Currently only the Ahousat Band holds a Woodlot Licence. Woodlot Licences provide the licensee with access to up to 400 hectares of Crown land for a renewable term of fifteen years. Licensees generally include some of their own land within the area; thus the Woodlot Licence is a scaled down version of the Tree Farm Licence in most respects. Present regulations explictly include native bands as candidates for the license. Both the Ministry of Forests and the Nuu-chah-nulth recognize the advantage of Woodlot Licences as potential training grounds for forest use and management.

Evaluations of the Nuu-chah-nulth forestry study and the ensuing program emphasize the effort that has been made to achieve a community-based approach.[18] In response to the significant geographic distances between member bands, coordination has been achieved through a forestry committee. The committee has given direction to the NTC's forestry manager and has played a leading role in various proceedings including an attempt to re-open consideration of several Tree Farm Licences renewed in the area during the late 1970s.

Co-management, in the sense that native groups participate in policy-making, is well-developed for Nuu-chah-nulth reserve lands. It is much less clear that anything approaching a policy role for the Nuu-chah-nulth has been achieved on off-reserve lands. The Meares Island situation and how it is eventually resolved will have a major impact on this possibility. The case of Meares Island, under claim by the Nuu-chah-nulth, is a sobering one because it indicates that allies can become adversaries if shared understandings of a basic nature do not underlie working arrangements.

4.2.3 The Musgamagw Demonstration Project: The Forest Component

The fisheries initiative of the Musgamagw has been described in the preceding chapter. The Integrated Resource Management and Development Demonstration Project of the Musgamagw Tribal Council (MTC) in the northern Vancouver Island area is a program of integrated resource management for the fishery and forestry sectors. This means that the lands and resources are managed so there is as much positive interaction and as little conflict in resource use as possible. Integrated resource management is an idea that has been promoted in British Columbia over the past decade. The Musgamagw, in cooperation with federal and provincial agencies, are testing the feasibility of this approach.

Despite the emphasis on integrated resource management in the MTC project, the forestry elements are as yet relatively discrete and can be discussed separately. The project foreshadows the "Allies and Adversaries" scenario because of the unusual degree of emphasis upon intergovernmental coordination. Although the MTC is hardly an equal partner in forest management and policy making, the demonstration project is directed at achieving such a state.

To reiterate briefly, planning for the project began in 1984 and start-up funding was established early in 1986. The central goal is:

To initiate a community based action oriented process of opportunity identification and planning in the forestry and marine areas from which projects and businesses appropriate to the cultural values and organizational capacity of MTC member bands, and which contribute to building self-reliance and community stability can be implemented.[19]

The project is a demonstration in two ways. First, it is meant to demonstrate that a community-based approach can succeed in both achieving social benefits and creating an integrated resource management system. Second — and it is with this that the MTC project charts an informative course in co-management — it is to demonstrate that "... interdepartmental and intergovernmental commitment to real, practical cooperation will ... make a positive contribution to the building of community self-reliance."[20] In other words, through the project the MTC is gently pressuring governments to change their relationship not only with native peoples but also among departments and governments so that cooperative management becomes possible.

Like the fisheries component, the forest aspects are framed against a general background of diminishing native participation on and off the reserves. The 1981-82 recession in the forest industry brought high unemployment among tribal members, just as it did for all forest workers in the province. An inventory of the Nimpkish Band (the largest band within the MTC) resources had been prepared in 1981 with the idea of initiating some forestry projects. Funding could not be secured. The conclusion reached by the MTC was that forestry ought to be pursued and that in doing so an approach reflecting a commitment to both a longer planning time horizon and a greater consideration of community needs was necessary. Here are some excerpts from the rationale for the forestry component:

Funding: Short term piecemeal funding is inappropriate for ... a long term forestry management and development program. . . .

Training: . . . the problem is one of programs being designed "downtown" and being delivered in inappropriate venues. . . . They need to be structured as on site training and geared to the specific characteristics of the client group. . . .

Infrastructure: . . .the recent high number of people involved from the Nimpkish Band in forestry has led to people trying to move their families out of Port McNeill for what amount to short term jobs. Understandably, these individuals and the Nimpkish Band are concerned about the social impact on the community. . . .[21]

The MTC project forestry elements are designed around several very specific objectives:

- completion of a forest inventory of lands both on and off-reserve (the boundaries of the off-reserve inventory have not been specified although the ultimate goal is to have a forest inventory for all lands within the claimed territory);
- preparation and submission of applications for Woodlot Licences for all member bands, based on preliminary inventory results;
- initiation of on-the-job training in a broad range of forest activities such as inventory and silviculture;
- development of organizational capacity especially in regard to entry into the business of intensive forestry operations.

The plans and activities of the MTC for the first two years of the five-year project included a broad range of forestry elements to meet these objectives. Budgetary problems were encountered so that not all of the intended actions were taken.

Forest inventories were completed for the 45 reserves (approximately 1,200 hectares) allotted to the five member bands of the MTC. The work was funded through the Indian Forest Lands Program which is part of the overall Canada-British Columbia Forest Resources Development Agreement. In fact, the Musgamagw inventory was the first project fully completed under the program. The inventories include estimates of timber volume, a calculation of the annual allowable cut and recommendations on required silviculture work for each reserve. Each band was advised of the nature of its opportunities and desirable cutting and management plans. The final report suggested that there should be no large scale harvesting until the plans and infrastructure for reforestation could be developed. A major emphasis for the first year was training.

The MTC project has also included efforts to initiate and strengthen working relationships with forest companies. One goal has been to establish the capability to seek and win contracts for intensive forestry management projects. Intensive forestry has become a popular idea with forest managers in many countries. The Canada-British Columbia Forest Resources Development Agreement includes funding for an Intensive Forestry Management Program. This entails a number of silviculture activities which can be performed by small firms or communities such as removal of brush and weeds, tree spacing and forest fertilization. The MTC project set an objective of winning contracts for juvenile spacing. The MTC staff, in conjunction with the Kingcome Band, negotiated with Scott Paper to provide that company with silviculture services on a Tree Farm Licence.

The demonstration project is intended to foster native involvement beyond field-level activities such as inventory, training and contracting; thus an explicit resource policy component is part of the project. The path that this component can take in fisheries is fairly clear since the federal government has been formulating a new policy on co-management. Within forestry, the policy involvement of the MTC is more difficult; the province has shown no inclination to share forest policy-making in any but the most customary—and limited—manners. Nonetheless circumstances have provided the MTC with an opportunity to enter this arena.

In 1986 controversy arose concerning the cutting plans of Whonnock Industries in the Kingcome Inlet watershed. The MTC demonstration project staff organized a series of meetings with the forest company, the bands and the Department of Fisheries and Oceans. Representatives of the Ministry of Forests for British Columbia attended several of these. The result of MTC's intervention was an agreement on Whonnock's plans that included reduction of logging in sensitive areas; environmental repairs and controls; terms that provided for Whonnock to sell some logs to the bands for processing in their portable sawmill; the opportunity for bands to bid on reforestation contracts; and some special consideration for band members in hiring for logging operations. In terms of the most positive images of the "Allies and Adversaries" scenario, what started as a typical confrontation was turned into a cooperative plan potentially benefitting all parties while protecting the environment.

The federal and MTC personnel most closely associated with the project express the view that the demonstration project is neither in conflict with comprehensive claims nor a way of "doing land claims by the back door." It seems reasonable, however, to assume that the project indicates the kinds of initiatives this native group could pursue if a comprehensive claims settlement were reached. The project is based upon a strong commitment to develop local participation in both the use and the management of forests. At the same time it recognizes the virtues of fostering cooperation with government and developing businesslike relationships with the private sector. Finally, the demonstration project is intended to invent and implement an approach to the management of resources which integrates respect for the fisheries resource while proceeding with forest harvesting.

4.2.4 The Washington State Timber/Fish/Wildlife Agreement

In looking for models that have potential applications in coping with forest resource conflicts few are so intruiging as the recent Timber/Fish/Wildlife (T/F/W) Agreement concluded in Washington State. Because native peoples have played a central role in this multilateral process it can be considered as a case which illustrates arrangements such as those pictured in the "Allies and Adversaries" scenario. Indeed, it represents a significant transformation of historic adversaries into allies.

Timber companies and other major corporations whose activities potentially affect native fisheries had for some years been exploring ways of cooperatively planning with treaty tribes. The reason was the Boldt rulings (see Chapter Three) which strongly suggested native rights in the fishery carried with them ancillary rights to protect fish habitat. The affirmation of native resource rights, in this instance, may be seen as a powerful incentive for development of joint planning among the major parties from other resource sectors.

As in British Columbia, there has been a long period of intense conflict in Washington State over the impacts of timber harvesting practices on other uses and values of the forests. The state's Forest Practices Board was established under the 1974 *Forest Practices Act* to serve as the principal arbiter of such disputes but, despite over a decade of regulatory experimentation, conflict continued to abound until early 1986 when yet another set of regulations was drafted. As in the past, industry felt these were too stringent; other groups including native ones complained of their leniency. A proposal for an alternative review process was made as a result of a meeting between the Northwest Indian Fisheries Commission and an industry organization, the Washington Forest Protection Association.

The Northwest Renewable Resources Center, the group that facilitated recent changes in fisheries management (see Chapter Three), was engaged to coordinate what became known as the T/F/W negotiations. The T/F/W negotiations eventually included approximately twenty organizations including native tribes, the Northwest Indian Fisheries Commission, the Columbia River Inter-tribal Fish Commission, several environmental advocacy groups, major forest firms and forestry lobby groups and the Washington State Departments of Ecology, Fisheries, Game and Natural Resources. An agreement was reached in 1986.[22] Substantive areas covered in the agreement include fish habitat protection, water quality improvement changes, wildlife habitat management, protection of archaeological and cultural resources and agreements on the general principle of and specific practices for intensive forest management. The implementation of this agreement entails the introduction of legislative and regulatory amendments under the *Forest Practices Act*; significant reorganization of the lead forest management agency, the Department of Natural Resources; the creation of an array of ongoing collaborative processes providing for cooperative monitoring of the T/F/W implementation; and the development of future management plans among the signers of the agreement.

It would be premature to assert that the T/F/W approach is effective and can be adapted to the Canadian context. Individuals within several ministries of the British Columbia provincial government have followed the process carefully and are presently considering its possible application. The most impressive aspect is that a signed agreement was reached and heralded as worthwhile by all participants. Stu Bledsoe from the Washington Forest Protection Association, an industrial advocacy group, comments:

From a purely business perspective, T/F/W will cost forestland owners less than new regulation.... But the benefits of T/F/W to industry are much, much more: an end to battles where nobody wins; a dedication to common sense field-oriented solutions....[23]

4.3 Homeland and Hinterland

No indigenous group in British Columbia or elsewhere has achieved a position in relation to forest resources which is close to that envisioned in the "Homeland and Hinterland" scenario. A locally-based forestry where the community is able to exercise a high degree of autonomous authority appears to be a difficult goal to achieve. One tribal group in British Columbia has been especially consistent in advancing a fairly detailed model of forest resource management and development based upon considerable authority over the resource. That group is the Nisga'a. Their approach to forestry may be the most informative harbinger of the resource regime which could arise if native groups asserted and received recognition for some form of inherent and independent jurisdiction over forests in comprehensive claims settlement areas. The Nisga'a are the only native group in the province actively negotiating a comprehensive claim with the federal government. This alone would justify paying attention to their approach to forest use and management. Their proposals, however, also represent some of the most detailed analysis any native or non-native communities have completed.

4.3.1 The Nisga'a Forestry Approach

The Nisga'a have been one of the most indefatigable of all the province's native groups in the pursuit of land claims (see Raunet 1984). Among their primary motivations in recent times has been the fear that the forests of the Nass River Valley will be irrevocably damaged by cutting under existing non-native tenure and provincial management. In their comprehensive claim the Nisga'a call for compensation for forest resources already removed from the territory and assert total ownership and control over the remaining forest resources. Marchak (1983), reporting on interviews conducted in 1978, notes the frequent assertion by area residents that "the forest is finished." The perceived threat to the resource, the forests' value to the Nisga'a and hopes for the future are summarized in a quotation attributed to a Nisga'a councillor:

They're ripping it out as fast as possible, and we're trying to stop them.... Our economic development depends on that timber. We've asked that the west side of the Nass be kept in proper condition. The saw logs they've got in the Terrace yard they're selling that to others, they don't need it. They're trying to wipe out the saw logs here as fast as possible. We ask them to slow down on that cutting. They say "no". What we want is to be partners in the Twin River and other operations. In this village there are a lot of experienced loggers who could take over a company very easily.[24]

In 1978 the Nisga'a prepared a detailed forest plan. It outlined a strategy for sustained yield management involving a partnership between present Nass Valley operators, the province and the Nisga'a.

The forest plan included reforestation and the construction of an extensive road network for access to high quality stands of timber. During the transition to Nisga'a management, forest companies were to be guaranteed a timber supply adequate to at least recover their investment in the region. The province rejected the plan.

In 1982 a further study was commissioned by the Nisga'a Tribal Council for a technical evaluation of forest management and practices in the Nass Valley. The final report documented severe mismanagement of Tree Farm Licence #1 dating back to the first commercial logging in the region in 1958.[25] Details were given of large scale soil damage, timber "highgrading" (taking the best quality and most accessible timber and leaving lower grades behind), lack of reforestation and inefficient utilization of felled timber. Estimates were provided of the resultant loss of jobs and other economic benefits to the Nass Valley.

The report presented an alternative approach that remains the basis of the Nisga'a proposal for the forestry component of a comprehensive claims settlement. Most fundamentally, it called for taking over much of Tree Farm Licence (TFL)#1 from the current licensee, Westar Timber, and implementing integrated resource management under a territorially-based government. The boundaries of the new TFL would include the northern portion of the current licence, plus a large tract in the Kalum Timber Supply Area. Reserve lands would be included as well. The Nisga'a would conduct a new forest resources inventory, perform extensive land rehabilitation and tree replanting, establish a nursery and process the timber at a local lumber and finished products plant. The proposed operations were estimated to yield a potential of 200 direct jobs in logging, silviculture and secondary manufacturing. By the report's calculations, another 350 service and support jobs would be created in the region, many of which would provide employment for non-natives. In a brochure used to explain the proposal, *Forests for People: A Nishga Solution*, the Nisga'a asserted: "Our solution is compatible with B.C. law and is one that will share the resources of the Nass with the people of Canada."

Concurrent with the promotion of its proposal the Nisga'a Tribal Council lodged a formal complaint with the British Columbia Ombudsman's Office. This complaint raised the issues of highgrading, overcutting and lack of reforestation. In 1985 the Ombudsman released a final report and agreed with the Nisga'a: "My staff and I discovered that the information we found in Ministry files largely supported the conclusions."[26]

The Ombudsman took note of the concerns expressed by several significant non-natives from the area, including both the legislative member from Skeena and the mayor of Terrace, the largest town in the vicinity. Without mentioning the Nisga'a, the Ombudsman recommended a change in the conditions of tenure and the possibility of a new tenure form designed especially for the rehabilitation of poorly managed forests. This was in accord with the objectives for intensive forest management laid out by the Nisga'a.

In responding to the Ombudsman both the Ministry of Forests and the operator, Westar Timber, emphasized two related points: the high dependency of the region on employment and other benefits from the Nass operations and the very weak financial condition of Westar's northern operations over the preceding several years. In response, the Ombudsman raised the issue of longer-term economic welfare:

With the standard of utilization which the Ministry has agreed to accept in which the good timber is taken and most of the pulp quality wood is left on the ground, and with the failure to ensure that harvested areas are properly reforested, I am afraid that in the not too distant future the forests of TFL #1 will have no economic value at all. When that happens not only will Westar Timber Ltd. cease operations but no other forest company will be interested in the area. In turn, there may be no employment for local communities.[27]

On this basis, the Nisga'a asked the Minister of Forests to transfer TFL #1 to them regardless of the status of the comprehensive claims question. They also attempted to purchase the licence from Westar but with no success. Westar did request and was granted a reduction of its TFL. The Nishga'a tried to combine the relinquished lands with higher quality areas to form a timber supply area. Instead, the Ministry awarded the licence to contractors from Terrace and Vancouver.

The tribal council currently employs a full-time Nisga'a forester who worked previously as a forest engineer with Westar. He was interviewed for this study and showed the researcher what he described as 2,500 hectares of potential highest grade timberland now covered in brush. To correct this situation, the Nisga'a propose to develop a tree nursery capable of producing 1.5 to 2.0 million seedlings annually. The Nisga'a, using the same rationale as the Musgamagw, have also advocated comprehensive watershed planning. The key argument is that if one government has authority over all resource development for a watershed and has a constituency including both forest and fisheries users (many Nisga'a carry out both activities seasonally), there is less likelihood of resource conflicts.

The watershed-based planning approach proposed by the Nisga'a is advanced along with a more general call for territorially-based governance emphasizing increased value-added components of primary activities such as forestry (cf. Aberley 1985). Nisga'a representatives stressed this orientation when responding to questions by researchers for this project about post-settlement resource use and management. They were adamant that non-natives would not be forced from their lands. In an interview for this book one tribal council member asserted that, "the non-Indian farm settlers of the Nass Valley have much more to fear from the province than they do from us." The same person pointed to the local school and medical diagnostic center, operated by the Nisga'a, but which serve all people of the Nass Valley, as examples of cooperation and concern for non-native peoples.

The picture formed of Nisga'a intentions in the forestry sector is one of using political strategies to increase their control over the resource. Like all other native groups, the Nisga'a are concerned with unemployment and related social problems which could be alleviated by forest-based development. However, they have a stronger inclination than many other groups to seek these benefits by directly challenging existing management and tenure arrangements. This strategy proceeds both in the forum of comprehensive land claims and in efforts to secure TFL #1. It is an example of efforts on the part of native peoples to restore a sustainable homeland from lands which they perceive, at present, to be mere hinterlands.

5. ...To The Future

The cornerstone of any discussion of forestry in Canada and particularly British Columbia is extraordinary riches from which flow major economic and social benefits. More recently, a series of problems have threatened this heritage. All of the major parties (the provincial and federal governments, industry, labour, environmentalists and native peoples) have separately recognized the values and conflicts that characterize forestry in the province today.

On many matters there is disagreement. Professional foresters and the forest industry, in general, believe that non-extractive uses such as parks or game reserves are significantly eroding the resource base (Ainscough 1979). Environmentalists disagree, arguing that a

legacy of poor forest management is responsible for decreasing th
quality of and the profits from the forests (Jones 1983). Governments differ with each other in their diagnosis of what contributes to
the sector's difficulties. Among native peoples there are also differing views because — and this may be the most compelling lesson for
those who seek to understand what might happen if comprehensive
claims settlements are reached — British Columbia's native peoples
have always walked a fine line between the harvesting and preservation of forest resources. The ambivalence was as recognizable in the
apologetic chants of canoe-makers in past times as it is today in the
tensions within bands when some members vie for commercial
timber harvests while others argue on behalf of older values.

In spite of important differences in interpretations, the various
groups agree on the broad categories of issues to be faced. For
purposes of discussion these can be organized in terms of the
economic, political and environmental dimensions of the forestry
and the native claims question.

5.1 Economic Dimensions

The broad category of economic implications of possible comprehensive claims settlements for the forestry sector can be discussed in
terms of three areas of particular concern: access to the resource,
survival of the industry as well as of individual firms, and patterns of
rent collection.

Native-sponsored research into possible new lands for native
forestry has confirmed the sobering conclusion that, in contrast to
the image of vast unspoken-for resource pools, British Columbia's
forest resources are more or less fully allocated. The implication is
that land transfers resulting from possible comprehensive claims
settlements would reduce the accessibility of forest resources for
non-natives, yet native leaders repeatedly deny third parties will be
disadvantaged. Despite such assertions, those third party interests
potentially affected are unconvinced.

In light of the fears among third parties, it is to be expected they
would seek something more binding than "mere rhetoric." As the
data which is recounted in the preceeding pages indicates, it is
possible to discover a number of cases in which the interaction
between natives and non-native logging firms indicates that a basis
for post-settlement economic cooperation and coexistence may
exist. The position of the Kwakiutl District Council in 1986 after
successfully winning an injunction against Deer Island logging is

interesting in this regard. In essence the Kwakiutl made a commitment to find either funds or alternative wood supplies for the logging firm restrained by the injunction.

The initiatives reviewed in this chapter reveal several situations where there are either formal partnerships in development, as with Hecate Logging, or close business ties between native and non-native enterprises. Both Tanizul Timber and the various Nuu-chah-nulth forestry operations involve the exchange of timber and services with non-native interests. The positive impact of the Nuu-chah-nulth activities on merchants of west Vancouver Island also provides evidence an augmented native role can be vital to non-natives. The Nisga'a proposal discussed above envisions at least a transitional period after possible comprehensive claims settlements when impacts of an increased native share on current non-native logging operators could be intentionally controlled to avoid disruption.

It is possible that after comprehensive claims agreements such relationships might sour, with native groups having the resources and additional assets to "go it alone." This is undeniable, but the evidence provided above indicates there is some basis for assuming that it is possible native groups and forestry firms may recognize each other's strengths in a post-settlement situation. The southeast Alaska case tends to corroborate this conclusion. These comments, for example, were made by the general manager of the Alaska Loggers Association:

Standing alone, the loggers, depending on government contracts would have perished if it wasn't for one thing — ANCSA (the *Alaska Native Claims Settlement Act*). Timberlands conveyed to Native Corporations were not subject to primary manufacturing (requirements) and, as such, could export round logs to foreign markets. . . . As this happened, loggers out of work, due to the domestic market slump were hired and absorbed by the Native Corporations to log their lands, for the lucrative export market.[28]

If comprehensive claims settlements are reached in British Columbia, all parties — native and non-native alike — may have to look for ways to support the efforts and meet the aspirations of each other, if economic prosperity for any one group is to be assured. One way in which the "pain" of any transfer of forest resources could be minimized would be to use British Columbia's existing forest tenure policy, even before possible claims settlements, to provide native groups with interim tenure so that they may further explore the benefits of being "Partners in Development".

Even if this is the case, there are still many concerns that non-natives have about the impact of increased native activity in the forest sector as the result of possible claims settlements. As noted, in response to questions from researchers for this investigation, forest executives raised concerns with regard to the capacity of native peoples to compete and survive in an unfriendly economic environment. There is evidence that small native-run businesses have encountered severe difficulties. One result is that some firms are reluctant to enter partnerships with native groups unless they maintain the controlling interest. This runs contrary to the aspirations native groups have to exercise greater control. The result can be a stand-off such as occurred between the Lytton Band and Lytton Lumber.

Some observations arising from the present study could temper pessimism over native capabilities to run or participate in competitive businesses, if claims settlements are obtained. The limited success of native firms must be seen against the background of unfavourable world conditions that have given a great deal of trouble to large companies as well. The fact that any native-operated forest enterprises have survived, notwithstanding the problems in the world economy, their relative inexperience and the fragmented and sometimes previously mismanaged resource base available to them, indicates that the issue is not simply small versus large or native versus non-native expertise in operations. It is one of multilateral relationships within the industry and the possibilities as well as the limitations of world markets. As shown in several cases such as those involving Hecate Logging, Cariboo Indian Enterprises and the Nuu-chah-nulth Tribal Council, the pooling of finances, expertise and resources by native and non-native firms can enhance both parties' chances of success, when economically viable enterprises are available.

There is no doubt that running a modern logging or milling operation does require enormous business and technical acumen. This is appreciated by native groups in light of the difficulties they have experienced in their pioneering initiatives. Consequently there is increased emphasis on hiring and developing expertise in the plans laid out by numerous groups including the Musgamagw, Nuu-chah-nulth and Nisga'a. Professional foresters have been retained and given a priority mandate of training tribal members. Similar developments are taking place in other resource sectors.

The collection and distribution of resource rents is another economic issue in the forest sector. The efficiency and equity of the province's system of collecting resource rents has been the subject of much analysis and debate (Pearse 1976, Marchak 1983, Schwindt 1987). These considerations are beyond the scope of analysis here, particularly since there are no relevant comparisons where native peoples in British Columbia have set their own revenue collection policies. It is clear that a net loss to the provincial government would occur if revenue rights to any significant forest resource base were transferred to native governments or corporations as part of comprehensive claims settlements. It is also clear that native claimants would want such revenue rights.

If this were to happen as a result of claims settlements and the new native "landlords" were to practice what they currently espouse in terms of a commitment to intensive forestry and good environmental practices, there might well be more direct reinvestments of resource rents in forests badly in need of renewal. It cannot be predicted whether this would actually happen with rents or with "back payments" for resources already removed, if settlements provided such benefits for native peoples. Native governments after claims settlements would face a bewildering array of demands for funding. There might be the temptation to extract maximum rents and to invest the revenues elsewhere than in long-term reforestation. There is some suggestion this may have happened in native-managed forests in southeast Alaska. The British Columbia experience is as yet too limited to allow predictions on whether this would happen here.

5.2 Political Dimensions

The recent increase of confrontation over resource use and the trend to link environmentalist and native rights issues easily lead to the belief that after comprehensive claims settlements such strife would be even more rampant. Given the structure of the forest industry and the aspirations of native peoples in British Columbia, it is understandable some level of conflict will continue to characterize the sector, whether or not comprehensive claims settlements are reached. The development of forest resources affects the health and status of most other natural resources. Forestry companies have millions upon millions of dollars invested in British Columbia. The provincial government has well-worked-out methods and systems for forest tenure and management. The province's forest industry is tied into world markets to a very high degree. These facts are not likely to change if comprehensive claims settlements are concluded in the province, nor will the assertions by native peoples of values that are often not as central to forestry development as those emphasizing monetary gain and secure markets. As these trends continue to predominate, so too will possible conflicts over the fate of British Columbia's forests. This is undeniable. This is one side of the story. There is another.

The research for this study indicates that comprehensive claims settlements would not greatly contribute to the likelihood of such conflicts and may even reduce this likelihood. There are both *a priori* and empirical bases for believing this to be a likely outcome. The interruption of logging by some native peoples through blockades and injunctions is largely attributable to the uncertainty regarding the scope and meaning of aboriginal title and rights. If a clear determination of the extent of title and rights were made, it would be less likely that forest companies would find themselves inadvertently operating on land native peoples wish to protect.

A related change tending to reduce the incidence of conflict if comprehensive claims settlements occur concerns the identification of special places. Native organizations and governments have put a high priority upon detailed resource inventories in which places of special cultural, spiritual and ecological value can be specified. Much more of the same could be expected if settlements were reached. If these places and their importance to native groups became better known as a result of post-settlement resource inventories, logging in other parts of the settlement area might proceed with little or no opposition. In such instances one could anticipate that disputes over logging versus other values might become more of an internal matter for bands and tribal councils.

Although it would be naive to suggest conflicts over forestry would disappear if comprehensive claims were settled, there are grounds for arguing that these conflicts would be handled more constructively. To date some native governments, for example, have chosen to deal with resource conflicts in a number of constructive and conciliatory ways. Several, such as the Musgamagw Tribal Council, have formally initiated integrated resource management projects. In a few instances native groups have played a mediative role. The example of the T/F/W Agreement in Washington State illustrates the kind of negotiated approach that could become possible if native rights are recognized in British Columbia within the context of comprehensive claims settlements.

5.3 Environmental Dimensions

As in the fishery sector, everyone in forestry readily agrees a strong priority must be placed on enhancing and restoring the province's timberlands. Analyses conducted for native peoples such as the Nisga'a and Nuu-chah-nulth have been harshly critical of past management practices both by the province off-reserve and the federal government on-reserve. Recently both the provincial and federal governments have recognized the onset of a potentially disasterous shortage of high-grade, accessible timber. They have begun to plan and provide funding for renewal.[29] How would potential comprehensive claims settlements affect these efforts to protect and enhance the health of the forest resource of British Columbia?

For many years the assumption was that significant investment of monies in forest management would be forthcoming only from larger companies with the commitment and ability to carry out forest renewal. The Canada-British Columbia Forest Resources Development Agreement (FRDA) is the most recent embodiment of a shift toward an alternative model of forest use and management which is labour rather than capital intensive. Indeed, a secondary justification of the benefits of the FRDA has been that the approach will permit more participation in the sector for small communities and native peoples. This approach is similar to that advocated by native peoples in several of the initiatives reviewed in this chapter. Intensive forest management is the recommended central strategy in the Nisga'a, Nuu-chah-nulth and Musgamagw projects. Its potential employment benefits are widely recognized by the management of small native enterprises such as Hecate Logging and Tanizul Timber. Not surprisingly there has been a strong positive response to the request for proposals under FRDA's Indian Forest Lands Program.

Provided that the funding is available, there is good reason to expect that forest renewal will be a priority after claims settlements because it can generate employment and because of the simple fact that native peoples do not generally have the opportunity to relocate their forest operations if mismanagement destroys the resource base. It could be argued that under certain incentive structures the pressures of "staying afloat" in the highly competitive corporate world of forestry may lead natives to activities that are no different from what some see as the worst kind of logging practices. There is little evidence that such a development might take place in British Columbia. There is a great deal of evidence that efforts to enhance and renew the forest resource might be intensified if comprehensive claims settlements were to take place in the province.

5
Non-Renewable Resources in British Columbia

1. Non-renewable Resources in British Columbia

British Columbia's non-renewable resource endowment and its use have been a major influence on the province's history and human geography.* Mining, particularly the gold rushes which swept through different areas of the province from the mid-to late-nineteenth century, catalysed the transition from fur trading to permanent settlement. Today, only forestry stands ahead of the non-renewable resource sector among the natural resource sectors of the British Columbia economy in aggregate economic impact.

The original peoples of the lands that became British Columbia had used non-renewable resources prior to contact. Nevertheless, the large-scale extraction of gold and other metals or the use of non-renewable fuels was not a large part of their culture. In contrast British Columbia native peoples have harvested fish and cut trees for economic and ceremonial purposes for centuries. Today, activity in these sectors has obviously changed but there is no major discontinuity in the uses made of fish and forests. This has not been the case in the non-renewable resources sector; native participation in this sector is both limited and without long precedent. This makes it more difficult to picture how this sector may be affected by comprehensive claims settlements. There are experiences, however, both in British Columbia and elsewhere which give a foretaste of possible patterns of non-renewable resource development, if comprehensive claims settlements were to be reached.

All natural resources share certain characteristics as far as their development and governance is concerned. At one level or another, they are scarce: sustainability is always an issue. They are all affected by market forces and former patterns of interaction in relation to development and governance. Non-renewable resources are no different in these respects from any other resources, but what is true about the development of natural resources in general is especially true about the development of non-renewable resources. These

---

* The term "non-renewable resources" is used in this chapter to include both fuel and mineral resources, that is, all inorganic, naturally occurring resources other than groundwater which can be recovered from the earth.

resources present great opportunities and their development also faces extensive constraints. Non-renewable resource development is often conducted on a large, and sometimes on a very large, scale. Much technical and financial capacity is needed. Given these characteristics, great certainty is also needed, yet other considerations make such certainty fragile. This is particularly the case in British Columbia at the present time.

Non-renewable resource development in the province, especially when it takes place in circumstances which touch upon native land and resource holdings or land and resources which are subject to native claims, raises many questions. Jurisdictional aspects are unclear, as is the authority of various groups, particularly that of native governments. The industry is, at best, hesitant about regulation, but other concerned parties frequently call for increased regulatory activity.

The comprehensive claims question presents further constraints as it heightens concerns about jurisdiction, regulation, consistency, technical and financial capacities as well as other issues. The resolution of comprehensive claims could reduce or augment these concerns. In this chapter, the grounds for this uncertainty will be explored. In addition, several cases will be discussed which will throw greater light on the possibilities and the opportunities as well as the constraints non-renewable resource development and management could face if comprehensive claims settlements were concluded in the province.

2. Native Peoples and Non-renewable Resources

Even though the native experience with the use of non-renewable resources in the province before recorded history was far more limited than with the fishery and forestry, these resources were used in many ways. Drucker (1963), for example, reports evidence of the prehistoric use of slate knives and the use of small quantities of iron in daggers, knives and chisels. There is no documentation of extractive mining prior to European contact, but the north coast natives hammered placer copper into large plaques called "coppers" and these were very important for ceremonial purposes.

When non-natives arrived, it did not take long for these circumstances to change. Coal was discovered near Fort Rupert on Vancouver Island in the 1830s and developers involved a native group in the extraction of non-renewable resources for perhaps the first time in what would become British Columbia. In this case the Kwakiutl retained control of surface coal extraction until Scottish miners were brought in to open underground workings in 1849:

The Kwakiutl who had never mined coal or even used it except occasionally as a pigment, very quickly saw the economic possibilities of such an enterprise for the group who controlled it. Finlayson writes: "They informed us that they would not permit us to work the coals as they were valuable to them, but they would labour in the mines themselves and sell us the produce of their exertions..." The Kwakiutl were determined to have the profits from the mines for themselves.[1]

During the Fraser River gold rush, natives unsuccessfully attempted to retain control of the gold that came from their territory. Fisher (1977) cites newspaper reports of natives trying to halt the progression of miners up the rivers and "attempting to impose taxes on those working ground claimed by the Indians."[2] Interracial tension grew due not only to intrusions into native land holdings such as village sites, fishing stations and cultivated areas, but also to the large numbers of mutally-antagonistic miners and natives working on the gold bars in close proximity: "One witness said that there were from sixty to seventy Europeans working alongside four or five hundred Indians at Hills' Bar alone in the summer of 1858."[3]

Over the next several decades native peoples persisted in their participation in placer mining in the interior of the province. Whenever gold discoveries occurred near their settlements, natives were certain to join in the quest. By the beginning of the twentieth century the mineral sector of the British Columbia economy was increasingly dominated by hard-rock subsurface mines. Individual natives joined in prospecting but the extent of their participation as hard rock miners has not been documented.

Elsewhere in Canada, the advent of major oil and natural gas finds on or near Indian reserves has led to significant native involvement. Bands in Alberta, Saskatchewan and more recently the Northwest Territories have responded both as economic participants and as political actors in decision making. In British Columbia there has been much less participation in non-renewable resource development with some notable exceptions such as the Fort Nelson Band whose experience is described below.

Until quite recently the most visible native involvement in non-renewable resource development in the province often has been in the form of opposition to particular developments. All of the major coastal claimant groups in British Columbia, for example, opposed the lifting of a moratorium on offshore petroleum development during hearings in 1985. Yet, even in this resource sector, one that lacks a long history of intense native activity, there is evidence that unequivocal opposition to development may not be the way of the future after comprehensive claims settlements.

3. Roles and Concerns

3.1 The Jurisdictional Situation

To understand the roles and perspectives of the various concerned parties in the non-renewable resources sector an overview of the current legal and constitutional framework is necessary. This overview is divided into discussions of the differing onshore and offshore regimes because of important distinctions between the two. As will be seen, the jurisdictional situation is complex and somewhat unsettled and, as such, provides considerable constraints for many groups in the development of the resource and the resolution of the comprehensive claims issue.

3.1.1 The Onshore Framework

In the terrestrial areas of British Columbia the jurisdictional position for non-renewable resource development is relatively straightforward. This is especially so because the province has, in general, followed a policy of retaining ownership of all non-renewable resources, granting only restricted rights to developers.[4] Apart from those limited lands and resources which have been alienated by the Crown and those lands to which title is held by the federal government (such as airports, military reserves, public harbours and Indian reserves), the provincial government's authority is based upon its proprietary position and its legislative jurisdiction.

Section 109 of the *Constitution Act, 1867* coupled with the British Columbia Terms of Union of 1871 confirms provincial ownership of public lands and resources. Section 92(5) of the *Constitution Act, 1867* provides the provinces with exclusive legislative jurisdiction over "the management and sale of public lands" and the new section 92A of the *Constitution Act, 1982* expands that jurisdiction. On provincial Crown lands, non-renewable resources are disposed of according to particular provincial statutes including the *Petroleum and Natural Gas Act*, the *Mineral Act*, the *Mining (Placer) Act*, and the *Coal Act*.[5] The implications for the comprehensive claims question are clear: the province will have to play some kind of role in negotiations and settlements if the use and management of onshore non-renewable resources is to be addressed.

More directly relevant to this study is the regime which currently applies on Indian reserves in the province. This regime is largely governed by the federal-provincial *British Columbia Indian Reserves Mineral Resources Agreement* of 1943. This Agreement was developed by the two governments as a means of resolving the question of mineral entitlements on reserves. The preamble to the agreement asserts that precious metals underlying reserves "belong beneficially to the Crown in the right of British Columbia." This, the preamble continues, creates an impossible situation for mining because of the close association of many deposits on and off Indian reserves. As a result, according to the agreement, the province is given charge of the development of all minerals on reserves, the term "mineral" being defined so as not to include coal, petroleum, natural gas or construction materials.

As a result of the 1943 Agreement, provincial administration is achieved by applying provincial mineral legislation to reserves provided that the base mineral interest is surrendered to the Crown in accordance with the *Indian Act* and provided that permission to enter or prospect is obtained from the Indian Agent. As well as applying provincial laws to reserves, the province retains 50 percent of any revenues received from the disposition of minerals. The remaining 50 percent is to be paid to the federal government in trust for the band concerned.

Problems have arisen between bands and the provincial government because of the use of the term "revenues" in the Agreement. The province takes the view that this includes rents, royalties and fees but not mineral taxes, thus the amount of revenues accruing to bands as the result of resource development on reserve lands would be sharply reduced. In these circumstances British Columbia bands have been reluctant to develop mineral resources on reserve. Recently, a process to amend the Agreement has been undertaken. This process is discussed later in the chapter. Because of disputes stemming from and surrounding the Agreement, there has been a significant lack of development of many non-renewable resources on reserve lands.

3.1.2 The Offshore Framework

In the offshore areas the main non-renewable resources of interest are oil and gas but offshore metal deposits also are involved. In some cases coastal native governments have made comprehensive claims which extend to the offshore and offshore resources. The federal government has agreed to negotiate offshore claims in its latest policy statement on the claims process.[6] There is nothing in principle to preclude an aboriginal title in the offshore although matters are undoubtedly more complex for the federal government because of its responsibilities under international law, for example.

With regard to offshore non-renewable resources the greatest difficulty lies in deciding where the province ends, since in the non-marine areas of the province provincial minerals legislation applies. Beyond this the applicable federal legislation is the *Canada Petroleum Resources Act.* Two decisions of the Supreme Court of Canada are important in considering the limits of provincial jurisdiction and the basis for federal jurisdiction: the *Offshore Minerals Reference* and the *Strait of Georgia Reference.*[7]

In the *Offshore Minerals Reference* the Supreme Court was asked to decide whether Canada or British Columbia has property in, rights to explore and exploit, and legislative jurisdiction with respect to the territorial sea and the continental shelf. The Court was unanimously of the view that, with respect to all these questions, Canada holds the rights. This was mainly because, at the relevant time (1871, when British Columbia entered Confederation), the continental shelf doctrine had not yet arisen and the territorial sea was considered to lie beyond the realm and therefore beyond the colony.

The *Offshore Mineral Reference* disposed of the federal-provincial jurisdictional issue for the territorial sea and the continental shelf but it did not determine where the territorial sea begins. The *Strait of Georgia Reference* confirmed that there are significant marine areas between the territorial sea and the land mass of the province and that these areas might belong to the province for two reasons. First, they might be inland waters as a matter of common law. In common law, inland waters include waters such as bays, estuaries, harbours and all waters *inter fauces terrae*, that is, waters "between the jaws of the land." Second they might be "inland" under the constitutive statutes of the province.

The particular issue in the *Strait of Georgia Reference* related to the lands beneath the straits of Juan de Fuca, Georgia, Johnstone and Queen Charlotte. The court found that the waters in question were annexed to the colony of British Columbia by imperial statute and that the colony brought these waters into the union with the colony of Vancouver Island in 1866 and thence into the union with Canada in 1871. This reasoning may be applicable to Hecate Strait. Whether it is or not, it should be apparent that other waters on the indented British Columbia coast may well qualify as provincial waters using a common law argument.

At the present time, the federal and provincial governments are negotiating an accord on offshore resource revenue sharing and management. The agreement may well be modelled upon the Nova Scotia and Atlantic accords and could apply to all offshore areas providing for one set of offshore resource legislation. For over a decade both governments had imposed a moratorium on offshore oil and gas exploration. Following the report of a joint environmental review, the moratorium was lifted in the late spring of 1987. Until an agreement is worked out, federal oil and gas and mining legislation will apply to the bulk of the offshore with provincial legislation applying to areas such as the Strait of Georgia.

In general, the jurisdictional situation regarding offshore non-renewable resources is full of uncertainties. This situation presents special constraints for those who attempt to clarify the possible consequences of comprehensive claims.

3.2 The Federal Government Perspective

The federal government can influence non-renewable resource development indirectly in the province through the government's powers of direct and indirect taxation and the power to regulate trade and commerce.[8] The federal government also influences this development through the fisheries-related powers noted in Chapter Three, the *Transportation of Dangerous Goods Act*, and more directly, through relations pursuant to section 9 of the *Atomic Energy Control Act*.

The most direct federal role in mining in British Columbia is on Indian reserves and federal Crown lands. As noted above, the federal-provincial *British Columbia Indian Reserves Mineral Resources Agreement* has governed the use and administration of reserve-based minerals except petroleum and natural gas, coal and various non-metallic resources since 1943. While the Agreement confirmed the applicability of provincial mining laws and regulations, it also provided the federal government's Indian Agent with a veto over development. Since the federal government sees the province's regime for capturing mineral resource rents as unlikely to benefit Indians, it has not supported development on British Columbia reserves (Dombroski 1985). Recent efforts to re-negotiate the 1943 Agreement reflect a major attempt on the part of INAC to assure substantial revenues for the benefit of natives from reserve lands.

Interviews by project researchers with Department of Indian and Northern Affairs Canada (INAC) officials revealed several areas of concern over future arrangements for non-renewable resource de-

135

velopment affecting native peoples. One theme was that any new arrangements for resource development should reflect an awareness that ore bodies do not respect reserve (i.e. political) boundaries. INAC would prefer to see an emphasis placed upon joint ventures between natives and industry which extend beyond boundaries. Joint ventures are seen as spreading the risk and allowing for a broader capture of the benefits of mineral development. There is also a concern for the needs of industry, regulatory consistency and a comprehensive and consistent system of taxation, royalty and administrative structures. All of these matters would have to be addressed if comprehensive claims settlements were reached in the province.

Energy, Mines and Resources, Canada (EMR) has very general concerns about non-fuel minerals in the offshore. A regulatory regime for those minerals is just beginning to take shape and EMR's intent is to involve as many interests, including the provincial government, as possible. The Canadian Oil and Gas Lands Administration (COGLA) administers the *Canadian Petroleum Resources Act*. COGLA anticipates a "Pacific Accord" with the resources managed jointly through a provincially and federally appointed board. How native interests would be included is unclear.

The concerns expressed by federal departments must be viewed in the light of the December 1986 INAC policy statement on comprehensive claims. This statement expressed the intent of enhancing the participation of native peoples in the development of non-renewable resources. It included the possibility of a native government receiving a percentage of the Crown's royalties derived from the extraction of non-renewable resources both on and offshore. The new INAC comprehensive claims policy anticipates that claims settlements could include native participation in environmental management, but these provisions do not imply resource ownership "... and will not result in the establishment of joint management boards to manage subsurface and sub-sea resources."[9] The risk which many people perceive is that such boards may create a balkanized regime for environmental and safety standards, employment and other issues.

3.3 The Provincial Government Perspective

As outlined in Chapter One, the province has consistently maintained that aboriginal title was extinguished before union with Canada or that extinguishment is strictly a federal responsibility. In either case, it does not view the use, management or the derivation of revenues from non-renewable resources as subject to native rights. Against the background of this formal stance, the province has played a role in reaching agreements on various issues in this field. Several instances are noted below.

Beyond the obvious "pocketbook" impact of losing mineral revenues if a comprehensive claims settlement were reached, there are several areas of concern for the provincial government. In fact, revenue loss may be seen as one of the less intractable problems. Past agreements concerning native peoples and non-renewable resources, both in the case of the Fort Nelson band with natural gas and petroleum (see below) and in the case of the 1943 Agreement for reserve lands, have resulted in revenue sharing arrangements. Regulatory authority, however, has remained with the provincial government. There are concerns on the part of the provincial government that more fundamental changes in the management regime and policy could drive away resource industries.

Specifically, as far as metals and coal are concerned, provincial regulators are worried about access to the mineral estate. Exploration must precede development and is very much an access-related activity. About ten percent of British Columbia is currently under intense mineral exploration. Provincial officials worry that a compensation system for mineral claim holders induced by a comprehensive claims settlement could be difficult to establish and expensive.

Also of concern to the province is the impact of comprehensive claims settlements on administration and title structure. Provincial regulators perceive administration to be most straightforward if full authority continues to rest with the province. In their view, the "worst case" would be for each native government which might agree to a comprehensive claims settlement to develop its own regulations and title system. Title structure, they argue, can have a significant impact on both the access to and the control of development. According to provincial officials joint or tiered title is particulary problematic. They fear that exploration would halt if non-natives were unable to stake claims and develop resources within a clear, unified regulatory system. They have particular concerns arising about the province's mine development process. Provincial regulators feel a great deal of time and effort has gone into creating the present provincial mine development review process and this effort would be wasted by the creation of a large number of tribal review procedures through comprehensive claims agreements.

For large projects provincial regulators worry that comprehensive claims settlements would cause greater uncertainty than now is

137

the case, that new regulatory systems would raise the cost of doing business, and that the resulting delays would deter development and investment. At the same time, officials interviewed for this study from the provincial Ministry of Energy, Mines and Petroleum Resources are positive about agreements between natives and industry which might fall within the framework of the provincial regulatory system. The agreement between Dome and the Lax Kw'alaams Band discussed below is an example cited by provincial officials as evidence of the potential for cooperative development involving native peoples and large non-renewable resource development companies.

Provincial petroleum regulators predict that the overall result of comprehensive claims settlements may be a slower pace of development resulting from a possible shift to a greater multinational involvement. In particular, they argue that the British Columbia petroleum sector currently involves many small companies who would not have the staff, technical expertise or the financial resources to address another layer of regulation.

These potential problems are perceived by some provincial officials to flow partially from the kind of native regulatory power and structures which might be created as the result of comprehensive claims settlements. Joint managment regimes, especially if they have to accomodate somewhat autonomous native governments, are not looked upon with favour by the provincial regulatory officials interviewed for this study. Nevertheless, the province does have a policy commitment to consult with native governments, and this has been evident in its recent support for direct communications between the industrial firms which undertake fuels and minerals development and the various bands. They maintain that the negotiation processes should not delay development and that public safety and the environment must be protected.

3.4 Native Perspectives

Natives do not speak with one voice any more than other parties concerned with non-renewable resource development, but, if their concerns could be expressed by one word, that word would be "control." Native peoples want control over non-renewable resource management. They see control as direct decision making about development and management and not as the indirect giving of advice to other decision-makers. In the words of Wedliedi Speck of the Kwakiutl District Council:

138

...the co-management that we are talking about is not...an advisory capacity...co-management to us is the recognition of sovereignty, is that when we sit around the table, we sit down as equals.[10]

This is not just a Kwakuitl view. The Tahltan, whose claim area includes part of mineral-rich northwestern British Columbia, are not prepared to continue to feel the helplessness of "outsider status."[11] Testimony by many native peoples at the 1985 provincial-federal hearings on offshore hydrocarbon exploration also reflected such feelings.

Native peoples in British Columbia express concerns about dangers to their way of life as well as a lack of power over non-renewable resource development. Fears of environmental damage from non-renewable resource development to the renewable resources which are the cornerstone of native traditions are, many native peoples assert, grounded in experience. The Haisla at Kitamaat, for example, say that their food source was the price they paid for the aluminium smelter at Kitimat. Effluent in the river from the smelter prevents harvest.[12] They have lost their salmon, they argue, and they must fight to save the Kemano oolichan, one of the last reliable oolichan sources in the Pacific northwest.

Underlying these feelings of powerlessness and loss is the stewardship relationship many native peoples feel they have with the environment. Several native leaders in interviews for this study emphasized the point that the difference between native peoples and non-renewable resource companies is that natives must live in the country after development. Tahltan people told project researchers that their belief in reincarnation means they will always be in the territory. Lack of stewardship today, they insisted, will literally come back to haunt them in the future.

Several other themes arise as native perspectives on non-renewable resource development are reviewed. One theme is that disaffection is not about non-renewable resource development *per se*, but about the processes surrounding such development, processes from which they feel they have been excluded. Another theme is that native peoples want broad benefits from economic development. They want to negotiate participation in all phases of resource development. Jobs, they feel, are not enough:

They won't be able to pacify us with twelve jobs. We want a change in all economic possibilities, not just training and development, but joint venture, equity participation...[13]

We will no longer be excluded from the political and economic life of this area. We want a say in the administration and planning of our joint futures, and we want to share in the proceeds of development.[14]

From the native viewpoint a non-renewable resource development project should not be assessed in isolation, but rather, it should be assessed according to its potential place in a native economic system which attaches more than a monetary value to renewable resources. Because of their ties to the territory and their salient responsibility to future generations, native peoples express an unwillingness to rely upon a single resource. They are especially leery of negative and irreversible impacts resulting from development. This attitude led to strong opposition by all coastal native groups towards the lifting of the moratorium on offshore petroleum exploration. At the 1985 hearings of the West Coast Offshore Exploration Environmental Assessment Panel, groups such as the Nuu-chah-nulth, Nisga'a, Kwakiutl and the Offshore Alliance of Aboriginal Nations repeated the same major concern: If risks to the marine environment can not be fully assessed, development should not proceed. Such outright native opposition usually occurs when they perceive that renewable resources are threatened by non-renewable resource developments.

3.5 Third Party Perspectives

In the non-renewable resources sector, the key third party interests are the industrial firms who undertake development. The private sector includes a great diversity of groups ranging in size from small exploration firms to the world's largest corporations. In addition to a variety of perspectives caused by size differences, there are variations which exist between developers in the major subsectors — the hardrock mining companies, the coal industry and the petroleum operators. Despite these differences there are cross-cutting themes which emerged in discussions for this study with representatives from firms in all of these categories. These revolve around:

1. uncertainty created by unresolved native claims;
2. predictions of balkanization and inconsistency in post-settlement regulation;
3. fears that claims will be settled "on the backs of the industry," i.e., that little or no compensation will be forthcoming from governments who transfer lands and resource entitlements to native claimants;
4. concerns that major existing or prospective mineral-rich areas will be permanently exempted from development after claims settlements;
5. apprehensions about the preparedness of native groups and individuals to participate in mineral resource development in spite of claimants' frequently expressed aims to do so.

The point made in Chapter Two that uncertainties regarding the ownership and management rights over resources are potentially discouraging to investors needs be re-emphasized in this context in particular. There are several major developments and exploration areas under consideration in British Columbia, including the Mount Klappan coal mines and several other large metallic mineral proposals in the northwestern region of the province. Industry representatives believe that unresolved aboriginal title could jeopardize investment in these activities. Counterbalancing these views, some oil and gas industry representatives contacted for this study noted that comprehensive claims settlements elsewhere — the western Arctic being a good example — have actually reduced uncertainty and its attendant costs. They see post-settlement resource regimes in British Columbia as having, at least potentially, similar advantages for industry, if they are compared to the regimes which characterize current situations.

The second theme voiced by industry representatives is based upon their belief that, after comprehensive claims settlements, resource development regulations might be too variable. They fear many small and different regulatory and taxation regimes which change at brief and irregular intervals. One spokesman from the petroleum subsector, for example, pointed out that rigs sometimes move around frequently and that it would be difficult and costly to adjust operating procedures almost every month to suit different native regulatory regimes.

The idea that comprehensive claims would be settled "on the backs of the industry" — a third theme — has been raised frequently by non-renewable resource developers both in discussions for this study and elsewhere.[15] The industry is concerned about inadequate levels of compensation which might accompany a politically-driven resolution of comprehensive claims.

Industry representatives fear that major areas might be withdrawn from any future production if comprehensive claims settlements were reached, because natives would see the land and resources as "sacred." The northern Australian situation is often cited. Industry representatives contend that new mineral exploration in that region has ceased, allegedly as a result of a newly-acquired aboriginal voice in decision making.[16] Most non-renewable resource developers acknowledge that native communities ought to be consulted to ensure protection of their lifestyles as well as fish and wildlife resources. Yet they worry that too much authority will be ceded by governments in comprehensive claims settlements and that development of valuable deposits of non-renewable resources will be vetoed.

141

The final theme which industry representatives express concerns the issue of the ability of native peoples to be full participants in the development process in a post-settlement regime. Many native groups seek guarantees of employment for their people and, in some cases, participation in business decisions for non-renewable resource developments. The question raised by some industrial developers concerns whether the training and education of native technical crews and managers would be adequate. To ensure that it is some mineral firms in other jurisdictions have initiated programs to enhance native participation. The Alberta based NOVA Corporation has been involved in several such efforts, for example.[17]

What do the current and emerging experiences of native involvement in non-renewable resource development both in British Columbia and elsewhere have to say regarding the concerns raised by industry as well as those of governments and native peoples themselves? Are these concerns indicators of permanent constraints on development opportunities? Or are they indicative of the mutual fears and ambiguities that have arisen because of uncertainties about jurisdiction and the dynamics of resource development in the absence of comprehensive claims settlements? And, as such, are these concerns a preface to significant efforts by the concerned parties to take advantage of non-renewable resource development opportunities? The following section provides relevant information and perhaps some tentative answers to these questions.

4. Current and Emerging Initiatives

As noted many times in this book, there are complex relationships concerning natural resource use and management emerging in the comprehensive claims question. Quite often groups — native and non-native — maintain formal positions that indicate one stance and, at the same time, engage in working relationships which indicate others.

Perhaps the most visible native stance in relation to non-renewable resource development can be seen in the reactions that arose in connection with two major marine inquiries over the past decade, those of the West Coast Oil Ports Inquiry and the West Coast Offshore Exploration Environmental Assessment Panel. In both cases, a selective or superficial reading of the many native briefs and submissions could give the impression that native peoples are irrevocably opposed to major projects based upon non-renewable resource development. To give one example, the language used by a native leader voicing misgivings over an oil tanker port in northern British Columbia was strong and uncompromising:

I want to mention here, I want to declare here, that the Indian people are the owners and have jurisdiction over marine resources on the west coast and, hence, claim our rights to manage, control and protect these and other resources from supertankers. Supertankers on our west Pacific coast is a sinister evil that has the potential of destroying our marine resources.[18]

At the hearings concerning offshore oil development every native organization advocated the retention of the moratorium that had been placed a decade earlier on any petroluem exploration.

It is easy to assume that this clearly indicates how native groups might be disposed towards non-renewable resource development if comprehensive claims settlements are reached. This conclusion is seriously misleading, for the fears that native peoples have vis-à-vis non-renewable resource projects are inextricably tied to the unresolved question of aboriginal title to lands and marine areas. The connection between the native opposition to offshore development and the lack of comprehensive claims settlements was brought up repeatedly at the panel hearings in 1985.

A range of current and emerging cases involving native peoples in non-renewable resource development and management are reviewed in the following pages. In these instances native involvement has been more tangible than the testimony in the inquiries into offshore petroleum transportation and exploration. As in previous chapters the cases are grouped under the three scenarios developed in Chapter Two. There is a dearth of examples in British Columbia of direct native participation in the management and/or development of mineral resources, but there are very relevant experiences elsewhere and these are included here.

4.1 Partners in Development

The "Partners in Development" scenario posits a future in which native governments primarily focus on deriving direct economic benefits from resources. The first case described in this section, revenue sharing at Fort Nelson, is quite clearly a current example of this kind. In this instance, the province, the band and the federal government were able to come to terms on the allocation of resource rents after years of acrimony. The other case discussed here involves a negotiated settlement between Chevron Canada Resources Limited and the community of Fort Good Hope. This agreement is viewed by many in the oil and natural gas sub-sector as an encouraging example of the kinds of economic arrangements possible when native communities and non-renewable resource developers have the opportunity and the incentives to plan cooperatively.

4.1.1 Revenue Sharing at Fort Nelson

One of the best known cases where a native group has participated in development exclusively in terms of deriving revenues is in the Fort Nelson area of northeastern British Columbia. In 1980 decades of controversy involving natural gas development on Fort Nelson Band reserves ended with an agreement on revenue sharing. A review of the case provides some sense of the opportunities and issues arising from this kind of arrangement.

Members of the Fort Nelson Band belong to the Slave tribe, signatories to Treaty 8. This 1899 treaty covers a vast area extending into the Northwest Territories, Alberta and Saskatchewan. The members of the Fort Nelson Band signed the treaty in 1915 but many years passed before the band's reserves were established in accordance with the treaty. By the early 1950s when band leaders began to push hard for the selection of reserves, the provincial government had already allowed petroleum exploration in the area and had given several companies permits for development. When the federal government asked British Columbia to make land available for the Fort Nelson Indian Band, there was opposition to the request and especially to any cession of mineral rights. Ultimately, the province acceded to the land transfer in 1961 but only in respect of surface ownership. The province continued to hold all mineral rights. The band agreed to the arrangement under protest and without prejudice to the prerogative to pursue a mineral claim.

In 1965 natural gas began to flow from fields within reserve lands. The Fort Nelson Band sought legal opinion and assistance from the federal government and the Union of B.C. Indian Chiefs but was advised that its case was not a strong one. On several occasions the band used blockades to bring the issue to the attention of resource developers, the province and the public. As a result of a blockade in 1971, petroleum companies agreed to pay some royalties directly to the band and these funds were used to prepare for an anticipated legal battle. In 1975 the band retained new legal counsel to seek a settlement — in or out of court. The province and the band subsequently began what was to be five years of negotiations culminating in an agreement in 1980. Federal approval of the arrangement was secured through the *Fort Nelson Indian Reserve Minerals Revenue Sharing Act* (SC 1980-81-82, c.38).

The terms of the 1980 agreement foreshadow the arrangements pictured in the "Partners in Development" scenario. Revenues are to be shared equally between Canada, on behalf of the band, and the province. These include monies from natural gas as well as from coal, petroleum and other minerals. The agreement, however, did not change the nature of proprietary and administrative rights: "The ownership, administration, control and power of disposition of coal, petroleum and natural gas underlying the Reserve are vested in the Province and all claims and rights thereto shall be subject to the laws of the Province..." [section (6)(1)]. There are no provisions granting the band any say whatsoever about the pace of development or the control of environmental or social impacts.

The band's involvement is strictly financial. The sums involved were very substantial since the agreement was retroactive to the beginning of gas production in the 1960s. Every band member, adult or child, received an immediate cash payment of $20,000. In 1980 the anticipated total revenues going to the band over the twenty-year production period was in the order of $120 million. This estimate has been reduced to $40 million in light of the reduced prices and rates of production recently besetting the oil and gas sub-sector.[19]

The consequences of this agreement other than the immediate and substantial prosperity enjoyed by band members are diverse. As noted, the total flow of revenues has not been as great as expected because of the reduced demand and prices for natural gas. By March 1987 the band had received revenues totalling approximately $33 million. Disposition of these funds has been varied. About 40 percent of the band's current assets are in interest-bearing accounts while 60 percent are in relatively conservative investments, or what has been described as "raw land and raw vegetables" including tracts elsewhere in the province as well as in the Fort Nelson area.[20] The band has set up Eh-Cho-Déné Enterprises, a contracting firm specializing in oil field facilities and land development. The band has also entered a partnership with the Westbank band in the Okanagan to construct and operate tourist-oriented facilities near Kelowna. In short, a diverse portfolio has been developed by the Fort Nelson Band. Social and community expenditures have also occurred including monies for housing, roads, power and water.

The band administration operates with an annual budget of about $1.5 million. It employs 45 people including six non-natives. Relationships with the non-native operators of the Fort Nelson gas fields have been cooperative. Non-natives of the area cited the on-reserve development (and thus indirectly the mineral revenue sharing agreement) as a source of spin-off benefits to the wider community during the recent downturn in oil and gas markets.

The political and jurisdictional implications of the Fort Nelson arrangement were a source of considerable controversy when the enabling legislation was reviewed by the Parliamentary Standing Committee on Indian Affairs and Northern Development.[21] Both the National Indian Brotherhood and the Union of B.C. Indian Chiefs testified against the agreement. Their opposition was based on the belief that a dangerous precedent was being established, a process whereby the provincial government could, in effect, "buy off" bands and the government of Canada. As the National Indian Brotherhood observed:

In effect, the Band and Canada are surrendering the claim to these minerals . . . and the province is prepared to pay a very substantial amount to obtain an unfettered title to the land and the minerals . . . Were I a provincial attorney-general reading this bill, I would learn from it that I could exploit minerals on an Indian reserve as I saw fit, negotiate when I saw fit, and purchase the right to the minerals long after I had sold them "just in case" they belonged to the band.[22]

Another objection concerned the negligible role of the band in decision making about the resource and the implementation of the arrangement. The agreement was not technically between the band and the province but between the government of Canada and the province. This was the case despite the fact that the Fort Nelson band had actually been a full participant in the negotiations. Noel Starblanket of the National Indian Brotherhood objected to the absence of a decision-making role for the band noting that, while the federal government is the trustee of native interests, native people are not in a position to challenge legally their trustee's performance.[23] He and others were concerned that the Fort Nelson agreement would be seen as a model for the resolution of other resource allocation controversies involving native groups and federal and provincial governments. Ultimately a clause was added to the enabling legislation to restrict its applicability to the Fort Nelson Band without prejudice to future settlements, but concerns about the kind of arrangements which characterize this case of economic partnership remain.

146

4.1.2 The Chevron/Fort Good Hope Agreement

A second and more recent case which provides an indication that "Partners in Development" type arrangements could emerge in this sector involves a negotiated settlement outside of British Columbia. In June 1987 Chevron Canada Resouces Limited of Calgary (hereafter, Chevron) and the community of Fort Good Hope, a Déné-Métis community in the Northwest Territories, negotiated a joint venture agreement for oil and gas exploration on a 405,000 hectare block of lands adjacent to the community. The circumstances of the agreement are somewhat unusual but they merit attenton as an example of a cooperative, community-oriented approach to the business of oil and gas development. While the agreement once again deals primarily with enhancing native economic participation, the community role is more diversified than in the Fort Nelson case.

As a result of the Berger inquiry into the construction of a northern pipeline, the lands around Fort Good Hope were withdrawn by the federal government from disposition under the prevailing oil and gas legislation. The lands have scarcely been explored but there has been some speculation that they may prove to have a geology similar to that of the adjacent, productive Norman Wells field. The considerable amount of interest in these particular lands resulted in an attempt by British Petroleum Limited (BP) to get the lands out from the freeze. To further its chances BP opened negotiations with the community believing that, if it had the community's consent, the order-in-council preventing disposition would be relaxed. By the summer of 1985 a deal had been worked out by the two parties.

At the time, others in the industry were critical of the deal. They believed it set a dangerous precedent and could result in inflated expectations by other native groups. They also objected to the method by which BP proposed to consumate the deal. For, having come to an arrangement with the band, BP believed that it ought to be able to obtain direct issuance of the petroleum rights in question from the federal government. Direct issuance would have allowed the Minister of INAC to grant an exploration agreement under the *Canada Oil and Gas Act* without putting the lands up to bids from all interested parties in the petroleum industry. Although this was permitted under the *Act* at the time, it was viewed as an exceptional measure not to be used to contravene the free market.

As a result of industry opposition, the Minister eventually decided that the lands should be put up for bid in 1985. Several companies submitted bids including Chevron and a BP-community joint venture. In the end the successful bidder was Chevron. The key feature of the community benefits part of Chevron's bid was an offer to assist the community in establishing a gravity and seismic company which would be given the contract for that portion of the work. Having been selected, Chevron then had to enter into negotiations with the community and, as a result, the scope of the proposed benefits was broadened dramatically, most importantly by the development of an equity participation proposal. An agreement was ultimately finalized in June 1987 after lengthy negotiations funded by Chevron and the federal government.

This agreement provides that the community will have the right to acquire a 20 percent interest in any production licences. The first 10 percent will be available on a very favourable basis since the cost will be fixed on the basis of prior investment costs. The second 10 percent is based on the value of the lands and facilities. In both cases the acquisition will be paid for from a portion of production revenues. The government gives the community an important say in the project management through an Operating Management Committee and various sub-committees. There is equal representation on all committees. Deadlocks are resolved by arbitration. The agreement continues to provide for a community seismic company getting all seismic-related contracts. All other contracts go though an Education, Training and Business Development Sub-committee and have to be issued on a competitive basis, but with a community, northern and then Canadian order of preference.

The agreement is seen by Chevron as a joint-venture agreement, separate and apart from the exploration agreement issued by the government. Although the government was kept informed, it had no formal role to play in the negotiations, and, at the time of writing, had yet to issue the formal exploration agreement or exploration licence.

On the face of it, the community obtained a favourable arrangement with Chevron, although some band members believe it to be less so than the one previously negotiated with BP. Chevron contributed geological and technical expertise as well as risk capital. The community had two things to offer: the value of cooperation and the veto which could arise from the withdrawal of the lands from disposition. It is important to note as well what the community did not contribute. It did not contribute the lands, for these lands are federal Crown lands disposed of under the *Canada Oil and Gas Act* and the *Canada Petroleum Resources Act*. More significantly for it, the community did not contribute its aboriginal title which remains untouched by the agreement.

The unusual background features of this agreement make it difficult to predict the extent to which it represents a model which could be used elsewhere. Chevron was certainly cognizant of the possibility that it was setting a precedent and anticipated an adverse reaction from industry which has yet to materialize. Chevron is well aware of the aspirations of the native people in British Columbia where the company is a major holder of petroleum rights in the offshore.

4.2 Allies and Adversaries

The major difference between the cases in this section and those in the preceeding one is that the native role shifts towards direct participation in political decision-making. In the experiences described below, the subject matter under negotiation is not restricted to the derivation or protection of direct economic benefits, as it would tend to be in instances such as those pictured in the "Partners in Development" scenario. These benefits are not ignored but the agenda includes much more: issues pertaining to environmental protection; the capture of indirect economic benefits; and the maintenance and enhancement of native community lifestyles. In negotiations on such issues native organizations begin to assume more of a governmental role in relation to third party interests as well as the provincial and federal governments.

The first two cases, involving the accord reached between Dome Petroleum Limited and the Lax Kw'alaams Band and the interactions between the Tahltan and Gulf Canada Resources Limited, centre upon negotiations about specific non-renewable resource projects. In each case a native government has negotiated directly with a corporation, with minimal direct involvement from either the provincial or federal governments. In these negotiations it has acted at least as much like a government as a partner in development. The last case considers discussions among native representatives as well as provincial and federal officials on the broad policy question of revising the 1943 *British Columbia Indian Reserves Mineral Resources Agreement* on revenue sharing. This section illustrates that governments — non-native and native — have complex and somewhat contradictory roles in relation to non-renewable resource development: they can help to create and foster development opportunities, but their actions and prerogatives can also act as constraints on such opportunities.

149

4.2.1 The Lax Kw'alaams Band and Dome Petroleum Limited

In the late 1970s Dome Petroleum Limited (hereafter, Dome) was one of several companies proposing to ship liquefied natural gas (LNG) to Japan from the northwest coast of British Columbia. The plant site selected by Dome and later approved by the provincial government was at Grassy Point on the Tsimpsean Peninsula. Adjacent to the Tsimpsean Indian Reserve, the site is about two and a half kilometres from the village of Lax Kw'alaams (Port Simpson). This remote village is accessible only by boat and seaplane and is home to about 1,000 band members who descend from nine tribes.

The Lax Kw'alaams Band would have been significantly affected by the Dome proposal. It does not own the surface rights, nor does it control access to the Grassy Point site, nor could it legally prevent the expropriation of reserve lands for the gas pipeline and a hydro-electric transmission line connected with the LNG project. However, federal policy is that the Minister of INAC will not approve easements or other encroachments on Indian reserves without band permission. This provided some leverage for the people of Lax Kw'alaams in negotiations with Dome as did the prospect of a gauntlet of public hearings and regulatory reviews faced by the company.

Dome believed that public opposition at any stage in the approval process could delay or even scuttle the project. According to the company's legal counsel:

Dome was well aware of native land claim issues. Any advancement of such a claim through the approval process or the courts could delay or terminate the project. The Berger enquiry had, in effect, terminated the MacKenzie Valley Pipeline. The National Energy Board requirement for a socio-economic agreement by Inter-Provincial Pipelines had delayed the construction of a pipeline south from Normal Wells by two years, and the Arctic Pilot Project became bogged down in a hearing before the National Energy Board to the extent that it was terminated.[24]

Both the band and Dome recognized that there would be some serious risks associated with the project. Public safety issues raised by LNG developments have been well-publicized. Nevertheless, the band recognized that the project could have substantial benefits and was aware that in other areas of Canada mega-project development had led to employment opportunties, construction of new public facilities, training programs and the like. Thus there were important incentives for Dome and the people of Lax Kw'alaams to negotiate.

With INAC and the provincial government's coordinator for Indian affairs playing a mediating role such as that envisioned in the

150

"Allies and Adversaries" scenario, preliminary meetings were held to explore the possibility of negotiations between the company and the band. Dome with 3,500 employees and revenues neighbouring $3 billion set off in the summer of 1981 to court the Lax Kw'alaams Band with its 24 employees and a budget of about $2 million. On October 14, 1983, just days before National Energy Board hearings on plant construction, the Lax Kw'alaams Band Council and Dome Petroleum Limited signed an agreement to:

... address the mitigation of Project impacts, (award) compensation for Project impacts that cannot be fully mitigated, (determine) the terms upon which Dome and others may secure easements for pipelines, powerlines, and roads surfacing the Project across Reserve land set apart for the use and benefit of the Band, and (resolve) other matters of mutual concern.[25]

The agreement was filed with the National Energy Board and representatives of the Lax Kw'alaams Band appeared before the Board to endorse the project and request, with their ally, Dome, that the agreement be incorporated as a condition of any certificate that the Board might issue.

The proposed Western LNG port was eventually put on the shelf along with the agreement, but the case remains a significant one for the subject of this book because it illustrates the potentially positive results of native government/corporate cooperation and the prerequisites of a negotiation process. Initially the band had refused to negotiate without its own information base. A funding agreement for $265,000 was signed in February 1982 to provide for the necessary studies as well as a liaison office and legal services. Those monies were supplemented by over $100,000 the band received from a two-year INAC program called the Resource Development Impacts Program. Based upon the information it gathered as a result of these initiatives, the band assessed the advantages and disadvantages of the project and chose to go ahead with the main negotiations. These were financed by a negotiations funding agreement signed in November 1982 which allowed independent experts to be hired to assist the negotiations committee.

After an initial period of formal negotiating sessions in which progress was quite slow, the process was restructured so that the lawyers for each side could undertake delegated negotiations. After a draft agreement was completed, internal review occurred both within the company and among the band council and members. Eventually, the band ratified the final agreement almost unanimously. Dome and the Lax Kw'alaams government could have become adversaries, but they remained allies throughout a complex negotiation process.

This agreement covered a very broad range of issues. Under the terms of compensation, Dome agreed to pay continuing expenses supporting the participation of Lax Kw'alaams in implementation. During the construction phase, payments of $275,000 annually were to be made, followed by $250,000 as the LNG plant went into full operation. An additional $400,000 was to be provided so that the band could conduct studies to monitor project impacts. The accord included terms dealing with the creation of employment opportunities and with training programs that would maximize benefits to band members during construction and operations. A wide variety of capital projects were to be provided by Dome, including transportation, recreational and medical facilities. A provision was included by which Dome made a commitment to maximize local business opportunities. Under terms related to fisheries and wildlife, the company agreed not only to mitigation and compensation but also to accept the burden of proof in cases of alleged damage to habitat or fish and wildlife populations.

In return the band granted the specific easements needed for roads, pipelies and transmission lines. They also agreed to support the project through the potentially tortuous path of regulatory reviews. An explicit section on comprehensive claims was included in the agreement. The band agreed to support the project notwithstanding any aboriginal rights and to respect pre-existing permits and rights if it acquired title to new lands on which project facilities were located. As a result, no re-negotiation would be required if comprehensive claims settlements changed land ownership and jurisdiction in the region. Correspondingly Dome acknowledged that the agreement in no way constituted a waiver of the Lax Kw'alaams Band's aboriginal title.

The Western LNG terminal was indefinitely postponed and as of 1987 Dome is no longer a participant. Nonetheless the case illustrates some of the ingredients and advantages of an approach which might become more commonly used if comprehensive claims settlements were to be concluded. First, it shows that, when a native government has leverage and an independent information base to help it understand its own and other parties' needs, mutually beneficial agreements are negotiable. Second, after initial difficulties, communication between Dome and the band was not precluded by the very different perspectives a major corporation and a small native government bring to the bargaining table. Third, even though the project has not gone forward, some of the benefits a native govern-

152

ment can attain from non-renewable resource development are already in evidence.

The studies commissioned for the project have helped the Lax Kw'alaams Band run its own logging program and establish credibility with business and financial institutions. In addition, the band was able to use the proposed economic development of non-renewable resources as a lever in the funding of renewable resource activities. The Lax Kw'alaams Development Corporation raised $0.5 million in five weeks in July 1985 for an enterprise which now exports raw logs and roe-on-kelp to Japan. Before, the people of Lax Kw'alaams merely sold timber; now they manage it and subcontract logging, booming and a dry log sort.

The agreement between Dome and the Lax Kw'alaams Band is already influencing other groups involved with non-renewable resource development in British Columbia. Explicit reference has been made to the case by groups such as the Offshore Alliance of Aboriginal Nations, the Council of the Haida Nation and the Nisga'a Tribal Council. The latter, for example, have outlined an approach for a very similar process to develop contracts with petroleum operators interested in offshore exploration.[26]

4.2.2 The Tahltan Tribal Council and
       Gulf Canada Resources Limited

In 1986 discussions were initiated between the Tahltan Tribal Council (TTC) and Gulf Canada Resources Limited (hereafter, Gulf) regarding a potential coal mine at Mount Klappan in northwestern British Columbia. Mount Klappan falls within territory included by the Tahltan in their comprehensive claim. The Mount Klappan anthracite coal project as proposed by Gulf is a major project with a production potential of 1.5 million tonnes per year. It could contribute significantly to primary as well as secondary employment and services in the region.

Details on the format and progress of the deliberations are limited because of their confidential nature. Nevertheless the participants have provided enough information and background material to indicate that this could become an interesting example of coordinated project planning. It should be emphasized at the outset that the provincial government's and Gulf's perspectives on the nature of the interaction differ from the Tahltan's — and from each other's. It is an open question, as will be seen, whether the final result comes closer to an "Allies and Adversaries" or a "Partners in Develop-

153

ment" type of arrangement. Certainly the TTC seeks the former.

The outcome of negotiations between the TTC and Gulf could be significant for several reasons. First, this case appears to be the most advanced and formalized interaction at present in British Columbia between a native government and a corporation in the non-renewable resources sector. There are numerous other mine proposals under review, most of which have potential consequences for particular native communities. The process and the outcome of discussions between Gulf and the TTC will undoubtedly become as well known to and influential with other native governments and corporations as the agreement between Dome and the Lax Kw'alaams Band. The case is also significant because northwestern British Columbia is presently the most attractive area in the province for new non-renewable resource development. The Tahltan's disposition towards mining (along with the somewhat differing attitudes of neighbouring groups such as the Carrier-Sekani, Gitksan-Wet'suwet'en, Nisga'a and Tlingit) may powerfully affect the course of development in that region.

The Mount Klappan project is currently within the province's mine development review process. This is a procedure whereby new mining ventures are subject to extensive multiple agency scrutiny. The province, with advice from INAC, now routinely identifies native peoples who might be affected by any proposal. Reports submitted to the provincial Mine Development Steering Committee are circulated for comment to the native governments concerned. The Tahltan have been particulary responsive to this opportunity and have made detailed commentaries on proposals.[27]

Negotiations between the TTC and Gulf began in autumn 1986. The goal, at least for the Tahltan, is to achieve a comprehensive project participation agreement dealing with a wide range of issues. These include avoidance of irreparable environmental damage, assurance that land claims will be unaffected, provision of job and training opportunities for all phases of the development, consideration of equity participation in the project, provision of maximal opportunities for Tahltan businesses as well as financial and managerial assistance from Gulf.

The tribal council's highest priority in initial discussions has been employment. The Tahltan have requested that Gulf establish a local personnel office. Based upon socio-economic assessments, the corporation has supported the Tahltan in their request for a regional employment outreach project and the need for upgrading and training. Furthermore, Gulf wrote to the federal government that:

In conjunction with Provincial and Federal agencies it is anticipated that a training program will be set up. Gulf is prepared to co-operate by providing 'on the job' training opportunities ... an (outreach) officer could assist both Gulf in its local hiring and also assist the communities in their interaction with resource projects.[28]

From Gulf's perspective the major subject for discussion is assistance to the Tahltan for establishing native-run firms which can provide on-site services. Gulf prefers to deal with native-owned corporations and is prepared to give business advice and training and to take bids locally so that native companies can compete more easily. Gulf is not in favour of preferential employment. The company views its involvement with the Tahltan as consistent with general corporate policies on improving relationships with local communities. The fundamental goal is to avoid confrontation. Gulf believes that support for major projects in remote areas, with non-native as well as native peoples, is enhanced through corporate programs which provide training, employment and local business opportunities.

Gulf is aware, however, that a comprehensive claim has been filed and accepted for negotiation in the territory which includes Mount Klappan. While the Tahltan may be seen as just another local community, their claim and the recent special attention the province has given to native governments in its mine development review process provide added incentives for negotiations. Gulf does not regard the process as one of negotiation with a governmental or quasi-governmental body. In the terms used in this book, the company sees the Mount Klappan discussions, at most, as aimed at developing a modest "Partners in Development" relationship. This may well be the outcome, but the aspirations of the Tahltan are to assume, minimally, a co-management role in resource decisions within the claimed territory. This was well-articulated in a recent policy statement by them.[29]

In April 1987 the Tahltan Tribal Council issued a general policy statement on resource development and management. In this document, the historic entrepreneurial spirit of the Tahltan, shown in their successful protection of their position as "middlemen" in trading within the region is noted. For forty years they were able to exclude the Hudson's Bay Company from establishing a trading post that would have disrupted the Tahltan network. The Tahltan's resource policy is the most explicit statement on co-management of non-renewable resources made by a British Columbia native group. The following lengthy quotation from the policy statement reveals a stance that is assertive of Tahltan authority yet still supportive of non-renewable resource development:

We wish to make it very clear that Tahltan people and the Tahltan Tribal Council are not inherently opposed to any specific type of business or resource development within our country. However we do feel strongly that any development within our tribal territory must adhere to some basic principles that the Tahltan Tribal Council has developed.

We appreciate that most private developers "just want to conduct their business". They do not want to have any discussions or participate in any actions that have overtones of aboriginal rights or native politics. We in one sense sympathize with developers because we, as businessmen, also experience frustration when politics begin to directly effect our business endeavours. However, the reality is that if our tribal objective of achieving substantial participation in business developments within our country is to be realized within a reasonable time, we must combine politics and business when dealing with developers. Developers will have to come to terms with this reality if they expect to function successfully within our territory (emphasis original).[30]

To achieve this the TTC requests developers to negotiate "project participation agreements." The policy statement lists the following elements which are to be included in such agreements:

1. assurance that the development will not pose a threat of irreparable environmental damage;
2. assurance that the development will not jeopardize, prejudice or otherwise compromise the outstanding Tahltan aboriginal rights claim;
3. assurance that the project will provide more positive than negative social impacts on Tahltan people;
4. provision for the widest possible opportunity for education and direct employment-related training for Tahltan people in connection with the project;
5. provision for the widest possible employment opportunities for Tahltan people with respect to all phases of the development;
6. provision for substantial equity participation by Tahltans in the total project;
7. provision for the widest possible development of Tahltan business opportunties over which the developer may have control or influence;
8. provision for the developer to assist the Tahltans to accomplish the objectives stated above by providing financial and managerial assistance and advice where deemed necessary.[31]

Neither Gulf nor provincial regulators necessarily accept the above as an agenda for current discussions. Nevertheless, the Tahltan's requirements and principles for non-renewable resource development provide an unusually specific list of the kinds of provisions native governments might seek in bargaining among "Allies and Adversaries" if comprehensive claims settlements are made.

4.2.3 The 1943 *British Columbia Indian Reserves Mineral Resources Agreement* Amending Discussions

In 1986 an effort was launched to redefine the arrangements by which minerals on reserves in British Columbia would be developed and managed. A noteworthy feature was that the effort involved tripartite discussions among the province, the federal government and native leaders. As such, these discussions provide a basis for examining the kinds of interactions which might take place if comprehensive claims settlements in the province were to result in conditions such as those outlined in the scenario "Allies and Adversaries."

The 1943 Agreement has been discussed in some detail earlier in this chapter (section 3.1). The problem which brought all parties to the table in 1986 was that the current framework actually discourages non-renewable resource development on reserve lands. There are two reasons for this: one is administrative, the other concerns revenue-sharing. By the terms of the 1943 Agreement any development on reserves would be administered by the province yet surface rights would remain with the federal government as trustees for the band. As a result, bands feared a potential loss of control while prospective mineral developers were faced with having to negotiate separately with at least two sets of regulators. The revenue-sharing problem stemmed from the fact that taxes were not included among the revenues to be divided equally under the Agreement, yet taxes are the major instrument used by the province to capture mineral rents. As Dombroski (1985) observes, under this arrangement the 50 percent split could leave bands with 50 percent of nothing.

As a result of these difficulties virtually no mining has been undertaken on British Columbia reserves in the four decades since the Agreement was ratified. Recent interest among some native governments in pursuing sole or joint mining ventures on reserve have helped to bring both governments and several band councils and native organizations together to re-examine the 1943 Agreement.

After several years of discussions between the provincial and federal governments, they decided to include native representatives. Tripartite meetings began with a working group composed of senior

157

officials from INAC, the Assistant Deputy Minister for Indian Policy and Programs for British Columbia (with the support of advisors from the provincial Ministry of Energy, Mines and Petroleum Resources) and several native representatives. The Okanagan, Sumas and Pavilion Bands were at the table on the native side in addition to several prominent native spokespersons from intertribal organizations. To date all parties have agreed that the provincial mining regulatory approach should be retained because it does appear to be working as a means of ensuring safety and environmental protection. Many bands have already been involved in reviews under this approach.

The working group has developed two options for administration and control. One is to amend the 1943 Agreement to allow bands which are legal entities (such as Sechelt) to assume complete administration and control of reserve mineral development and to determine with the province and developers how provincial mining regulations will apply to reserve land. The second option is to repeal the Agreement and to amend the *Indian Mining Regulations* which apply in most other provinces to include British Columbia. This would allow for the application of provincial legislation unless it conflicts directly with the *Indian Mining Regulations*.

Three new revenue-sharing options have been proposed in addition to the problematic status quo. One would be a 50 percent sharing of mining taxes and royalties between the province and the bands. A second option would be to allocate 100 percent of these monies to the bands, a situation similar to that in the Prairie provinces. The third option would be to transfer 100 percent of all mining taxes and royalties plus federal and provincial income taxes to the bands.

While it is no small feat that these groups have been able to generate a discrete set of alternatives, the discussions have underscored how far the parties remain apart. The attempt to design province-wide regulations has come up against contending jurisdictional concerns on the part of the parties involved as well as a diversity of native perspectives. Not only do native governments differ in their attitudes towards mineral development, but they also vary in the likelihood that significant discoveries will be made on their lands. The incentive to conclude negotiations is much less for native bands whose lands are not especially promising in terms of minerals. It is worth quoting from the minutes of one meeting of the native participants:

Finally, it became apparent at this meeting that none of the Indians present felt themselves to be representatives of larger communities. All present spoke for their Bands alone. In order to properly canvass the Indian community on the subject of amendment of Mineral Legislation, it is crucial that all Bands receive the package informing them of progress to date and possibilities for change. There is little point in meeting with the Committee again until this project is carried out.[32]

To date, there has been no resolution of the issues involved. It is still not clear if the various groups who have participated in the discussions have done so as allies or adversaries. In terms of reaching agreement on mineral policy issues there are mixed signs in this experience. The negotiations have allowed differences in perspective to surface. The diversity on the native side presages situations in which many rather than one negotiating forum may be required for non-renewable resource management if comprehensive claims settlements take place.

Perhaps the broadest implication of this attempted amending process is that the native drive for subsurface ownership is not premised on a desire to shut down mining or for radical changes in how mining is regulated once the decision has been made to proceed. It suggests that, although comprehensive claims settlements might change the administration and distribution of the benefits of non-renewable resource development, at least some native governments would have a keen interest in seeing that development continues. In this sense, the amending process for the 1943 Agreement indicates that native governments in British Columbia may be quite willing to be allies rather than adversaries in the development and management of non-renewable resources.

4.3 Homeland and Hinterland

The "Homeland and Hinterland" scenario envisions a high degree of native autonomy in regulating and undertaking natural resource development within clearly demarcated regions of native ownership of and jurisdiction over resources. The nature and purposes of non-renewable resource development make a true "Homeland and Hinterland" scenario problematic in the eyes of most industry and government representatives. There is scant precedent in Canada for native governments having paramount authority over the full range of non-renewable resource governance such as revenue raising, permitting, development and regulation. Nevertheless, this scenario pictures arrangements which are often suggested by native spokespersons when addressing the comprehensive claims question.

To shed some light on what a "Homeland and Hinterland" scenario might be like in the non-renewable resources sector, it is necessary to look to two examples from outside the province. The first case included in this section concerns the use and management of lands within the area covered by the *Inuvialuit Final Agreement* where the highest level of native authority obtains. These are the so-called section 7(1)(a) lands, in reference to the section of the final agreement where provision is made for them. The recent conclusion of a development agreement with Esso Resources Canada Limited has provided an early test of how the Inuvialuit may use the authority recognized in its settlement.

The second case is from Alaska's North Slope Borough. In this area a local government whose leaders and electorate are almost entirely native Inupiat have formulated coastal zone plans intended to govern non-renewable resources. The North Slope Borough may well be the closest approximation to a "native homeland" in North America at present. The case of the Inupiat coastal plan provides some indication of now native governments might seek to use and control non-renewable resources under a "Homeland and Hinterland" scenario.

4.3.1 The Inuvialuit Final Agreement

In 1984 eight years of comprehensive claims negotiations between the federal government and the Inuvialuit of the western Arctic culminated in a final agreement.[33] If the management of lands for which the Inuvialuit have greatest authority is considered, some appreciation may be gained of the dimensions of a "Homeland and Hinterland" regime. The key elements of such a resource management regime and how it has worked in the case of a development proposed by Esso Resources Canada Limited are examined here.

Under section 7, the *Inuvialuit Final Agreement* creates a tiered land rights system. Under this Agreement the Inuvialuit are granted fee simple ownership to an Inuvialuit Settlement Region of about 90,000 square kilometres of land in the western Arctic and Cape Bathurst. The first land rights category, usually referred to as 7(1)(a) lands after its location in the agreement, within this region includes about 13,000 square kilometres and provides for non-renewable resource rights ownership. In this inner core, the Inuvialuit have special powers and rights with respect to non-renewable resources. These Inuvialuit powers and rights tend to replace those of the federal government. In the remaining area the Inuvialuit do not have rights to oil and gas, coal, native sulphur, base or precious metals. They do have rights to some industrial and carving materials such as

160

soapstone, limestone, sand and gravel, as well as hunting and fishing rights.

The ultimate responsibility for matters related to the supervision, management and administration of the Inuvialuit lands rests with the Inuvialuit Regional Corporation. Title is vested in the Inuvialuit Land Corporation and the area is administered by the Inuvialuit Land Administration (ILA). Both are divisions of the Regional Corporation.

This agreement's treatment of third party existing non-renewable resource rights and the conditions for continued and new subsurface activity are particularly important. Existing subsurface and surface rights in the Inuvialuit Settlement Region are retained, including the right to renewal. Many of these existing rights are on 7(1)(a) lands and their re-negotiation and administration are to be transferred to the Inuvialuit, subject to agreements with non-renewable resource companies.

Both existing and new non-renewable resource rights are subject to applicable Canadian and Territorial laws governing private lands. In the case of new rights, the Inuvialuit Land Administration may set terms and conditions which exceed general environmental and safety standards. New non-renewable resource developments are also subject to an environmental screening process to determine whether proposals should be assessed and reviewed by an environmental impact review board composed of federal, territorial and Inuvialuit government members.

The Inuvialuit also control access to existing non-renewable resources on or across Inuvialuit lands. Although developers' access is guaranteed, such access is subject to compensation charges and to the negotiation of participation agreements which set the terms and conditions of land use. What distinguishes these agreements from other access agreements is their breadth. They may provide for:

- the costs associated with any Inuvialuit Land Administration inspection of the development work sites and the nature and scope of such inspection;
- wildlife compensation, restoration, and mitigation;
- employment, service and supply contracts;
- education and training; and
- equity participation or other similar types of participatory benefits.

The *Final Agreement* also provides for non-renewable resource development undertaken by the Inuvialuit themselves. Within the settlement region, the Inuvialuit Development Corporation may develop royalty-free coal for community and regional industrial use.

Subsurface rights on 7(1)(a) lands are subject to concession agreements for the exploration and production of coal, oil and minerals. For oil and gas, these replace the exploration agreements under the Canadian Oil and Gas Lands Administration (COGLA) and may have stronger but not weaker environmental and safety terms and conditions. COGLA retains responsibility for monitoring and enforcing the national drilling regulations on all lands in the settlement region.

The real test of the implications of the *Inuvialuit Final Agreement* for non-renewable resources is in the kind of arrangements that can actually be reached between the native land owners and non-native developers. In 1986 a concession agreement allowing Esso Resources Canada Limited (hereafter, Esso) to explore and produce oil and gas on Inuvialuit 7(1)(a) lands south of Tuktoyaktuk was ratified. This was the result of over two years of effort involving a series of increasingly specific negotiations and agreements.

In 1983 and 1984 a memorandum of understanding was developed, an agreement likened by some observers to a marriage contract in which Esso and the Inuvialuit agreed first that a relationship was possible and second on the general principles they would observe. Next, in 1985 a general economic cooperation agreement was signed with provisions on native economic participation, consultation procedures, how contract bidding would be carried out and training for natives in areas of technology and management. This agreement also included quite specific elements such as a commitment by Esso to buy a fixed amount of service from Aklak Air, an Inuvialuit company.

The 1986 concession agreement replaced Esso's exploration agreement under the *Canada Oil and Gas Act* which otherwise would not have expired until June 1987. The Inuvialuit attached several new conditions to the agreement including the exclusion of almost 130 square kilometres of land for environmental reasons and the inclusion of the Inuvialuit Petroleum Corporation as a co-signatory. The concession agreement has a 30-year term with provision for successive cooperation agreements, renewable every two to five years. Also included are arrangements to govern surface access for Esso and its contractors, access fees, land relinquishment, royalties, work requirements and review as well as appeal procedures. Four elements of the agreement are particularly interesting.

First, in accordance with the 1984 *Final Agreement*, the Esso lease is governed by Canadian and Territorial laws and its operation and management may be amended to conform to additional Inuvialuit

162

rules. Such amendments may trigger re-negotiation, which if unsuc-cessful, could be referred to arbitration. Second, Esso and its associates are required to prevent, mitigate and compensate for present and future wildlife harvest loss. Third, the concession agree-ment provides for direct Inuvialuit involvement in exploration and production through the Inuvialuit Petroleum Corporation. Finally, the petroleum corporation is granted the preferential right to buy oil and gas for local use over and above its share of production. In other words, through the agreement, local residents are to have a small oil refinery and cheaper fuel.

The implications of the above developments shed light on how a "Homeland and Hinterland" scenario might unfold in British Co-lumbia in relation to the use and management of non-renewable resources. The Inuvialuit and Esso were able to conclude an agree-ment less than two years after the comprehensive claims settlement and the agreement even covered the core lands for which the Inuvialuit has most authority. Native homelands, to some degree, apparently can still be corporate hinterlands even when the rules and players of the game are dramatically changed. In fact, the *Inuvialuit Final Agreement* more generally reflects the old adage, *plus ça change, plus c'est la même chose*. Its provisions were not a shock to industries operating in the Beaufort Sea. Rather they echoed the kinds of terms negotiated previously under the *Canada Oil and Gas Act*. The major difference is that resource development industries must negotiate, reach agreements and work on implementation with native governments.

Many of the same corporations who operate in the western Arctic are also active in British Columbia, directly or through their sub-sidiaries. These corporations believe that the claims agreement with the Inuvialuit can reduce delays in permitting and bring an end to the uncertainty over title and the regulatory regime. It would be a mistake to extrapolate and suggest that industry has nothing to fear from the creation of fairly autonomous zones of native non-renew-able resource management. Quite possibly some native governments operating within "homelands" might choose to slow or scale down resource mega-projects. What the Inuvialuit case does indicate is that there are no *a priori* grounds for assuming this outcome.

4.3.2 Coastal Zone Planning in Alaska's North Slope Borough

One of the most autonomous native-run governments in North America is the North Slope Borough of Alaska. Although the borough government is not racially-defined, the population and leadership is predominantly Inupiat, close ethnic relatives of the neighbouring Inuvialuit in the Canadian Arctic. The borough comes as close to a "Homeland and Hinterland" arrangement as any jurisdiction in North America. Thus the directions taken by the borough in coastal planning related to non-renewable resource management may be useful indicators of the features of the kind of arrangements pictured in this scenario as they might unfold in a post-claims settlement regime.

The borough's history is tightly interwoven with non-renewable resource development in the region. The huge Prudhoe Bay oil find of the late 1960s brought changes and the potential for massive social dislocation to one of the continent's most isolated areas. The *Alaska Native Claims Settlement Act* of 1971 was a legislative response to these issues and to industry's concern that Alaskan natives might launch litigation which could delay oil field production and pipeline construction. Fearing that the legislative settlement of the land claims question would not in itself provide the North Slope region with sufficient local control over Prudhoe Bay's impacts, natives of the area promoted the idea of a borough government.[34]

Despite state government reluctance and considerable opposition from the oil industry, the North Slope Borough (NSB) was incorporated in 1972. In 1974 the NSB achieved home rule status giving it further broad legislative powers. Separately, amidst much controversy, the borough was able to acquire taxation powers applicable to the Prudhoe Bay oil field. A settlement of $5 million for revenues already generated by Prudhoe Bay funded political and administrative development in the borough's early years.

Literally built on oil revenues, the NSB has placed highest priority over the years on playing as strong a role as possible in the regulation of non-renewable resource activities. With many of the most important dimensions of the Prudhoe Bay development already decided before it came into existence, the NSB focused attention on the offshore. Some offshore tracts had been leased for petroleum exploration by 1974 and much larger lease sales were imminent as the "energy crisis" and a rise in oil prices stimulated interest in the Arctic Ocean and the nearby Beaufort Sea. The fact that drilling rigs were already in the Canadian Beaufort region disturbed NSB leaders and further quickened their search for means of exerting control over offshore development.[35]

In 1977 the NSB initiated coastal zone planning primarily as a means of preparing for the offshore activity. Federal and Alaska state legislation had provided incentives for local governments to prepare coastal plans as a means of protecting the environment and resolving or avoiding resource use conflicts. For the Inupiat of the North Slope, the framework seemed an ideal opportunity. Not only would funds be available for coastal planning but, once approved and in place, local coastal plans would have to be respected by federal and state agencies.

NSB coastal planning is one indication of the principles and approach that a native-run government might use in managing non-renewable resource developments.[36] The first version of the NSB coastal plan, drafted and submitted for state and federal review by early 1980, illustrates the nature of Inupiat aspirations. What happened subsequently sheds light on the difficulties and compromises such aspirations face even when something similar to "Homeland" powers have been achieved.

The NSB coastal program of 1979-80 consisted of a series of background documents, statements of policies and standards, and a Coastal Management Ordinance for implementation purposes. The NSB prepared inventories documenting critical resources, heritage areas, existing use patterns and the like. They gave special attention to documenting the subsistence lifestyle of the North Slope Inupiat. They established a zoning system delineating several kinds of districts to which standards and project review procedures of differing stringency applied. Within a broadly defined coastal zone, there were to be four districts: a petroleum service base and production district, a geophysical hazard district, a conservation district and a deferred development district. Petroleum development and ancillary facilities were to have a place on the North Slope, but it was to be one with clear geographic boundaries.

Thirty-two specific policies were set down to guide coastal zone activities; twenty-five dealt expressly with petroleum-related issues. These included a policy of very gradual development of new fields and another that called for deferring oil leasing beyond the barrier islands. The latter policy directly challenged lease sales which both the state and federal governments had scheduled at that time. Highly detailed performance standards were delineated for all aspects of oil exploration. Controls were formulated for onshore as well as offshore drilling. Outside of the designated petroleum service base and production district, special permits were to be required from the NSB for any petroleum-related activities. Again, this flew in the face of industry and state plans for opening new areas of exploration in several areas adjacent to the Prudhoe Bay field. Finally there was a policy that, in all decisions, subsistence was to be considered the highest priority use in the NSB coastal zone irrespective of all other detailed goals, standards and area designations.

Several state agencies and the entire oil and gas industry took vehement exception to the broad thrust as well as the particulars of the NSB coastal program. The geographic area was seen as too broad; the reach of regulation excessive; and the idea intolerable that subsistence activities would always prevail when in conflict with other uses. Despite numerous meetings aimed at resolving differences, the NSB coastal program faced enormous opposition and, anticipating rejection, the borough government withdrew the program in 1980.

Over the next few years the goals and even many of the policies and procedures inherent in the coastal program were not abandoned. An interim ordinance had actually been in effect by late 1979 and was used as a regulatory tool until 1983. During that time, numerous oil industry activities were subject to NSB review. Many meetings were held between borough officials and industry representatives to render specific proposals more acceptable to NSB. State agencies, oil companies and the NSB met often to discuss revisions of the coastal program.

In late 1980 the NSB began to develop a comprehensive plan and land management regulations to cover all of the borough's territory rather than just the coastal zone.[37] The plan went into effect in January 1983 replacing the interim ordinance. Since then it has served as the basis for a great deal of negotiation between industry and the NSB over non-renewable resource activities. One NSB official argues that through this experience, "(t)he Borough has shown that it will not act in an arbitrary and capricious manner and that it recognizes the multiple uses of the land within its boundaries."[38] Industry and state representatives contacted for the present study did not contradict this assessment.

The significance of what the NSB has tried to accomplish, indeed what it has accomplished, in gaining respect and legitimacy among other regulators and developers in the non-renewable resources field cannot be overstated. The NSB also exerts a great deal of influence on native groups outside Alaska especially through its role as prime instigator and financer of the Inuit Circumpolar Conference. It is interesting that the borough government is formally independent of, but has evolved concurrently with, the corporate structure created by the land claims legislation. In fact, the Arctic Slope Regional Corporation, formed as a result of the *Alaska Native Claims Settle-*

ment Act, is subject to the NSB's land use and coastal zone controls, much as any other corporate actor in the region.

In sum, the borough government has assumed broad powers within the Inupiat homeland. It has tried to advance as strong a position as possible to protect traditional subsistence activites and yet it has been able to reach accommodations with and benefit from the operations of major non-renewable resource companies. This suggests once again that arrangements such as those pictured in the "Homeland and Hinterland" scenario need not imply paralysis for resource development.

5. ...To the Future

What are the implications of these current and emerging initiatives for non-renewable resource development if comprehensive claims are settled in British Columbia? The indications emerging from these experiences are less determinate than in previous chapters, for it is hard to find examples where mining and oil and gas activity have fully developed with native participation. In some instances, the assumption of economic or political roles by native peoples has come where development had already begun such as Fort Nelson and the North Slope Borough. In others, projects with substantial native involvement from the start have not proceeded sufficiently. This is the case, for instance, with the Inuvialuit/Esso agreement, the Western LNG terminal and Mount Klappan coal. World petroleum and minerals markets also have fluctuated widely in recent years with the result that the plans of industry have been unstable with or without native participation. The suspended Western LNG project, for example, left both Dome Petroleum Limited and the Lax Kw'alaams Band with an agreement that was not implementable. How the relationship would have fared through the construction stage, what the political, economic and environmental consequences might have been, are questions which remain totally speculative.

Nevertheless, the evidence recounted in this chapter does indicate some important and perhaps surprising trends, trends which may well emerge if there are comprehensive claims settlements in British Columbia. The direct and active involvement of native peoples in the development and management of non-renewable resources can and often does present developers with constraints, but in a surprising number of instances, once the nature of this involvement is clarified and regularized, it can also facilitate many opportunities to proceed with the business of resource extraction and use.

167

In this category there are two major issues as far as non-renewable resource development is concerned: the effects of possible comprehensive claims settlements upon developers' access to resources and the implications of the settlement of these claims for revenue collection and distribution. Of greatest concern to the third parties associated with non-renewable resource development is the question of whether access to resources would be maintained in the aftermath of comprehensive claims settlements. Broad native support for continuing a moratorium on offshore exploration is sometimes cited as evidence of a general antipathy towards the non-renewable resources sector as a whole. In light of the data and discussions presented above, this assumption is not well-founded.

The fear that existing leaseholders would be summarily driven from their mines and wells, especially if native title were affirmed by settlements, is not based on any precedents which could be documented in the course of this study. It seems probable that in British Columbia, as in the *Inuvialuit Final Agreement* in the western Arctic, no settlement would be reached without protection of the existing mineral rights of third parties. The Government of Canada would be most unlikely to agree to major displacements involving large multinational companies. Native groups are at pains to indicate that they also do not seek such an outcome.

Repeatedly, native representatives in British Columbia have been clear that their major concern in non-renewable resource development is a lack of control. As they see it, mega-projects have the potential to disrupt traditional and modern rural lifestyles and to damage the renewable resources upon which their communities depend for food and commerce. The people of these communities have no alternative lands or livelihoods and therefore strongly emphasize the risks.

As indicated in the foregoing pages, where information and relevant knowledge can be acquired by a group of native people who are affected by a specific project, as in the Lax Kw'alaams/Dome negotiations, projects became more acceptable to them. Ironically, the more control natives have the less likely it is that development might be frozen. Compare, for example, the vehement opposition of coastal natives in British Columbia to offshore petroleum exploration and the accommodations which have been reached between developers and natives in Alaska and in the Canadian Arctic.

The Inuvialuit reached a prompt and businesslike agreement with Esso for development on their 7(1)(a) lands. The Inupiat of the

North Slope Borough have taxed and regulated but not opposed Prudhoe Bay development. In these instances a resolution of the native claims question did bring more certainty and encouraged non-renewable resource development. In both cases, however, native governments have sought permanent exemption of certain areas from non-renewable resource development. The concession agreement between Esso and the Inuvialuit identified an environmentally sensitive area where petroleum was not to be developed. More broadly the North Slope Borough's coastal and land use plan included zones exclusively for subsistence and preservation. The implications for a British Columbia in which comprehensive claims settlements have been reached are clear: while a broad moratorium or exclusion of development after claims is unlikely, some limitations applicable to particular areas might be anticipated.

The other key economic issue is revenue collection and sharing. Native governments in British Columbia, as elsewhere, are naturally interested in getting as large a share as possible of royalties, taxes and the like from non-renewable resources. Pragmatic arrangements such as the Fort Nelson one, involving a 50/50 split of revenues between native governments and the province, have been possible in the past. These arrangements, however, were for relatively small areas of Indian reserves. The province might not be as agreeable to the same formula if it were to apply to greatly expanded native territories in a post-settlement regime. Instead, if any agreement were to be reached, it would probably at most entail a tiered approach as in the Inuvialuit claim.

Whatever approach to revenue sharing that might be taken in comprehensive claims settlements, there seems little likelihood that a major absolute increase in rents would occur. No native government in British Columbia is likely to have title to a mineral or petroleum deposit so attractive that terms and fees could be dictated to would-be developers. Excessive financial demands would lead to corporate decisions simply to invest elsewhere. It is more likely that native governments seeking a higher return from non-renewable resources would look to equity participation such as the Tahltan seek in the Mount Klappan development or ancillary business opportunities such as those pursued by the Fort Nelson Band.

5.2 Political Dimensions

The issues most often raised in connection with the political dimensions of non-renewable resource management after comprehensive claims settlements are: potential fragmentation of resource management among many small jurisdictions; excessive and burdensome regulation; and a high incidence and intensity of political conflict among governments and user groups. What do the current and emerging initiatives reviewed in this chapter reveal about these issues?

Given the evidence, it might be posited that as result of comprehensive claims settlements in British Columbia, many different regimes for non-renewable resource development and management would develop. The existence of numerous small and different regulatory regimes could mean added difficulties for industry as adjustments in operating and accounting procedures would be needed for any move between native jurisdictions. This situation could be mitigated by the fact that, after settlements and with passing time, an increasing convergence on a common approach to management might occur as successful and flawed administrative models became common knowledge.

Industry might play an important role in this. On the corporate side, for example, major corporations with years of involvement with native communities in Alberta and the Canadian North have already transferred some of that experience to British Columbia. As outlined in this chapter both Dome Petroleum Limited and Gulf Canada Resources Limited brought to their discussions with the Lax Kw'alaams Band and the Tahltan, respectively, models of interaction and agreements from the Arctic region. A similar process could well take place between native governments if claims settlements in British Columbia generated many different regulatory regimes under the authority of these governments. If it did not, then fears of fragmentation could well be justified.

A second related issue is the nature and extent of regulatory change if settlements on comprehensive claims were reached. It appears, from the native/corporate agreements described here, that native governments bring a fairly common agenda to the bargaining table in terms of preferred regulations and conditions. If comprehensive claims settlements did come about these governments might well be relatively active regulators and, as such, they might be seen by corporate interests as tending towards excessive regulation.

The Inuvialuit, the Lax Kw'alaams Band, and the Tahltan all profess a major concern that the environment be fully protected. The Inuvialuit under their claims settlement can make environmental regulations more stringent (but not less so) than applicable federal laws. This was apparently not required in the concession agreement with Esso Resources Canada Limited. The Lax Kw'alaams

170

Band successfully bargained for some additional restrictions and conditions in their agreement with Dome Petroleum Limited. Perhaps the most interesting example was the provision that, in the event of habitat loss or fish stock reduction, the onus of proof would be with the company: that is, Dome Petroleum Limited would have had to establish that its activities were not responsible for observed changes. In the Tahltan case there is also evidence that some added forms of regulation would be in place if native governments were given more regulatory authority. On the basis of these experiences, it might be posited that, in post-settlement regimes, native governments might be active but not unreasonable regulators seeking to balance economic benefits with other values.

British Columbia has experienced heightened levels of resource conflict in all sectors in recent years. The third area of concern about the political dimensions of possible comprehensive claims settlements is that they will result in a possible worsening of relationships between the concerned parties in the non-renewable resource sector. The cases presented here suggest that the incidence and intensity of conflict may actually diminish if native governments are more actively involved in non-renewable resource management after claims settlements.

A strong trend for direct face-to-face negotiations between natives and non-renewable resource developers has taken place throughout North America as companies and native communities, with or without government participation, have negotiated the details of non-renewable resource projects in dozens of cases. Negotiated agreements between industry and native groups have some important advantages over litigation or bureaucratic mediation as ways of resolving differences. They provide an opportunity for reaching a better understanding of each others' perceptions and for learning about the technical and social complexities associated with major developments. As noted above, the Lax Kw'alaams/Dome agreement has become well known among native groups and non-renewable resource developers in British Columbia. It has influenced the aspirations of the Tahltan and the disposition among the Nisga'a and Haida to consider similar procedures. The result of direct face-to-face negotiations in the long run could well be a decrease in the frequency and intensity of disputes over non-renewable resource activities.

5.3 Environmental Dimensions

There are two broad concerns over the environmental implications of possible comprehensive claims settlements with regard to non-renewable resource development and management. First, and most important to most native peoples, is the protection of the renewable resources, particularly fish and wildlife. A greater voice in non-renewable resource decisions is seen by native peoples as essential to ensuring habitat protection. A second issue, and one that was discussed in Chapters Three and Four, is that of sustainability. For a non-renewable resource sustained yield is ultimately not possible, but a great deal of deliberation has occurred in many jurisdictions over achieving as complete as possible utilization of deposits in distinction to "highgrading." What implications can be drawn from the cases outlined here regarding these issues?

In discussions for this study with native leaders in British Columbia surprisingly little dissatisfaction was encountered with the way that mine proposals are reviewed or with existing environmental controls.* The current system of environmental regulation for land-based non-renewable resource development appears to be acceptable to native peoples (except, of course, for the lack of native control over the process). The same cannot be said for some other resource management activities such as those relating to timber harvesting and hydroelectric developments.

This acceptability of onshore arrangements cannot be generalized to include the environmental regulation for offshore development. In this case almost every native group, and certainly all with coastal locations, has objected to a perceived lack of information on and preparedness for offshore development. On the basis of the testimony before the Environmental Assessment panel, it must be concluded that, if a land claim, or rather a sea claim, were to be settled and a relatively autonomous native jurisdiction affirmed, further postponement of offshore development could result. All coastal native groups seem deeply committed to enhancing community welfare through fisheries-based development. The risk, however small, that these plans face from potential blow-outs or pipeline ruptures

---

* As this book went to press in 1988 controversy flared over mining in Strathcona Park on Vancouver Island. Two tribal councils, the Nuu-chah-nulth and the Kwakiutl joined to oppose new mineral exploration. It should be noted, however, that mines outside the park boundaries have not precipitated major opposition from these groups. Furthermore, one of the Kwakiutl District bands currently leases reserve waterfront to the major company operating within Strathcona Park. These mixed responses to mineral development underscore the difficulty of predicting native responses to mining after claims settlements.

weighs heavily on the minds of today's native leaders and would probably continue to do so in a British Columbia where comprehensive claims settlements had taken place. If such settlements were to take place in the province, development of non-renewable resources in the offshore could well be constrained by concerns about the health of renewable resources.

At the conclusion of the forestry chapter, the point was made that one effect of the settlement of comprehensive claims could be an incentive for fuller utilization and further processing of resources remaining in non-native tenure. More would have to be made from less. To a degree the same argument might be applied in the non-renewable resources sector. Already the past decade's heightened concerns about mining's effects on the land base have led to evolution of new technologies, for example the so-called in-situ mining. This technique, whereby rocks are leached at the mine site with the mineral-laden water then pumped and processed, has the potential of producing high yields with less land disturbance than older techniques. This is but one more example of how the constraints presented by the comprehensive claims question may as yet provide new opportunities for the key parties — native and non-native alike — in the non-renewable resource development industry.

6

After Native Claims?

1. Implications of Settlements

As a result of the findings reported in this book, three implications of possible comprehensive claims settlements may be identified. The first has to do with cooperation rather than confrontation. While the direct discussion and negotiation of comprehensive claims has almost reached an impasse, there are numerous examples detailed in the preceeding pages of people, whether they be native peoples, the federal or provincial governments or third parties, working co-operatively in relation to fishery, forestry or non-renewable resources. Contrary to impressions which could arise from the claims negotiation process, mounting litigation and increasing resource disputes, concerned groups have often worked to establish mutually beneficial relationships. There is an "underside" of the comprehensive claims question which indicates that, if settlements come about, these groups may well be able to build on the basis of emerging involvements in a much more cooperative way than several current events might indicate.

As the different parties presently interact — and this is a second general implication — they do so with a broad and shifting variety of economic and political strategies. This would probably continue in post-settlement regimes. In many instances, for example, native peoples seek to develop resources for economic benefits and work cooperatively with non-natives. Occasionally they rely upon governments as mediating agents or coordinating bodies. At other times, they use direct action, litigation or independent resource development approaches. Native peoples are not alone in this tendency. Everyone employs a mixture of approaches to attempt to benefit from and control resource development. In fact, the strategies taken by each reflect those taken by others. The result is a web of interactions which cannot be simplified in terms that just represent industry, federal government, provincial government or native peoples' stated aspirations.

This leads to a third general implication: If comprehensive claims settlements were reached in the province, the character of resource development and management would probably differ significantly from sector to sector and from region to region, depending upon such factors as local, provincial and world markets; past patterns of interaction; and the shape of the settlements themselves. This third conclusion will be explored further, but it is important to note here that comprehensive claims settlements would not have a uniform effect upon all parts of the province or upon all natural resource sectors. Diversity, always a characteristic of British Columbia, would continue and perhaps even intensify.

2. Resource Sector Analysis

2.1 The Fishery

The fishing industry in British Columbia is plagued by long-standing problems: year-to-year fluctuations in the size of salmon runs, damage   resulting from the development of other resources, an overabundance of commercial interests seeking to harvest the resource and uncertain markets. Historically native peoples have had a high level of concern with the sector. They are disturbed by a decline in their participation in the industry and the destabilization of the resource because of what they perceive as poor management. Native peoples have not been alone in their concerns. Non-native commercial interests fear a loss of access and a declining resource if natives are given increased powers of control. The federal and provincial governments have expressed uneasiness about perceived threats to their jurisdictional powers.

In Chapter Three evidence was presented indicating consistent and patterned interaction between native peoples, governments and industry. Some of the cases which were discussed could well foreshadow the conditions envisioned in the "Partners in Development" scenario. Attempting to increase their share of economic benefits, native peoples sought special fishing licences and harvesting rights. The activities of companies such as the Northern Native Fishing Corporation and community economic development efforts associated with the Salmonid Enhancement Project were accented. Fort Babine Enterprises and the Big Qualicum Project were also reviewed. Special attention was given to the Tahltan fishery strategy which is based on efforts to establish the Tahltan presence in the Stikine River commercial fishery while fostering good working relationships with independent non-native fishermen.

Native peoples are seeking progress through the enhancement of their commercial efforts. In many cases they work positively with governments. In others they work profitably with non-native commercial interests. Provided with the opportunity, native people have

175

indicated that they are ready and, indeed, anxious to be "Partners in Development."

Native peoples also have raised questions about the long-run management of the fishery. They have identified training priorities that cannot be met in the context of specific commercial operations and have pointed to the need for strategic planning and an adequate information base. They have advocated integrated resource management. Sometimes conflicts have arisen because they have wanted to develop the resource in ways that clash with the aspirations of other groups. In the face of these conditions, native peoples have participated in a set of governmentally-oriented strategies. These have led to initiatives which indicate comprehensive claims settlements might produce circumstances similar to those in the scenario "Allies and Adversaries."

The Musgamagw Tribal Council (MTC), for example, has sponsored a demonstration project which stresses inter-governmental coordination as well as the generation of more effective relationships with the private sector. The project has taken an integrated resource management approach to both forestry and fisheries. Seeking to deal with conflicts over the development of the resource, the MTC has worked with other groups as allies rather than adversaries. The Haida have indicated their wish to take a similar approach. The B.C. Aboriginal Peoples Fisheries Commission and the Interior Indian Fishing Commission have provided a basis for coordination among native organizations and governments in order to deal with issues spanning a multiplicity of jurisdictions.

None of these initiatives have taken place within the context of a comprehensive claims settlement or a conclusive ruling by the courts on aboriginal fishing rights. It is necessary to look outside of British Columbia to find examples of what has happened under these circumstances. The outcome of the *James Bay and Northern Quebec Agreement* and the aftermath of the Boldt decision in Washington State indicate conditions similar to those envisioned in the "Allies and Adversaries" scenario may arise if settlements are reached.

Not all native peoples have indicated a willingness to engage in fisheries co-management regimes as they are usually understood. Native governments such as those of the Nisga'a, Kwakiutl and Gitksan-Wet'suwet'en have asserted an aboriginal right to govern the fishery as well as to benefit from it. These groups are not seeking systems of co-management under the authority of the federal or provincial governments. They do not want to be allies or adversaries in a circumstance where jurisdiction is unclear. They want their jurisdiction to be fully and clearly recognized as well as guaranteed shares of the fishery. They are seeking arrangements much like those pictured in the scenario "Homeland and Hinterland".

The evidence concerning the fishing sector indicates that many current and emerging initiatives suggest circumstances pictured in each of the scenarios used in this book. After comprehensive claims settlements, where possible, native groups would stress economic imperatives. They would want jobs and income for their communities. They would want to be "Partners in Development."

If patterns of consistent and disruptive conflict or negative impacts from the development of other resources were to arise, then native peoples and the other concerned parties might be forced by events to adopt other strategies, to focus on governance as well as commercial issues. In these instances alliances might be formed around common concerns such as the health of fish stocks or adversarial relationships around more divisive issues such as special access and harvesting privileges. As this occurs circumstances similar to those presented in the scenario "Allies and Adversaries" could predominate.

Given the high likelihood of such a situation as well as the increasing concern of native peoples with self-government, it is not inconceivable that they would continue to push strongly for arrangements such as those pictured in the "Homeland and Hinterland" scenario, whether or not settlement packages provided for them. The forces influencing such a development would be strongly affected by the attitudes and stances of all participants and not just native peoples. If non-natives found it possible to accommodate the aspirations of native peoples within existing industrial and political frameworks, then moves by native peoples toward "Homeland and Hinterland" type conditions might not be perceived by them to be necessary.

Whichever scenario might predominate in the fisheries sector if settlements took place, several matters are clear. There would be more certainty about the ownership of and jurisdiction over the resource. There also would be some displacement of non-natives from the resource base. This displacement could be ameliorated by the enhancement of stocks, the creative use of those parts of the fishery which are currently unutilized or underutilized and structural changes in the industry, but it is undeniable that it would take place.

The pace of resource development might be slowed somewhat in the short-run, because of changed priorities among affected groups as well as new processes of regulation and resource conservation. In the long-run, the pace might be strengthened, particularly if events encouraged new directions in resource use and processing. As far as jurisdiction is concerned, it would remain somewhat fragmented, but it is currently fragmented and settlements might provide a basis for more systematic cooperation and coordination or, minimally, recognized mediation processes between decentralized agencies of resource governance.

Good environmental conditions in relation to the resource would be a continuing concern for everyone. There is no evidence that increased native participation in the industry would have a negative impact on conservation.

2.2 The Forests

The forests are presently the most important natural resource sector in the British Columbia economy. Traditionally, native peoples used the forests in many ways. They showed great reverence for trees, relying upon them as a material basis for their way of life. They worked both as labourers and independent contractors as the timber industry spread across the province. Changes in technology, the economy and government policies had a strong impact on them, adversely affecting the viability of small operations and employment opportunities.

Given the size of the forestry sector and the impact of its development upon other resources and community life, the fate of this sector would be a matter of great concern if comprehensive claims settlements were reached in the province. Native peoples would want guaranteed access to and benefits from the resource and a decisive role in its management. They would place greater emphasis upon the role of environmental and community values than some of the other parties.

Non-natives might be concerned about the possibilities that forest resources would be less efficiently and completely used; that governmental responsibilities would become too complicated; and that the economic health of the province would be affected adversely. In recent years these concerns have been heightened as native peoples have opposed logging activity in many places throughout the province, including the South Moresby area of the Queen Charlottes, Meares Island, the Stein Valley and Deer Island.

Representatives of most native organizations interviewed for this study indicated there is some form of commercial forestry activity in which they would like to engage. In many instances they have sought to be "Partners in Development" with non-natives. This was true in the early days after contact. It is true today. Despite limited access to the resource and the effects of a recession, Cariboo Indian Enterprises (CIE), for example, has continued to survive and compete in this demanding industry. In the instance of Hecate Logging, a co-venture has been forged between a native band holding a Forest Licence and a non-native company requiring access to timber. In the Fraser Valley, Scott Paper has maintained a long-standing arrangement with the Matsqui Band for access to cottonwood on its reserve.

Sometimes increased access to forest resources is not enough to assure prosperity. Management and conservation issues concerning reforestation and the effects of logging on other resources may arise. Additional skills may be required for managing large enterprises or accomodating cross-cultural differences. Whatever the circumstance, long-term planning and cooperation between governing entities are necessary. More than being "Partners in Development" is needed.

After claims settlements native peoples might be involved in a variety of arrangements such as those envisioned in the "Allies and Adversaries" scenario. Tanizul Timber, for example, has operated a Tree Farm Licence, under provincial jurisdiction, since 1981-82. The Timber/Fish/Wildlife arrangement in Washington State indicates negotiated agreements can lead to positive co-management arrangements. The forestry aspects of the Musgamagw Tribal Council demonstration project also point to such possibilities. Integrated resource management is an approach which encourages close alliances rather than adversarial relationships.

The implications of the experiences related to the Nuu-chah-nulth Tribal Council forestry program have been more mixed than those of Tanizul, for example. On reserve, where the powers of its member bands have been clearer if still limited, the tribal council has been able to forge alliances in the development and management of the resource. In some instances, tribal council personnel also have been contracted to do restorative and other silvicultural work for non-native forest firms off-reserve. Controversy relating to the logging of Meares Island also has arisen.

No indigenous group in British Columbia has established arrangements in the forestry sector close to those envisioned in the "Homeland and Hinterland" scenario. In the province the Nisga'a have put forward an approach corresponding most closely to such arrangements, consistently proposing that their ownership and control be recognized and territorially-based governance, guided by community rather than market imperatives, be instituted.

As initiatives in this sector indicate, native peoples, both within and outside of the province, are taking a variety of strategies as they seek a larger role in development and management. If comprehensive claim settlements were concluded, these trends would continue. Claims settlements would probably involve substantial monetary compensation as well as provisions for expanded ownership, assured employment opportunities and special access to forestry resources. Such outcomes would provide a real basis for native involvement in logging and wood processing operations. Native peoples would seek "Parnerships in Development" where they could identify opportunities for more jobs and, in some cases, revenues through rent collection.

After settlements native peoples might go beyond approaches oriented strictly toward economic benefits and assert political goals as well. Native peoples have increasingly articulated the need to balance environmental and community values with ones relating to material gain. As a result of these and other concerns, they would seek, in many cases, to emphasize the governance as well as the development of the resource in arrangements such as those pictured in the "Allies and Adversaries" and "Homeland and Hinterland" scenarios.

The general arrangements for the governance of the forest industry might remain the same, but trends toward integrated resource management and community-based forestry would increase. Concerns about the sustainability of the resource and the effects of its development on other resources would also become more central. Settlements would generally result in greater certainty and this would have a positive impact on the pace and direction of development, particularly in the medium -and long-term.

Diversity would be the rule, but there are clear indications certain features would characterize the sector as a whole. Native peoples would have more extensive and assured access to the resource. They would have more capital and, in many instances, greater guarantees of employment. Non-native interests would experience some displacement from the resource, but they could alleviate the resulting problems, to a degree, through the use of expertise and capital in co-ventures with native controlled corporations and governments. Environmental matters would continue to be a source of conflict, particularly between native governments and other industrial interests.

2.3 Non-renewable Resources

The development of non-renewable resources often involves small and medium-sized companies, but frequently it takes multinational companies such as Gulf Canada Resources Limited, Dome Petroleum Limited and Chevron Canada Resources Limited to provide the capital and expertise to enable development to proceed. Companies such as these, each of which is involved in a case reviewed in Chapter Five, need certainty, certainty about jurisdictional, regulatory, environmental and other matters.

The needs and claims of native peoples often seem like one more constraint industry must face as it attempts to explore for and extract non-renewable resources — a constraint which can tip the balance against fragile and costly development deals. In British Columbia uncertainty is particularly the case, because native peoples have no tradition of and little recent experience with extensive non-renewable resource development. Nevertheless there are some current and emerging initiatives involving native peoples, both in British Columbia and elsewhere, which provide insights into what could happen if comprehensive claims were settled. Significantly such instances are ones in which developments promise very substantial revenues.

In the case of the Fort Nelson Band of northeastern British Columbia, the province and the band were able to reach a revenue sharing agreement by which monies from natural gas are divided equally between the province and Canada, the latter receiving the revenues on behalf of the band because of the circumstances established by the *Indian Act*. The Fort Nelson Band's involvement in this arrangement is strictly financial. In ways which presage the kind of arrangements pictured in the "Partners in Development" scenario, the band has not focused on political or other matters of jurisdiction or regulation. Rather, it has used its monies to establish a diverse investment portfolio, economic development enterprises and community infrastructure.

The Déné-Métis community of Fort Good Hope in the Northwest Territories has also been able to enter into a partnership to improve its economic well-being through oil and gas development, acting with Chevron Canada Resources Limited in a joint venture agreement. Chevron is a major holder of petroleum rights in the British Columbia offshore. Instances such as the Fort Good Hope case point to the possiblity that in a British Columbia where settlements have been obtained, non-renewable resource development would proceed, even in situations characterized by continuing political uncertainties, if investment opportunties promise the advantage of healthy profits for all involved.

The cases included in Chapter Five under the heading "Allies and Adversaries" tell a more mixed story. A high degree of government involvement and an accentuation of the political dimensions in the development and management of non-renewable resources may raise costs, heighten uncertainties and reinforce constraints. This will not be true in every instance. In the case of the Dome Petroleum Limited/Lax Kw'alaams Band agreement, the two parties were able to conclude a mutually acceptable agreement. External economic factors intervened, making the proposed liquefied natural gas terminal unprofitable at present, but Dome and Lax Kw'alaams had joined as allies in an effort to foster development.

In the Tahltan Tribal Council/Gulf Canada Resources Limited case, the provincial government and Gulf have seen the situation surrounding a potential coal mine at Mount Klappan in northwest British Columbia in fundamentally different ways than the Tahltan have. Negotiations have proceeded, but there has been little agreement on the Tahltan role. Gulf takes it to be similar to that of any other community affected by coal development. The Tahltan assert a stronger role as a government with authoritative decision-making power. It is not clear how far discussions can proceed in the light of these differences. The outcome of these discussions could be indicative of how much conflict may be anticipated if comprehensive claims settlements come about.

The discussions of changes to the 1943 *British Columbia Indian Reserves Mineral Resources Agreement* have not been fruitful to date. Contending jurisdictional concerns and a diversity of native perspectives have made agreement difficult to achieve. Nevertheless, it is important to note that the involvement of native governments has not been based on their desire to hamper the development of non-renewable resources or radically to change regulatory practices.

People sometimes allege that non-renewable resource development would be hampered severely by comprehensive claims settlements which cede significant authority to native governments. Behind this view are fears that a native veto on development would strangle economic enterprise. The cases reviewed under the heading "Homeland and Hinterland" in Chapter Five provide a basis for disputing this perspective, at least as far as development involving large multi-national firms may be concerned. The Inuvialuit/Esso interaction in the western Arctic and the coastal zone planning initiatives in Alaska's North Slope Borough indicate strong jurisdictional powers on the part of native governments may be a preface to healthy non-renewable resource development activities. Esso's attitude regarding Inuvialuit lands, for example, was clear: once it understood the ground rules for development, it was ready to do business.

Native peoples have been willing to engage in non-renewable

resource development for economic as well as other benefit.
bring strong environmental concerns to negotiations and de
ment projects, but they are also aware of the large benefits dev
ment can often bring. Where environmental matters and poss
negative impacts on other resources are not seen as paramou
native peoples have been open to development initiatives.

As far as the pace of development after settlements, a significant
variable may be certainty about the nature of management regimes
rather than the source or sources of the authority underlying these
regimes. If this is the case, then arrangements such as those pictured
in the "Partners in Development" and "Homeland and Hinterland"
scenarios may be each much more accommodating to non-renewable
resource development than those pictured in the "Allies and Adversaries" scenario.

A fundamental difference in the "Partners in Development" and
the "Homeland and Hinterland" scenarios revolves around the
political dimensions of these visions of a British Columbia in which
claims have been resolved. One might suppose that development
would proceed in more active ways in a "Partners in Development"
than in a "Homeland and Hinterland" situation. This may not be
the case at all. In either situation, native peoples might be willing to
do business with industry. The crucial difference may not be based
upon who has political authority. It may be based on the that
authority's ability to provide a workable foundation for development.

If comprehensive claims settlements were to take place, non-
renewable resource development, with the possible exception of
offshore projects, would, for the most part, benefit, as long as these
settlements do not result in the creation of an extensive array of
regulatory and review mechanisms where authority is shared. If this
were to be the case then the uncertainty which characterizes many
non-renewable resource development efforts in a British Columbia
without comprehensive claims settlements might continue.

3.   Critical Uncertainties

3.1 Economic Dimensions

Throughout British Columbia native peoples are seeking an expanded share of the resources they have traditionally used as well as
revenues, jobs and other economic gains arising from the development of non-renewable resources. In the absence of comprehensive
claims settlements, they seek these benefits in a wide variety of ways,

but they continue to assert that the only real solution to their economic problems would involve a solution to the claims question.

If settlements are reached, the benefits that could come to native peoples may take the form of recognized ownership of or special access to resources. Direct monetary compensation from development could also be involved. In some instances, native peoples may want to take a much more direct role in the management and business of resource development. In others, they may, for one reason or another, seek to benefit from rent collection. In almost all instances, they would seek more employment possibilities.

Benefits for some invariably involve costs for others. Who would bear these costs? Probably no notion about the future is so provocative of emotion as the idea that, after settlements, non-native interests might be abruptly cut off from the resources presently providing their livelihood. This notion is not supported by the facts. Native organizations and native governments have often gone to great lengths to reassure non-natives of their intentions to ease the pains which may come from resource re-allocation. In addition many native groups, particularly in the fisheries sector, have sought to enhance current resource bases or develop new ones rather than displace non-natives from existing ones. The Haida, for example, are focusing their fisheries strategy on presently unutilized or under-utilized marine species in an effort to create new wealth. The Qualicum and Chehalis Bands are currently developing substantial operations based on the harvesting of surplus stocks. The Nisga'a place great emphasis upon reforestation.

Where native peoples seek access to resources which are presently being developed and managed mainly by non-natives, they often emphasize a desire to strengthen community harmony by including non-natives. The Nisga'a, for example, are adamant that non-natives would not be forced to leave their lands after a settlement, arguing that the latter have much more to fear from the province and current industrial practices. There are many instances where close business ties have been established between native and non-native enterprises, particularly in the forest industry.

There can be no denial of the fact that there would be significant displacement if settlements were concluded. The resource pool may be expanded or better managed. Cooperative ventures between native and non-native groups may take place. Such ameliorating measures might occur, but, at least in the short-run, the considerable costs of settlements would have to be borne by non-native interests. Constitutional or legal developments might affect the division of these costs, but they would not reduce their overall impact.

The distribution of the benefits and costs of comprehensive claims settlements would have implications for the pace and direction of resource development. Many non-native groups contend that even with massive subsidies native-run firms are likely to fail. They cite actual instances of failure and express a sense that complex and uncertain world markets outstrip the capabilities of small independent firms, native or not. Yet, in many instances native firms have succeeded. The operations of Hecate Logging, the Northern Native Fisheries Corporation and Tanizul Timber are examples of this.

There are some indications that the pace of development might be augmented in the long-run and that such development might also take new directions if settlements were reached. The Chehalis Band and the Nuu-chah-nulth Tribal Council's smoked fish products have had a good reception in the United States market. The Gitksan-Wet'suwet'en have articulated a desire to develop new products for international export based upon their inland fishery strategy. Co-operative relationships between large corporations and native peoples could facilitate development in every resource sector.

While there are hints that the pace of development could be enhanced by settlements, there are other indications that development could be disrupted, at least in the short-run. If settlements were reached, native governments and organizations would be likely to maintain their current priority of assisting band members to prepare for employment and business opportunities. They could, for example, place emphasis on the training of people who are otherwise unemployed. The stress placed on training by the Nuu-chah-nulth and Musgamagw Tribal Councils, Tanizul Timber, Hecate Logging and Cariboo Indian Enterprises indicates this may be the case. Such an emphasis, apart from its other consequences, may slow down development in the short-run as time is spent preparing people for new roles.

Other signs point to additional factors which could result in some short-term slowing of resource development if settlements were reached. Native peoples have strong environmental concerns. They decry what they define as soil damage, timber "highgrading," a low degree of emphasis on reforestation, and the inefficient utilization of felled timber. The search for and substitution of new technologies and practices could well have positive long-run benefits, but in the short-run much delay would take place. Moreover, some valuable parts of the resource base may be removed from development if places such as Meares, Deer and Lyell Islands are withdrawn and given protected status. Non-renewable resource development in the offshore could also remain problematic.

Such concerns and possiblities should not lead to incorrect conclusions. Native peoples, for the most part, do not want the province to be preserved as a "pristine wilderness." It was not a pristine wilderness at the time of contact with non-natives. Native peoples in what is now known as British Columbia have traditionally developed and managed fishery, forestry and other natural resources. As the initiatives reviewed in this book indicate, they are continuing to do so. In fact, over the past ten years or so, native involvement in natural resource development has grown with great rapidity. All indications are that, as they continue to press for comprehensive claims settlements, natives will continue to seek economic benefits based upon natural resource development. They are equally likely to continue this strategy after claims settlements and, in the not so long-run, such an outcome might well have a very positive effect on the province's economy.

3.2 Political Dimensions

Politics and economics are often hard to separate, especially in British Columbia where the government is deeply involved in the management and development of natural resources. This would be no less the case if comprehensive claims settlements were reached. Such settlements would affect the incidence of political conflict over the costs and benefits of economic enterprises. They might affect the size, complexity and level of decision making of governments and public bureaucracies. They would also affect jurisdictional arrangements, particularly in relation to the regulatory functions of government.

The issue of regulation would continue to be a contested one after comprehensive claims settlements. Experiences in other jurisdictions indicate this. In the case of the fishery in Washington State, the affirmation of native rights led directly to the development of more stringent regulations. Such examples should be contrasted with instances where the resource-related activities of native peoples have indicated that they would not allow regulatory concerns to interfere with good investment and development opportunities. Companies dealing with resource development in the Inuvialuit territory, for example, have found no increase in red tape or in the stringency of controls.

In British Columbia a similar spread of experiences can be found. The people of the Fort Nelson Band, for example, did not become involved in regulation as they reached and implemented a revenue-sharing agreement with the provincial government. Other instances indicate trends toward more regulation if comprehensive claims settlements are concluded. Many native governments and organizations are seeking guaranteed shares of the fisheries, for example. To re-address the question of inter-user allocations of a scarce resource might entail more extensive as well as more costly regulatory mechanisms.

In this context, it is important to consider the fishing by-laws developed by the Gitksan-Wet'suwet'en. These by-laws are intended to be primary in relation to the regulations of any other government. Such an approach indicates that some native governments would use increased regulatory mechanisms if comprehensive claims settlements were reached. The fishing industry and those third parties who have direct concerns about the province's fishery may perceive this as an excessive amount of regulation. Many native peoples may see this as a justifiable adjustment of their presence in a resource regime which is already highly regulated. In either case, the level of political interaction around the resource would probably rise.

The extent of government involvement in the management and development of natural resources is one matter that raises concerns in the shadow of settlements. The possible decentralization and proliferation of post-settlement governance systems is another. If comprehensive claims settlements are reached, there may be an increase in the sheer number of tribally-based agencies and commissions involved in resource governance. The possibilities of balkanization are there, but the choices lie with the concerned parties. Models exist in Washington, for example, of the creation of agencies to coordinate tribally-managed fisheries. Such integrative organizations might develop in British Columbia.

Administrative complexity sometimes arises because of jurisdictional complexity. Many tribal groups increasingly espouse a view of the native claims question which places matters of jurisdiction, of the authority to govern, with matters of ownership and resource use at the forefront of their claims. The Nisga'a, Gitksan-Wet'suwet'en, Nuu-chah-nulth and Kwakiutl, for example, have put forward resource management proposals which emphasize their claims to independent and inherent jurisdiction over their territories.

If comprehensive claims settlements come about, they might give rise to new regulatory and governance arrangements with a much greater native presence than is currently the case. As a result the governance of natural resources could become more extensive and more decentralized at the same time. The results of such developments for the provincial political system, in terms of its viability and the confidence of the citizenry in it, may well be substantial.

Comprehensive claims settlements could bring many benefits. They could bring more certainty and provide native peoples with a sense that long unfinished business finally has been settled in a just manner. They would, however, not bring an end to conflict over the development of British Columbia's fishery, forests and non-renewable resources. Different groups in resource development will always see development and management challenges in different ways. When native peoples are involved this is particularly the case because of their unique cultural and historical interests and values. Claims settlements would change many things, but they would not and could not change this fundamental fact.

3.3 Environmental Dimensions

Perceptions of the attitudes that native peoples have concerning the environment often have a contradictory flavour to them. Some contend native peoples would elevate environmental concerns to a disproportionate level if claims settlements were to take place in the province. Others argue native peoples would disregard environmental values if they had the chance to cash in on profitable endeavours. Some people have suggested that, if comprehensive claims are resolved in such a way that native peoples are recognized as having greater authority over the regulation of resource use, they will have difficulty controlling the actions of their tribal members. Some people are also very concerned that post-claims native communities may face financial demands for newly-acquired responsibilities and that these demands will provide a strong incentive to abuse environmental resources.

The evidence in British Columbia is more positive than these fears suggest. There is a cultural commitment among the native peoples to environmental protection. The Gitksan-Wet'suwet'en, the Kwakiutl, the Nisga'a, the Nuu-chah-nulth and other tribal groups have each emphasized their traditional concern for maintaining the productivity as well as the quality of the resource base. Emerging initiatives among native peoples also exhibit a concern for these matters. The Musgamagw Tribal Council's demonstration project, for example, has featured an approach which integrates fisheries and forest development on the basis of efforts to protect and enhance the environment.

With their view that the forest lands of the west coast of Vancouver Island have not been sufficiently replanted, the Nuu-chah-nulth have exhibited similar concerns. Analogous motivations underlie Nisga'a forestry proposals. The Gitksan-Wet'suwet'en argue

188

strongly that methods of resource extraction can be altered by introducing an "inland fishery" which would be both productive and respectful of the needs of the resource to be maintained and enhanced. Many similar examples could be cited. In each of these cases native peoples have attempted to develop a much more comprehensive grasp of the resource base and its limitations as well as its possibilities than they feel other groups have done. These patterns, attitudes and intentions would carry over into post-settlement regimes, presenting other concerned parties with an opportunity to place greater emphasis on environmental quality, renewal and enhancement.

Yet, native peoples must not be seen as having a single-minded concern with the environment. Many environmentalists take comfort in and many resource developers have fears arising from the notion that comprehensive claims settlements could possibly mean the removal of significant parts of the provincial land base from any extractive use. This is most unlikely. While it is true that native governments generally express concern for particular special places which may hold high resource values, they have also indicated a keen interest in acquiring timber rights and enhancing community development on the basis of logging and wood processing. Native peoples, like many other British Columbians, have strong concerns for the environment, but they also have pressing economic needs.

4. A Future of Diversity

If there is any one impression which arises over and over again from this study, it is of diversity in terms of resource sectors, governmental attitudes and jurisdictions, and the aspirations and approaches of native peoples. If uncertainty prevails in British Columbia while the comprehensive claims question remains a matter of unfinished business, diversity may well be a central concept for understanding a British Columbia in which the comprehensive claims question has been addressed and become the focus of settlements representing accommodations by a variety of interests.

Natural resource development would continue to be the critical element in British Columbia's economy. The business of natural resource development would go on, but it might not entirely be business as usual. The politics and economics of development would change as would its environmental aspects. Native peoples might have a much expanded role in the governance process. They might be able to free up or block access to portions of the resource base.

189

They may require a more intense concern about the physical environment.

These trends would change the direction and pace of natural resource development, but not in a way which would fundamentally alter the economy or governance of the province. Things would change. That is certain; but the changes would produce neither the bright and simple world for which many wish nor the threatening tomorrow many fear. On the contrary, economic relationships and outcomes, political conflicts and accommodations, and environmental limits and challenges would still be diverse and seen in many different ways by different interests. Here is one of the most important lessons which may be learned from a study such as this: comprehensive claims settlements may bring many changes, but they would not bring a new world marked by either disaster, decline and disintegration or by unbridled success and Utopian harmony.

The research for this study provides a basis for several conclusions regarding the possible implications of comprehensive claims settlements in British Columbia for the development and management of fishery, forestry and non-renewable resources. Three broad conclusions may be identified:

1. Contrary to impressions which may be gained from observations of the federal comprehensive claims negotiation process and several examples of litigation or confrontation, natives and non-natives in many instances have worked to establish mutually beneficial relations which could well provide a basis for positive and cooperative arrangements, if settlements are obtained.

2. As they interact in the development and management of natural resources, concerned groups do so on the basis of a complex and mutually-influenced variety of economic and political strategies, ranging from partnerships designed to maximize economic benefits to governmental coordination and regulation to independent action of one sort or another. They would probably continue to do so in a British Columbia where claims were settled.

3. The character of resource development and management currently differs from sector to sector and, to a somewhat lesser degree, region to region, depending upon a range of factors. If settlements were to come about this pattern would continue and possible even intensify. Settlements would not have an equal impact across the board. Diversity not uniformity would be the rule.

Beyond these general conclusions some more specific ones concerning the economic, political, and environmental dimensions of the outcomes of possible claims settlements may also be identified:

1. In the short-run the pace and direction of resource development might be disrupted somewhat as new relationships were established. In the long-run resource development may well be enhanced. This is particularly true of the forestry and non-renewable resource sectors. Such an outcome in the fishery sector would depend on the possibility of accompanying structural changes.

2. There would be some displacement of non-native interests from access to the resource base, particularly so in the fishery and forestry sectors. This outcome could be ameliorated by efforts to utilize undeveloped and underdeveloped resources as well as an increased emphasis on the enhancement of the resource base.

3. Governance in relation to resource management would become somewhat more extensive, decentralized and integrated. Once again this would probably be more true of the fishery and forestry sectors than of the non-renewable resource sector.

4. In the short-run, conflict concerning resource use might increase. In the long-run, it would probably be reduced.

5. The health and enhancement of the resource base would become a matter of higher priority.

Comprehensive claims settlements would bring more certainty to British Columbia's natural resource sectors. Settlements might result in many benefits and costs, but they would not fundamentally change the nature of British Columbia's economy. The province could still rely on natural resource development as the key to its prosperity.

FOOTNOTES

INTRODUCTION

[1] P. W. Beck, "Corporate Planning for an Uncertain Future," Long Range Planning 15 (August 1982), p. 18.

[2] Beck, pp. 13-17. See also Elizabeth Parr-Johnson, "Policy Making in Uncertainty," Policy Options 5 (July 1984), pp. 44-47.

[3] Beck, p. 15.

[4] Quoted in Pierre Wack, "Scenarios: Uncharted Waters Ahead," Harvard Business Review (September-October 1985), p. 74.

[5] Parr-Johnson, pp. 44-47.

[6] Wack, p.77.

CHAPTER 1
COMPREHENSIVE CLAIMS AND NATURAL RESOURCES

[1] See "Reserve Sought for Indians," *Vancouver Sun* (June 16, 1987).

[2] Indian and Northern Affairs Canada, *Outstanding Business: A Native Claims Policy* (Ottawa: Minister of Supply and Services Canada, 1982), p.19.

[3] Wilson Duff, *The Indian History of British Columbia: Volume 1. The Impact of the White Man*. Anthropology in British Columbia Memoir No. 5 (Victoria: Provincial Museum of Natural History and Anthropology, 1964), pp. 38-45.

[4] This is discussed in Rolf Knight, *Indians at Work: An Informal History of Native Indian Labour in British Columbia, 1858-1930*. (Vancouver: New Star Books, 1978). For regional treatments see James K. Burrows, "'A Much-Needed Class of Labour': The Economy and Income of the Southern Plateau Indians, 1897-1910," *BC Studies* 71 (Autumn 1986),pp. 27-46, and Maureen Cassidy, *From Mountain to Mountain: A History of the Gitksan Village of Ans'pa yaxw* (Kispiox, B.C.: Ans'pa yaxw School Society, 1984).

[5] Examples of these early protests can be found in: *British Columbia, Report of Conferences Between the Provincial Government and Indian Delegates from Fort Simpson and Naas River*. (Victoria: Richard Wolfenden, 1887), "Return to an Order of the Legislative Assembly for all correspondence relating to the recent Indian troubles on the North-West Coast" B.C. *Sessional Papers* for 1885, pp. 277-287; British Columbia Attorney General, "Copies of correspondence in and out re the Skeena River Uprising 1888," Provincial Archives of British Columbia.

[6] Paul Tennant, "Native Indian Political Organization in British Columbia, 1900-1969: A Response to Internal Colonialism," *BC Studies* 55 (Autumn 1982), p. 16.

[7] *Statement of the Government of Canada on Indian Policy* (Ottawa: Queen's Printer, 1969).

[8] Quoted in: Task Force to Review Comprehensive Claims Policy, *Living Treaties: Lasting Agreements, Report of the Task Force to Review Comprehensive Claims Policy* (Ottawa: Department of Indian Affairs and Northern Development, 1985), p. 12.

[9] Task Force, p. 12.

[10] Task Force, p. 13.

[11] *In All Fairness* (Ottawa: Department of Indian and Northern Affairs, 1981).

[12] House of Commons, Canada, *Minutes of Proceedings of the Special Committee on Indian Self-Government* (Ottawa: Queen's Printer, 1983).

[13] *Living Treaties...*, p. 13.

[14] *Living Treaties...* , pp. 12-13.

[15] "Comprehensive Land Claims Policy," Indian Affairs and Northern Development, Dec. 18, 1986, pp. 5-6.

[16] "Comprehensive Land Claims," p. 6.

[17] "Comprehensive Land Claims," p. 6.

[18] "Comprehensive Land Claims," p. 7.

[19] "Comprehensive Land Claims," pp. 8, 9-10, 13.

[20] Task Force on Program Review, *Improved Program Delivery, Indians and Natives: A Study Team Report* (Ottawa, Supply and Services Canada, 1986), p. 255.

[21] Program Review, p. 254, 253.

[22] British Columbia Ministry of Attorney General, Secretariat for Indian Policy and Programs, "Indian Land Claims in British Columbia" (typescript, Dec. 1985), p. 5.

[23] "Comprehensive Land Claims...," p. 12.

[24] *Financial Post* (January 24, 1987).

CHAPTER 2
SCENARIOS: FROM THE PRESENT TO THE FUTURE

[1] See, for example, *James Bay and Northern Quebec Agreement Implementation Review* (Ottawa: Indian Affairs and Northern Development, 1982); Wendy Moss, Practically Millionaires? A Report on the Implementation of the James Bay and Northern Quebec Agreement (Ottawa: National Indian Brotherhood, 1981); and The Western Arctic Claim: A Guide to the Inuvialuit Final Agreement (Ottawa: Indian Affairs and Northern Development, 1984).

[2] For a description of the administrative implications of the James Bay and Northern Quebec Agreement see I. LaRusic, *Negotiating a Way of Life; Initial Cree Experience with the Administrative Structure Arising Out from the James Bay Agreement* (Montreal: Indian Affairs and Northern Development, 1983).

[3] "This Land is Whose Land," Maclean's 97 (June 1, 1981), pp. 49-61.

CHAPTER 3
THE FISHERY: A SPECIAL RESOURCE

[1] Peter Pearse, *Turning the Tide: A New Policy for Canada's Pacific Fisheries*. Final Report of the Commission on Pacific Fisheries Policy (Vancouver: The Commission on Pacific Fisheries Policy, 1982), p. 156.

[2] Philip Drucker, *Indians of the Northwest Coast.* (Garden City, N.Y.: Natural History Press, 1963), p. 3.

[3] Letter from George Hunt to Franz Boas, quoted in D. J. Gillis & Associates & W. McKay Associates, *Economic Development Planning for the Kwakiutl District*, Volume 1, Report to the Kwakiutl District Council (no date).

[4] Nuu-chah-nulth Tribal Council. Presentation to the West Coast Offshore Exploration Environmental Assessment Panel (1985), p. 41.

[5] In May 1985, the Federal Court of Appeal overturned a ruling by Justice Collier (Federal Court of Canada) that had limited the Department of Fisheries & Oceans' authority to allocate among user groups.

[6] Canada. Department of Fisheries and Oceans, "A Policy Proposal for a B.C. Indian Community Salmon Fishery." Released for Discussion by the Minister of Fisheries & Oceans and the Minister of Indian Affairs & Northern Development (March 13, 1986), p. 4.

[7] "Policy Proposal," p. 4.

[8] Canada. Department of Fisheries and Oceans, "Native Comprehensive Claims Policy Review Submission." (October, 1985).

[9] *R. v. Fowler*.

[10] *Indian Act*, R.S.C. c. 10, s. 81(1)(o).

[11] Enforcement of the Squamish fisheries by-law passed in 1976 has twice been challenged in terms of conflict with the *Fisheries Act* and has prevailed both times in British Columbia County Court. The most recent of these cases was *R. v. Joseph and Lewis* (1986) 2 *C.N.L.R.* 108.

[12] Christine Cummins, Michael Friedlaender, Douglas Williams, *Impact of the Salmonid Enhancement Program on Native People*. (Vancouver: Environment Canada, Fisheries and Marine, 1978), p. 64.

[13] *Sparrow v. R.* (1986) 9 *B.C.L.R.* 300, at 317-318.

[14] Pacific Fishermen's Defense Alliance, "Canada's Fisheries... in Crisis," Information Booklet (Surrey, B.C.: Pacific Fishermen's Defense Alliance, 1986), p. 5.

[15] Fisheries Council of British Columbia, *Submission of the Fisheries Council of British Columbia to the Task Force on Comprehensive Claims Policy* (Vancouver: September 1985), p. 1.

[16] Among the many sources advocating fleet reduction was the Pearse Commission inquiry into the Pacific Fisheries.

[17] A. D. Rank, "Assessment of the Community Economic Development Program." Report to Fisheries and Oceans, Canada (May 1982), p. 6.

[18] Information on the Fort Babine experience is based primarily on discussions with Pat Michelle of Fort Babine Enterprises (November 1986) and on a brief Mr. Michelle presented to a meeting with the Gitksan-Wet'suwet'en in November 1986 hereafter cited "Presentation Outline."

[19] "Presentation Outline," p. 1.

[20] For a discussion of this position see Mike Morrell, "The Struggle to Integrate Traditional Indian Systems and State Management in the Salmon Fisheries of the Skeena River, British Columbia." Paper presented to the U.B.C. School of Community and Regional Planning Fisheries Co-Management Confernce (May 6, 1986).

[21] See Morrell, "The Struggle to..."

[22] See Cummins, p. 86.

[23] Letter from Hon. Pierre De Bane to D. Elliot (Executive Director, Pacific Trollers Association), reprinted in *Current* (PTA Newsletter, December 1983).

[24] "Chief hails bounty from inland fishery," *Vancouver Sun* (January 31,1986).

[25] *Ibid*.

[26] See Tahltan Nation Development Corporation, "Creating an Industry from a Way of Life: The Comprehensive Development Strategy of the Tahltan Nation" (1986).

[27] Tahltan, p. 17.

[28] Tahltan, p. 18.

[29] Tahltan, p. 18.

[30] Tahltan Tribal Council, "A Fishery-Based Economic Development Strategy," (April 1986), p. 9.

[31] Musgamagw Tribal Council, "Integrated Resource Management and Development Demonstration Project Model," Alert Bay, B.C., (1985), p. 2.

[32] Discussed in Miles Richardson, "The Fisheries Co-management Struggle in Haada Gwaii," Paper Presented to the Fisheries Co-management Conference, U.B.C. (May 6, 1986).

[33] Richardson, p. 7.

[34] Richardson, p. 7.

[35] See B.C. Aboriginal Peoples' Fisheries Commission, "Mechanisms for Consultation on Native Fisheries with Native Peoples of British Columbia." Final Report, DSS Contract 01SB. FP501-4-5611. (1984/5), p. 1.

[36] Canada. Department of Fisheries and Oceans, "Discussion Paper on Options for Restructuring the Pacific Fisheries Consultation Process, (August 1986), p. 4.

[37] Interior Indian Fisheries Commission, "Presentation to the Honorable Tom Siddon, Minister of Fisheries and Oceans and Honorable David Crombie, Minister of Indian and Northern Affairs" (March 17, 1986), p. 1.

[38] J. Harper, "The Economic Effects of the Boldt Decision." Report to DFO Contract FP-802-3-2304 (1984), p. 2.

[39] F. L. Gaffney, "Beyond Boldt: When Ten Years of Lawsuits Failed to Add Another Steelhead," *Trout* (Winter 1986), p. 53.

[40] Gaffney, p. 52.

[41] Fikret Berkes, "Co-Management and the James Bay Agreement." Paper prepared for the Fisheries Co-Management Conference, U.B.C. (Vancouver, May 8-10, 1986), p. 7.

[42] Berkes, p. 9.

[43] Information on the draft initialled agreement between the federal negotiator, Mr. Fred Walchli and the Nisga'a Tribal Council became public in July 1987, sparking renewed protest on the part of the Pacific Fishermen's Defense Alliance and the Fisheries Council of B.C. Details on the agreement presented here are based on several articles appearing in *The Fisherman* (July 1987).

[44] See, for example, Department of Fisheries and Oceans, "A Policy Proposal..."

[45] Marvin Shaffer, "Fisheries Co-Management as a Component of Watershed Co-Management." Paper presented to the Fisheries Co-management Conference, U.B.C. (May 6, 1986), p. 7.

[46] Kwakiutl District Council, "Kwakiutl Sea Claims: Baseline Information and Proposals for the Commercial Fisheries." Discussion Draft (1984), p. 25.

[47] *Ibid*.

[48] Kwakiutl Territorial Fisheries Commission, Constitution, section 2(4) (undated).

[49] See Morrell, p. 13.

[50] Morrell (1985), p. 181.

[51] See Neil J. Sterritt, "An Ancient Respect for the Land," *Vancouver Sun* (Sept. 9, 1985).

[52] Morrell (1985), p. 187.

[53] Photocopies of this definition were circulated by Neil Sterritt at a meeting between the Gitksan-Wet'suwet'en Tribal Council and the Skeena Watershed Sportsfishermen's Coalition, 22 November 1986.

CHAPTER 4
THE FORESTS: THE LEADING RESOURCE SECTOR

[1] Phillip Drucker, *Indians of the Northwest Coast* (Garden City, N.Y.: Natural History Press, 1963), p. 6.

[2] Rolf Knight, *Indians At Work* (Vancouver: New Star Books, 1978), p. 200.

[3] Canadian Forestry Service and British Columbia Ministry of Forests, *Canada-British Columbia Forest Resource Development Agreement (1985-1990)* (Victoria, B.C.: Canadian Forestry Service and British Columbia Ministry of Forests, undated).

[4] An overview of British Columbia forest tenure alternatives is presented in B.C. Ministry of Lands, Parks and Housing. *Land Allocation Terminology* (Victoria: Queen's Printer, 1979).

5 "Lytton Indians Join Opposition to Stein Logging," *Vancouver Sun* (September 13, 1985).

6 Quoted in "Stein Logging Debate: Profit vs. Loss," *Vancouver Sun* (January 14, 1986).

7 See for example, "B.C. Must Settle Land Claims, MB Executive Says," *Vancouver Sun* (April 19, 1985).

8 Ron Rose, "The Fight for the Forests," *B.C. Outdoors* (May 1986), p. 35.

9 Earl Smith, "Financing Native Forest Activities," in *Native Reliance Through Resource Development* ed. W. F. Sinclair, Proceedings of International Conference, "Toward Native Self-reliance Renewal and Development," held in Vancouver, August 19-24, 1984 (Vancouver: Hemlock Printers, 1985), p. 121.

10 Chief Louis Julian is quoted on this matter in "Cooperative Forestry: One Band's Approach to Forest Management," *Tree Talk* (Summer 1986), p. 3.

11 Ed John, "The Tanizul Timber Company Ltd.," in *Native Reliance Through Resource Development*, p. 113.

12 Ministry of Forests, "Conditions for Tree Farm Licence 42," (1981).

13 John is quoted in J. Friesen & S. Mitchell, "Profits for People," *B.C. Business* (June 1985), pp. 10-20.

14 T. M. Thompson, & Associates, "Management and Working Plan #1, TFL 42," Prepared for Tanizul Timber Company Ltd., Victoria, 1983, p. 8.

15 Thompson, p. 76.

16 West Coast Information & Research Group, "The Nuu-chah-nulth Forestry Study," Prepared for the Nuu-chah-nulth Tribal Council, Port Alberni, 1980, p. 19.

17 West Coast, p. 21.

18 Bob Kuiper, "Nuu-chah-nulth Forestry Program: A Case Study of Community-based Planning and Implementation Project Model," (Vancouver, INAC Planning Section, October 1985).

19 Musgamagw Tribal Council, "Integrated Resource Management and Development Demonstration Project Model," (Undated mimeo), p. 11.

20 Musgamagw Tribal Council, p. 2.

21 Musgamagw Tribal Council, p. 19-20.

22 "Timber/Fish/Wildlife: A Report from the Northwest Renewable Resources Center," Volume I, Number One (Summer 1987).

23 T/F/W/, p. 6.

24 Quoted in Patricia Marchak, *Green Gold: The Forest Industry in British Columbia* (Vancouver: University of British Columbia Press, 1983), p. 337.

25 Silva Environmental Consultants, "Report to the Nisga'a Tribal Council," (1985).

26 Ombudsman of British Columbia, "The Nisga'a Tribal Council and Tree Farm Licence No. 1," Public Report No. 4 (1985), p. 7.

27 Ombudsman, p. 38.

28 J. Galea, "The Impacts of ANSCA on the Forest Products Industry," paper presented at Indian Land Claims Seminar, Association of British Columbia Professional Foresters, Vancouver, January 27, 1987, p. 5.

29 The *Forest Resource Development Agreement* program (see note 3 above) includes an analysis of timber supply problems recognized by both governments. This assessment is based on studies independently conducted by each which predict serious shortfalls in supply, e.g., Environment Canada, *The Need for Forest Renewal and Management in British Columbia* (Victoria, 1983) and the B.C. Ministry of Forests, *Forest and Range Resource Analysis* (Victoria, 1985).

1   Helen Codere, *Fighting with Property: A Study of Kwakiutl Potlatching and Warfare, 1792-1930* (Seattle: University of Washington, 1950), pp. 22-23.

2   *Daily Victoria Gazette*, 20 August 1858. Cited in Robin Fisher, *Contact and Conflict* (Vancouver: UBC Press, 1977), p. 100.

3   Robert M. Ballantyne, *Handbook to the New Gold Fields* ... (Edinburgh: A. Strahan, 1858), cited in Fisher, p. 100.

4   See R. E. Cail, *Land, Man and the Law: The Disposal of Crown Lands in British Columbia, 1871-1913* (Vancouver: U.B.C. Press, 1974).

5   RSBC 1979, c.323; RSBC 1979, c.259; RSBC 1979, c.264; and RSBC 1979, c.51.

6   Indian and Northern Affairs Canada, *Comprehensive Land Claims Policy* (Ottawa: INAC, 1986).

7   [1967] S.C.R. 792 and [1984] 4 WWR 289 (SCC).

8   See J. Peter Meekison, Roy J. Romanow & William D. Moull, *Origins and Meaning of Section 92A: The 1982 Constitutional Amendment on Resources* (Montreal: The Institute for Research on Public Policy, 1985) for a view of the provisions of natural resource management under the Constitution Act, 1982.

9   Indian and Northern Affairs Canada 1986, p. 14.

10   Quoted in *Offshore Hydrocarbon Exploration* 1986, p. 85.

11   Interview, George Asp, Land Claims Researcher, Jerry Asp, Tahltan Development Corporation; Vern Marion, President, Tahltan Tribal Council, August 1986 (hereafter cited as Tahltan interview).

12   Interview, Charles Shaw, Kitamaat Band, OSAANS meeting September 1986; Clarence Nyce, Band Manager; Gerald Amos, Chief Councillor, Kitimaat Band, September 1986.

13   Tahltan interview.

14   Presentation by Heber Maitland, Chief Councillor, Haisla Nation, to the NDP Caucus, April 22, 1978.

15   See for example, Mining Association of Canada, "Economic Renewal and Canadian Mining: A Submission to the Government of Canada by Canada's Mining Industry," January 1985.

16   For a discussion of the situation in northern Australia, see S. McGill & G. J. Crough, *Indigenous Resource Rights and Mining Companies in North America and Australia* (Canberra: Australian Government Publishing Service, 1986), p. 9.

17   See Ron Scrimshaw, "Native Business Opportunities" in *Native Reliance Through Resource Development*, ed. W. F. Sinclair. Proceedings of International Conference, "Towards Native Self-reliance Renewal and Development" (Vancouver, August 19-24, 1984). Vancouver: Hemlock Printers, pp. 39-41 for a description of NOVA's native training programs.

18   George Manuel, Testimony to West Coast Oil Ports Inquiry, Transcript Proceedings, West Coast Offshore Exploration Environmental Assessment Panel (25 November 1985), Volume 16, pp. 2578-79.

19   "Frustration is Boom Industry in this Oil Patch," *Vancouver Sun*, 25 February 1987.

20   "Most of Band's Gas Money pumped into Buying Land," *Vancouver Sun*, 2 March 1987.

21   Minutes of Standing Committe on Indian Affairs and Northern Development, (10 July 1980), Issue #13.

22   National Indian Brotherhood, Memorandum on Bill C-26, (undated), p. 2.

23 Noel Starblanket, President, National Indian Brotherhood, testimony in Minutes of Standing Committee on Indian Affairs and Northern Development, 10 July 1980, Issue No. 13.

24 Murray Smith, "The West Coast LNG Project: Path of Least Resistance," in *Indian-Provincial Government Relationships*, ed. Menno Boldt, J. Anthony Long & Leroy Little Bear, proceedings of a Conference on Indian-Provincial Government relationships (University of Lethbridge, April 22-25, 1986), p. 98.

25 Smith, p. 99.

26 Submission of the Nisga'a Tribal Council to the West Coast Offshore Exploration Environmental Assessment Panel, October 1985. Executive Summary.

27 Interview with Ray Crook, Chairman, Mine Development Steering Committee, August 1987.

28 Letter from Manager, Coal Division to the Regional Office of Employment and Immigration Canada in Terrace. Dated October 15, 1986 and included in Tahltan Development Corporation, *Creating an Industry from a Way of Life*, January 1986. Outreach Project Proposal.

29 Tahltan Tribal Council Resouce Development Policy Statement (signed by Vernon Marion, President Tahltan Tribal Territorial, April 7, 1987), pp. 2-3.

30 Tahltan Tribal Council, p. 2-3.

31 Tahltan Tribal Council, p. 3-4.

32 *Notes from Indian Group Meeting B.C. Indian Minerals Negotiations*, September 29, 1986.

33 The full text of the agreement is presented in Indian and Northern Affairs Canada, *The Western Arctic Claim: The Inuvialuit Final Agreement* (Ottawa: Ministry of Indian and Northern Affairs, 1984).

34 An excellent authority for early developments in borough government is G. McBeath & T. Morehouse, *The Dynamics of Alaska Native Self-Government* (Lanham, Maryland: University of America, 1980).

35 "Mayor Eben Hopson's Warnings to the People of the Canadian Arctic" Testimony before the MacKenzie Valley Pipeline Inquiry (Photocopy, obtained from North Slope Borough, Barrow, Alaska, no date).

36 The account of the 1979-80 coastal planning experience in the North Slope Borough is based primarily on N. Dale & P. Wessling, *Northern Shore Zone Management Part II: CZM in Alaska and the North Slope Borough*, (Unpublished study for the Department of Indian and Northern Affairs, March 1981).

37 S. Anjum, "Land Use Planning in the North Slope Borough," in *National and Regional Interests in the North*, Proceedings of the Third National Workshop on People, Resources and the Environment North of 60 (Ottawa: Canadian Arctic Resources Committee, 1984), pp. 269-89.

38 Anjum, p. 287.

Bibliography

Aberley, Doug. 1985. *Bioregionalism: A Territorial Approach to Governance and Development of North Western British Columbia.* M.Sc. Thesis, University of British Columbia.

Adams, John W. 1973. *The Gitksan Potlatch: Population Flux, Resource Ownership and Reciprocity.* Toronto: Holt, Rinehart and Winston of Canada.

Ainscough, Grant L. 1979. "The Dragons and St. Georges of the Coastal Forest." *Coastal Resources of B.C.* ed. by A. H. J. Dorcey. Vancouver: Westwater Resource Centre:77-109.

Anjum, Shehla. 1984. "Land Use Planning in the North Slope Borouth," in *National and Regional Interests in the North*, Proceedings of the Third National Workshop on People, Resources and the Environment North of 60°. Ottawa: Canadian Arctic Resources Committee:269-89.

Anon. 1983. Report of Fishermen's Survival Conference. Dec. 10, 11, 1983.

Anon. 1984. "Kwakiutl Sea Claims: Baseline Information and Proposals for the Commercial Fisheries." Discussion Draft.

Asch, Michael. 1984. *Home and Native Land: Aboriginal Rights and the Canadian Constitution.* Agincourt: Methuen Publications.

Bankes, Nigel. 1983. *Resource-Leasing Options and the Settlement of Aboriginal Claims.* Ottawa: Canadian Arctic Resources Committee.

"Battling to See Who Owns B.C." *Western Report* 1 (January 27, 1986):18-22.

Beck, P. W. 1982. "Corporate Planning for an Uncertain Future," *Long Range Planning* 15 (August):13-17.

Berger, Thomas R. 1977. *Northern Frontiers, Northern Homeland: Volume II: Terms and Conditions.* Ottawa: Department of Supply and Services.

———. 1983. "Native History, Native Claims and Self-Determination," *BC Studies* 57 (Spring):10-23.

———. 1985. *Village Journey: The Report of the Alaska Native Review Commission.* New York: Hill & Wang.

Berkes, Fikret. 1986. "Co-Management and the James Bay Agreement." Paper prepared for the Fisheries Co-Management Conference. University of British Columbia. May 8-10, 1986.

B.C. Aboriginal Peoples' Fisheries Commission. 1984/85. "Mechanisms for Consultation on Native Fisheries with Native Peoples of British Columbia." Final Report, DSS Contract 01SB.FP501-4-5611.

British Columbia Indian Minerals Negotiations. 1986. "Notes from Indian Group Meeting, September 27, 1986."

British Columbia. Ministry of Attorney General. 1888. Copies of correspondence in and out re the Skeena River Uprising 1888. Provincial Archives of British Columbia, Victoria.

————. ————. Secretariat for Indian Policy and Programs. 1985. *Indian Land Claims in British Columbia*. p. 5.

————. Ministry of Lands, Parks and Housing. 1979. Land Allocation Terminology. Victoria.

————. 1887. *Report of Conference between the Provincial Government and Indian Delegates from Fort Simpson and Naas River*. Victoria: Richard Wolfenden.

————. Stein Basin Study Committee. 1975. *The Stein Basin Moratorium Study: a report submitted to the Environment and Land Use Committee/ Stein Basin Study Committee*. Victoria: Stein Basin Study Committee.

Brody, Hugh. 1981. *Maps and Dreams: Indians and the British Columbia Frontier*. Vancouver: Douglas and McIntyre.

Burrows, James K. 1986. "A Much-Needed Class of Labour: The Economy and Income of the Southern Plateau Indians, 1897-1910," *BC Studies 71* (Autumn):27-46.

Cail, Robert E. 1974. *Land, Man, and the Law: The Disposal of Crown Lands in British Columiba, 1871-1913*. Vancouver: University of British Columbia Press.

Canada. Environment Canada. 1983. *The Need for Forest Renewal and Management in British Columbia*. Ottawa: Minister of Supply & Services Canada.

————. ————. 1986a. *A Policy Proposal for a B.C. Indian Community Salmon Fishery*. Background Documentation released for discussion by the Minister of Fisheries and Oceans and the Minister of Indian Affairs and Northern Development. March 13, 1986.

————. Fisheries and Oceans Canada. 1986b. *Discussion Paper on Options for Restructuring the Pacific Fisheries Consultation Process*.

————. House of Commons. 1983. *Indian Self-Government in Canada: Report of the Special Committee*. Ottawa: Queen's Printer.

————. ————. 1969. *Statement of the Government of Canada on Indian Policy 1969*. Ottawa: Queen's Printer.

————. ————. 1973. *Statement on Claims of Indian and Inuit People*. Press Release. August 1973.

————. ————. 1975. *The Historical Development of the Indian Act*. Ottawa: Planning and Research Branch.

————. Indian Affairs and Northern Development Canada. 1976. *An Approach to the Government-Indian Relationship*. Unpublished manuscript.

————. ————. 1978. *Native Claims: Policy, Processes and Perspectives*. Ottawa: Queen's Printer.

————, ————. 1981. *In All Fairness: A Native Claims Policy*. Ottawa: Queen's Printer.

————. ————. 1982. *James Bay and Northern Quebec Agreement Implementation Review*. Ottawa.

————. ————. 1982. *Outstanding Business: A Native Claims Policy, Specific Claims*. Ottawa.

————. ————. 1982. *Selected Annoated Bibliography on B.C. Indian Policy and Land Claims*. Ottawa: Treaties and Historical Research Centre, Research Branch.

————. ————. 1983. *Review of the Comprehensive Claims Process*. Ottawa: Audit Branch.

————. ————. 1984. *The Western Arctic Claim: A Guide to the Inuvialuit Final Agreement*. Ottawa.

————. ————. 1985. *Living Treaties: Lasting Agreements. Report of the Task Force to Review Comprehensive Claims Policy*. Ottawa.

————. ————. 1986. *Comprehensive Land Claims Policy*. Press Release, December 18, 1986. Ottawa.

————. ————. *Northeastern Quebec Agreement*. Ottawa.

————. Task Force on Program Review. 1986. *Improved Program Delivery, Indians and Natives: A Study Team Report*. Ottawa.

Cassidy, Maureen. 1984. *From Mountain to Mountain: A History of the Gitksan Village of Ans'pa yawx*. Kispiox, B.C.: Ans'pa yaxw School Society.

Chamberlin, J. E. 1975. *The Harrowing of Eden: White Attitudes Toward Native Americans*. New York: Seabury Press.

Chambers, Alan D. & J. MacLeod. 1980. "Can British Columbia's Sustained Yield Units Sustain the Yield?" *Journal of Business Administration* 11:103-114.

Clement, Wallace. 1986. *The Struggle to Organize: Resistance in Canada's Fishery*. Toronto: McClelland and Steward.

Codere, Helen. 1950. *Fighting with Property: A Study of Kwakiutl Potlatching and Warfare, 1792-1930*. Seattle: University of Washington Press.

Cooper, Jim. 1985. "Cariboo Indian Enterprises." in *Native Reliance Through Resource Development*. ed. W. F. Sinclair. Proceedings of

International Conference. "Towards Native Self-reliance Renewal and Development," August 29-24, 1984. Vancouver: Hemlock Printers:114.

Council of Forest Industries of British Columbia. 1986. *Native Indian Land Claims in British Columbia: A Background Paper*. Vancouver: COFI.

Council of the Haida Nation. 1985. Presentation to House of Commons Standing Committee on Fisheries and Forestry. Prince Rupert: April 2, 1985.

Cove, John J. 1982. "The Gitksan Traditional Concept of Land Ownership," *Anthropoligica* 24:3-17.

Crough, G. J. 1986. *Indigenous Resource Rights and Mining Companies in North America and Australia*. Canberra: Australian Government Publishing Service.

Cumming, Peter A. and K. Aalto and Neil Mickenburg. 1972. *Native Rights in Canada*, 2nd ed. Toronto: Indian-Eskimo Association of Canada and General Publishing.

Cummins, Christine, Michael Friedlaender & Douglas Williams. 1978. *Impact of the Salmonid Enhancement Program on Native People*. Vancouver: Environment Canada, Fisheries and Marine.

Dale, Norman. 1986. "Getting to Co-Management: Social Learning in the Redesign of Fisheries Management." Paper prepared for the Fisheries Co-Management Conference. University of British Columbia. May 8-10, 1986.

––––––. and P. Wessling. 1981. *Northern Shore Zone Management Part II: CZM in Alaska and the North Slope Borough*. Unpublished study for the Department of Indian and Northern Affairs, March 1981.

Daniel, Richard. 1980. *A History of Native Claims Processes in Canada, 1867-1979*. Ottawa: Research Branch, Department of Indian and Northern Affairs.

Doerksen, D. 1987. Letter to membership of Northern Trollers Association 18 January 1987.

Drucker, Philip. 1963. *Indians of the Northwest Coast*. Garden City, N.Y.: Natural History Press.

Duff, Wilson. 1969. "The Fort Victoria Treaties." *BC Studies* 3 (Autumn): 3-57.

––––––. 1964. *The Indian History of British Columbia: Volume 1. The Impact of the White Man*. Anthropology in British Columbia Memoir No.5. Victoria: Provincial Museum of Natural History and Anthropology.

Fashler, R. A. & Andrew R. Thompson. 1983. "Constitutional Change and the Forest Industry." in *Canada and the New Constitution*. Vol. 2. ed.

S. M. Beck & I. Bernier. Montreal: Institute For Research On Public Policy:55-87.

Feit, Harvey. 1984. "Conflict Arenas in the Management of Renewable Resources in the Canadian North: Perspectives Based on Conflicts and Responses in the James Bay Region, Quebec," in *National and Regional Interests in the North.* Proceedings of the Third National Workshop on People, Resources and the Environment North of 60°. Ottawa: Canadian Arctic Resources Committee:435-58.

Fisher, Robin. 1971. "Joseph Trutch and Indian Land Policy." *BC Studies* 12 (Winter):3-33.

———. 1977. *Contact and Conflict: Indian-European Relations in British Columbia, 1774-1890.* Vancouver: The University of British Columbia Press.

Fisheries Council of British Columbia. 1985. Submission of the Fisheries Council of British Columbia to the Task Force on Comprehensive Claims Policy. Vancouver, September 1985.

Friesen, J. and S. Mitchell. 1985. "Profits for People." *B.C. Business* (June):10-20.

"Frustration is boom industry in this oil patch." *Vancouver Sun* (25 February 1986).

Gaffney, F. L. 1986. "Beyond Boldt: When Ten Years of Lawsuits Failed to Add Another Steelhead." *Trout* (Winter):51-53.

Galea, J. 1987. "The Impact of ANCSA on the Forest Products Industry." Paper presented at the Indian Land Claims Seminar, Association of British Columbia Professional Foresters. Vancouver, January 27, 1987.

Gillis D. J. & Associates & W. McKay & Associates. n.d. *Economic Development Planning for the Kwakiutl District.* Volume 1. Report to the Kwakiutl District Council.

Grainger, Martin. 1964 [1908]. *Woodsmen of the West.* Toronto: McClelland and Stewart.

Green, E. R. 1983. "Cathedral Grove." *Saturday Night* (June):52-59.

Harper, J. 1984. *The Economic Effects of the Boldt Decision.* Report to Department of Fisheries and Oceans Contract FP-802-3-2304.

———. 1982. *Indian Fisheries Management in the State of Washington: A Working Document.* Report to Indian and Northern Affairs Canada.

Hawley, Donna Lea. 1984. *Indian Act Annotated.* Calgary: Carswell.

Hopson, Eben. n.d. "Mayor Eben Hopson's Warnings to the People of the Canadian Arctic." Testimony before the MacKenzie Valley Pipeline Inquiry. Photocopy.

Hopwood, Al. 1985. "A National Indian Forestry Program." in *Native Reliance Through Resource Development*. ed. W. F. Sinclair. Proceedings of International Conference, "Towards Native Self-reliance Renewal and Development." August 19-24, 1984. Vancouver: Hemlock Printers:109-112.

Indian Claims Commission, Research Resource Centre. 1975. *Indian Claims in Canada: An Introductory Essay and Selected List of Library Holdings*. Ottawa: Information Canada.

Interior Indian Fisheries Commission. 1986. Presentation to the Honorable Tom Siddon, Minister of Fisheries and Oceans and Honorable David Crombie, Minister of Indian and Northern Affairs, March 17, 1986.

John, Ed. 1985. "The Tanizul Timber Company Ltd." in *Native Reliance Through Resource Development*, ed. W. F. Sinclair. Proceedings of International Conference, "Towards Native Self-reliance Renewal and Development." August 19-24, 1984. Vancouver: Hemlock Printers:112-114.

Jones, Trevor. 1983. *Wilderness or Logging?: Case Studies of Two Conflicts in B.C.* Vancouver: Federation of Mountain Clubs of B.C.

Knight, Rolf. 1978. *Indians at Work: An Informal History of Native Indian Labour in British Columbia, 1858-1930*. Vancouver: New Star Books.

La Rusic, I. 1983. *Negotiating a Way of Life: Initial Cree Experience with the Administrative Structure Arising from the James Bay Agreement*. Prepared for the Research Division, Policy, Research and Evaluation Group, Department of Indian Affairs and Northern Development. Montreal: ssDcc inc.

LaViolette, Forrest E. 1961. *The Struggle for Survival: Indian Cultures and the Protestant Ethic in British Columbia*. Toronto: University of Toronto Press.

Levy, David A. and Kenneth J. Hall. 1985. *A Review of the Limnology and Sockeye Salmon Ecology of Babine Lake*. Vancouver: Westwater Research Centre, the University of British Columbia in cooperation with the British Columbia Ministry of Forests, Forest Service, Prince Rupert Forest Region.

Lysyk, Kenneth. 1973. "The Indian Title Question in Canada: An Appraisal in the Light of Calder." *Canadian Bar Review* 51: 450-80.

————. 1982. "The Rights and Freedoms of the Aboriginal Peoples of Canada," in *The Canadian Charter of Rights and Freedoms*, eds. Walter S. Tarnopolsky and Gerald A. Beaudoin. Toronto: Carswell:467-88.

McBeath, G. and T. Morehouse. 1980. *The Dynamics of Alaska Native Self-Government*. Lanham, Maryland: University of America.

204

Madill, Dennis. 1981. *British Columbia Indian Treaties in Historical Perspective*. Ottawa: Research Branch, Indian and Northern Affairs Canada.

———. 1982. *Selected Annotated Bibliography on British Columbia Indian Policy and Land Claims*. Ottawa: Treaties and Historical Research Centre, Research Branch, Corporate Policy, Indian and Northern Affairs Canada.

Maitland Heber. 1978. "Presentation by Heber Maitland, Chief Councillor, Haisla Nation, to the NDP Caucus, April 22, 1978."

Manuel, George and Michael Poslums. 1974. *The Fourth World: An Indian Reality*. Toronto: Collier-MacMillan.

Marchak, M. Patricia. 1983. *Green Gold: The Forest Industry in British Columbia*. Vancouver: University of British Columbia Press.

Meekison, J. Peter, Roy J. Romanow and William D. Moull. 1985. *Origins and Meaning of Section 92A: The 1982 Constitutional Amendment on Resources*. Montreal: The Institute For Research On Public Policy.

Mining Association of Canada. 1985. "Economic Renewal and Canadian Mining: A Submission to the Government of Canada by Canada's Mining Industry."

Morrell, Mike. 1986. "The Struggle to Integrate Traditional Indian Systems and State Management in the Salmon Fisheries of the Skeena River, British Columbia." Paper presented to the Fisheries Co-Management Conference. University of British Columbia. May 6, 1986.

Morrison, William R. 1983. *A Survey of the History and Claims of the Native Peoples of Northern Canada*. Ottawa: Department of Indian Affairs and Northern Development.

———. 1984. *Under the Flag: Canadian Sovereignty and the Native Peoples in Northern Canada*. Ottawa: Research Branch, Department of Indian Affairs and Northern Development.

Morse, Bradford W., ed. 1985. *Aboriginal Peoples and the Law: Indian, Métis and Inuit Rights in Canada*. Ottawa: Carleton University Press.

Moss, Wendy. 1981. *Practically Millionaires? A Report on the Implementation of the James Bay and Northern Quebec Agreement*. Ottawa: National Indian Brotherhood.

"Most of Band's gas money pumped into buying land." *Vancouver Sun* (2 March 1987).

Musgamagw Tribal Council. 1985. *Integrated Resource Management and Development Demonstration Project Model*. Alert Bay, B.C.: Musgamagw Tribal Council.

National Indian Brotherhood. n.d. "Memorandum on Bill C-26."

Nisga'a Tribal Council. 1985. "Submission to the West Coast Offshore Exploration Environmental Assessment Panel, October 1985, Executive Summary."

Northwest Renewable Resources Center. n.d. "The Joint Management Project Phase I Report to the National Institute for Dispute Resolution." photocopy.

———. 1987. "Timber/Fish/Wildlife: A Report from the Northwest Renewable Resources Center." Volume I, Number One.

Nuu-chah-nulth Tribal Council. 1985. Presentation to the West Coast Offshore Exploration Environmental Assessment Panel.

Odam, J. 1985. "Three Major Forces Threaten Future of Industry, Observers Say." *Vancouver Sun* (7 October 1985).

Ombudsman of British Columbia. 1985. *The Nisga'a Tribal Council and Tree Farm Licence No. 1.* Public Report No. 4.

Pacific Fishermen's Defense Alliance. 1986. "Canada's Fisheries...in Crisis: Information Booklet." Surrey, B.C.: Pacific Fishermen's Defense Alliance.

Parr-Johnson, Elizabeth. 1984. "Policy Making in Uncertainty." *Policy Options* 5 (July):44-47.

Pearse, Peter H. 1976. *Timber Rights and the Forest Policy in British Columbia.* 2 vols. Royal Commission on Forest Resources. Victoria: Queen's Printer.

———. 1982. *Turning the Tide: A New Policy for Canada's Pacific Fisheries.* Final Report of the Commission on Pacific Fisheries Policy. Vancouver: The Commission on Pacific Fisheries Policy.

Pinkerton, Evelyn. 1984. "Intercepting the State: Dramatic Processes in the Assertion of Local Co-management Rights." Paper presented to Society for Applied Anthropology, March 1984.

———. 1983. "Taking the Minister to Court: Changes in public opinion about forest management and their expression in Haida land claims." *BC Studies* 57:68-85.

Pynn, L. 1986. "Proposed Indian Fish Take Doubled with Ottawa Plan." Vancouver Sun (20 June 1986).

Ralston, H. Keith. 1965. *The 1900 Strike of Fraser River Sockeye Salmon Fishermen* M.A. Thesis, University of British Columbia, Vancouver.

Rank, A. D. 1982. "Assessment of the Community Economic Development Program." Report to Fisheries and Oceans, Canada, Pacific Region. May, 1982.

"Reserve Sought for Indians." *Vancouver Sun* (16 June 1987).

"Return to an Order of the Legislative Assembly for all Correspondence Relating to the Recent Indian Troubles on the North West Coast," *B.C. Sessional Papers for 1885*:227-287.

Richardson, Miles. 1986. "The Fisheries Co-management Struggle in Haada Gwaii." Paper presented to the Fisheries Co-Management Conference, University of British Columbia. May 6, 1986.

Rose, C. 1985. "Ottawa Urges Preservation of South Moresby Parkland." *Vancouver Sun* (7 February 1985).

Rose, R. 1983. "Indians Seek Greater Control of Fishery Resources." *Vancouver Sun* (29 November 1983).

———. 1986. "The Fight for the Forests." *B.C. Outdoors* (May):34-35, 40.

Sanders, D. E. 1983. "The Rights of the Aboriginal Peoples of Canada." *Canadian Bar Review* 61(1):314-38.

Schwindt, R. 1987. "The British Columbia Forest Sector: Pros and Cons of the Stumpage System," in *Resource Rents and Public Policy in Western Canada*. eds. T. Gunton & J. Richards. Halifax: The Institute For Research On Public Policy.

Scrimshaw, Ron. 1984. "Native Business Opportunities." in *Native Reliance Through Resource Development*. ed. W. F. Sinclair. Proceedings of International Conference, "Towards Native Self-reliance Renewal and Development." August 29-24, 1984. Vancouver: Hemlock Printers:39-41.

Sewell, D. 1986. "Co-Management of the Recreational Chinook Fishery in the Strait of Georgia." in *Native People and Renewable Resource Management*, the 1986 Symposium of the Alberta Society of Professional Biologists: 96-107.

Shaffer, Marvin. 1986. "Fisheries Co-Management as a Component of Watershed Co-Management," Paper presented to the Fisheries Co-Management Conference, UBC., May 6, 1986.

Shebbeare, R.A. 1985. "Training and Development of Native People on the Forest Industry," in *Native Reliance Through Resource Development*. ed. W. F. Sinclair. Proceedings of International Conference, "Towards Native Self-reliance Renewal and Development." August 19-24, 1984.
Vancouver: Hemlock Printers:117-119.

Sinclair, William F. 1985. *Native Self-Reliance through Resource Development*. Proceedings of International Conference "Towards Native Self-Reliance Renewal and Development." August 19-24, 1984.

Slattery, Brian. 1982-83. "The Constitutional Guarantee of Aboriginal and Treaty Rights." *Queen's Law Journal* 8:232-73.

Slocan Valley Community Forest Management Project. 1976(7). *Final Report*. Winlaw, B.C.: Slocan Valley Resource Society.

Smith, Earl E. 1985. "Financing Native Forest Activities." in *Native Reliance Through Resource Development*, ed. W. F. Sinclair. Proceedings of International Conference. "Towards Native Self-reliance Renewal and Development" August 19-24, 1984. Vancouver: Hemlock Printers:119-121.

Smith, Murray. 1986. "The West Coast LNG Project: Path of Least Resistance." in *Indian-Provincial Government Relationships*. ed Menno Boldt, J. Anthony Long and Leroy Little Bear. Proceedings of a Conference on Indian-Provincial Government Relationships. University of Lethbridge. April 22-25, 1986).

Squamish Indian Band Council. 1981. "Submission to the Pearse Commission on Pacific Fisheries Policy." (June 26, 1981).

Supply and Services Canada. 1985. *What the Constitution Says about Aboriginal Peoples*. Ottawa.

Tahltan Nation Development Corporation. 1986. *Creating an Industry from a Way of Life: The Comprehensive Development Strategy of the Tahltan Nation*.

Tahltan Tribal Council. 1986. *A Fishery-Based Economic Development Strategy*.

Taylor, John Leonard. 1983. *Canadian Indian Policy during the InterWar Years, 1918-1939*. Ottawa: Department of Indian Affairs and Northern Development.

Tennant, Paul. 1982. "Native Indian Political Organization in British Columbia, 1900-1969: A Response to Internal Colonialism." *BC Studies* 55 (Autumn 1982):3-49.

———. 1983. "Native Indian Political Activity in British Columbia, 1969-1983." *BC Studies* 57 (Spring 1983):112-136.

"This Land is Whose Land." *Maclean's* 97 (1 June 1981):49-61.

Thompson, Andrew R. 1981. *Environmental Regulation in Canada: An Assessment of the Regulatory Process*. Vancouver: Westwater Research Centre.

Thompson, T. M. & Associates. 1983. "Management and Working Plan #1, TFL 42." prepared for Tanizul Timber Company Ltd., Victoria.

Union of British Columbia Indian Chiefs. 1974. *The Lands We Lost: A History of Cut-off Lands and Land Losses from Indian Reserves in British Columbia*. Prepared by Rueben Ware. Vancouver: Land Claims Research Centre, Union of B.C. Indian Chiefs.

Upton, L. F. S. 1973. "The Origins of Canadian Indian Policy." *Journal of Canadian Studies* 8:51-61.

Wack, Pierre. 1985. "Scenarios: Uncharted Waters Ahead," *Harvard Business Review* (September-October):77.

Weaver, Sally M. 1981. *Making Canadian Indian Policy: The Hidden Agenda 1968-70*. Toronto: University of Toronto Press.

West Coast Research and Information Centre. 1981. *Nuu-chah-nulth Forestry Study*. Report to the Nuu-chah-nulth Tribal Council.

Appendix I

Organizations and Agencies Which
Provided Information and Interviews

Native Governments and Organizations
 Alkali Lake Band
 Alliance of Tribal Nations
 B.C. Aboriginal Peoples Fisheries Commission
 Cariboo Indian Enterprises
 Carrier-Sekani Tribal Council
 Chehalis Band
 Council of the Haida Nation
 Council of the Tsimshian Nation
 Cree Regional Authority
 Ehattesaht Band
 First Nations of South Island Tribal Council
 Gitksan-Wet'suwet'en Tribal Council
 Gitwangak Band
 Grand Council of the Cree
 Hagwilget Band
 Kispiox Band
 Kitimaat Band
 Kootenay Indian Area Council
 Kwakiutl District Council
 Lax Kw'alaams Band
 Lillooet Tribal Council
 Lytton Band
 Moricetown Band
 Musgamagw Tribal Council
 Native Brotherhood of British Columbia
 Native Self-Reliance Association
 Nimpkish Band
 Nisga'a Tribal Council
 North Coast Tribal Council
 Nuu-chah-nulth Tribal Council
 Sto:Lo Tribal Council
 Tahltan Tribal Council
 Tanizul Timber Company Limited

Municipal and Regional Government Agencies
 Alberni-Clayoquot Regional District
 New Hazelton

Village of Hazelton
Mission
Mount Waddington Regional District

Government of British Columbia Agencies
Agriculture and Fisheries
Economic Development
Energy, Mines and Petroleum Resources
Forests and Lands
Intergovernmental Relations

Government of Canada Agencies
Canada Employment and Immigration Commission
Canada Oil and Gas Lands Administration
Energy, Mines and Resources
Fisheries and Oceans
Indian and Northern Affairs Canada
Regional Economic and Industrial Expansion

Interest Groups and Associations
British Columbia Wildlife Federation
Canadian Petroleum Association
Coal Association of Canada
Council of Forest Industries of British Columbia
Fisheries Council of British Columbia
Gulf Trollers Association
Mining Association of British Columbia
Pacific Fishermen's Defense Alliance
Pacific Trollers Association
Skeena Watershed Coalition
United Fishermen and Allied Workers' Union

Private Firms/Crown Corporations
Canada Tungsten
Cassiar Mines
Crow's Nest Resources
Crown Forest
Dome Petroleum
Echo Bay Mines
Esso Resources Canada Limited
Gulf Canada Resources Limited
Lytton Lumber
MacMillan Bloedel

NOVA
Petro Canada
Westar Timber

U.S.-based Groups and Organizations
Alaska Department of Natural Resources
Bering Straits Coastal Management District (Alaska)
California Fish and Game Department
Cenaluiruit Coastal Management District (Alaska)
Columbia River Inter-Tribal Fish Commission
Northwest Gillnetters' Association
Northwest Indian Fisheries Commission (Washington)
Northwest Power Council (Oregon)
Oregon Fish and Game Department
Pacific Coast Federation of Fishermen's Association (California)
Quinault Nation (Washington)
Washington Department of Fisheries

Appendix II

*Summary of Contents of Comprehensive Claims
in British Columbia as Prepared by the
Native Affairs Secretariat of the Province*

This material was prepared by Ruth Mongomery, a Director with
the Native Affairs Secretariat of the Province of British Columbia,
from federal government material. A copy of the précis of each claim
and letters requesting verification of the accuracy of the précis were
sent to each of the claimants. All points of clarification raised by the
claimants who responded were incorporated.

The following accepted claimants verified the accuracy of their
précis:

Nisga'a Tribal Council
Kitwancool Band
Nuu-chah-nulth Tribal Council
Heiltsuk Nation
Kaska Dena Council
Carrier Sekani Tribal Council
Alkali Lake Band
Kootenay Indian Area Council

Accepted claimants who did not verify the accuracy of their précis
include:

Kitamaat Village Council (Haisla Nation)
Association of United Tahltans
Nuxalk Nation (Bella Coola)
Nazko-Kluskus Band
Taku Tlingit (Atlin Band)
Allied Tsimshian Tribes
Council of the Haida Nation
Council of the Tsimishian Nation, and
Nlaka' pamx Nation (Thompson Salish)

The Gitksan-Wet'suwet'en Tribal Council acknowledged the request for verification, but declined outlining any possible inaccura-
cies pending the determination of their claims case in the courts.

With regard to comprehensive claims rejected by the Government
of Canada and claims under review, the Kwakiutl First Nations and
the Homalco Band verified the accuracy of the précis of their claims.
The Musqueam and Sechelt Bands did not respond to the request for
verification.

COMPREHENSIVE CLAIMS
IN BRITISH COLUMBIA

1. *Nisga'a Tribal Council*
   (Population approximately 5,000)
   (Claim accepted by Federal Government in 1974)

The Nisga'a Indians assert "title" to more than 5,000 square miles in Northwestern, B.C. centering on the extensively-timbered Nass River Valley. Non-Indian settlements of any size in the claim area include Alice Arm, Kitsault, Stewart and Nass Camp.

The Nisga'a are described as one branch of the Tsimshian-speaking peoples, the others being Tsimshian proper, (Prince Rupert and the Lower Skeena River), and Gitksan (Hazelton and the Upper Skeena River). The bands represented by the Nisga'a Tribal Council have a combined population on reserve of approximately 3,500 and are:

Gitlakdamix (New Aiyansh)
Lakalzap (Greenville)
Canyon City
Kincolith

Approximately 1,500 Nisga'a live off-reserve. Main forms of employment are in the logging and fishing industries, as School District (No. 92), Band Council and Tribal Council staff.

The Nisga'a have consistently stated they have "no interest in selling their land in exchange for extinguishment of title" (Nisga'a Position Paper 1976). Their position is they own all the resources in the claim area. Notwithstanding the above, the Nisga'a are committed to negotiate with governments of Canada and B.C. on the principles of sharing and co-existence. The objective is to define with certainty the powers and benefits each party will have.

They say they are interested in joint Government-Nisga'a economic development programs such as: the eventual construction of the CN line from Terrace to Meziaden Lake, forestry development, mining projects and fish processing plants. They do not rule out agreements with private companies.

The Nisga'a want to retain their exclusive hunting and fishing rights subject to the requirement to set up Nisga'a management and conservation committees. Compensation for past resource extraction is sought from both levels of government.

The Nisga'a main resources are the timber in the Nass River Valley and the fisheries. A major concern is that these resources not be depleted prior to a settlement.

2. *Kitwancool Band*
   (Band population 366)
   (Claim accepted by Federal Government in 1977)

The Kitwancool Band claims unextinguished aboriginal title to territory in Northwestern B.C. The claim covers an area approximately 130 miles long and 60 miles at its widest starting from a point 7 miles north of Kitwanga on Highway 37. The only village is Kitwancool.*

Kitwancool Indians are culturally a part of the Gitksan division of Tsimshian-speaking peoples. However, they have long maintained a position of independence from all other bands and have not joined the Gitksan Wet'suwet'en in their claim and litigation. The Kitwancool never agreed to accept reserves and have never accepted any part of the $100,000 "B.C. Special" funds established in 1927 in lieu of treaty payments.

The Kitwancool claim compensation for timber losses since 1920, continued royalties on natural resources, hunting and fishing rights, highway compensation, housing and education assistance.

* Elder spokesman Peter Williams was granted an Honorary Doctor of Laws degree from the University of Victoria in 1984. He is one of the five Kitwancool residents who served time in Oakalla prison in 1927 for obstructing Dominion Government surveyors who were attempting to survey the reserves in their area.

* Although the claim submitted gives no indication of the area of the claim, provincial officials estimate it totals over 3,000 square miles.

3. *Gitksan-Wet'suwet'en Tribal Council*
   (Combined population approx. 4,500)
   (Claim accepted by Federal Government in 1977)

The Gitksan-Wet'suwet'en Indians, through their Tribal Council, claim "ownership, protection and control" over more than 20,000 square miles in Northwestern B.C. on the Upper Skeena and Bulkley Rivers.

Comprised of two cultural groups, the Gitksan are part of the threefold Tsimshian-speaking peoples while the Wet-suwet'en are the western most branch of the Athapascan Carrier Indians. Because they have lived in close proximity and by now enjoy many shared cultural and family ties, they act as a united body. The villages represented by the Tribal Council are:

Gitksan	*Wet'suwet'en*
Gitwangak (Kitwanga)	Moricetown
Kitsegulka	Hagwilget
Kispiox	
Glen Vowell	
Gitanmaax (Hazelton)	

Kitwancool is a Gitksan village but has chosen to remain independent and is not represented by the Tribal Council. Hazelton and Smithers are major non-Indian settlements located in the claim area.

The Gitksan-Wet'suwet'en Tribal Council claims sovereignty over the land claim area based on use and occupancy since time immemorial. They see a just settlement of their land claim as the basis to enable them to exercise "sovereignty" in the fields of education, social and economic development, land use, conservation and local and regional government. They claim they rejected the reserve system and openly occupied their aboriginal lands as required by their season pursuits. The Gitksan petitioned the federal government in 1908 regarding their land claims, and have been active, particularly in the last decade, in pursuing support for their claim.

As well as the Comprehensive Claim, the Gitksan-Wet'suwet'en initiated legal action against the Province for a declaration of sovereignty over the claim area. The case commenced on May 11, 1987, and will resume in September after summer recess.

4. *Kitamaat Village Council (Haisla Nation)*
   (Band population 1,053, plus approximately 1,000 non-status Indian included as beneficiaries)
   (Claim accepted by Federal Government in 1978)

The Haisla Nation is an amalgamation of two groups of Northern Kwakiutl Indians, the Kitamaat, whose principal village was situated at the head of Douglas Channel; and the Kitlope, whose main community was at the head of Gardner Canal.

After amalgamation in the 1950's, the Kitlope took up residence at Kitamaat.

The claim area includes the Power Plant at Nechako and the towns of Kitimat and Kemano.*

* Although the claim submitted gives no indication of the area of the claim, provincial officials estimate it totals approximately 4,000 square miles.

216

5. *Association of United Tahltans*
   (Band population 488 status plus approx. 2,000 non-status
   Indians included as beneficiaries)
   (Claim accepted by Federal Government in 1980)

The Tahltan Indians of Northwestern Interior B.C. first gave notice in respect of their aboriginal rights by means of a declaration in 1910. The present day United Tahltans (composed of the Tahltan and Iskut bands) claim a large area of land based on traditional use and occupancy throughout most of northwestern B.C., and extending into the southern Yukon. Telegraph Creek, Dease Lake and Cassiar fall within their claimed area.*

The United Tahltans belong to the Déné or northern Athapascan Indians who were traditionally a nomadic big game-hunting people whose hunting territories were far-ranging. This may explain the overlapping of their territorial boundaries with those of other tribes, in particular the Nisga'a, Gitksan-Wet'suwet'en, Kaska-Dena and Taku Tlingit.

The United Tahltans differ from some of the other bands in that the Tahltans are not claiming sovereignty over land, but are asking the federal government to present them with a settlement proposal. Among the items they want included in the proposal are:

(1) Specific land areas within their tribal territory to be allocated in perpetuity;
(2) Guaranteed Tahltan participation in programs to preserve the ecology of their tribal territory;
(3) Assurances that the Stikine River not be damned or diverted so as to affect their annual salmon supply;
(4) Guaranteed and protected hunting and fishing rights;
(5) Tahltan Tribal Government;
(6) Economic development programs.

They also seek tax concessions, natural resources development participation, Tahltan involvement in education, monetary and other compensation.

NOTE: The United Tahltans are not seeking settlement from the provincial government at this time.

* Although the claim submitted gives no indication of the area of the claim, provincial officials estimate it totals approximately 42,000 square miles.

6. *Nuu-chah-nulth Tribal Council*
    (Band population approximately 4,000)
    (Claim accepted by Federal Government in 1983)

The Nuu-chah-nulth Tribal Council represents 15 bands on the western half of Vancouver Island. Historically known as Nootka Indians, the Nuu-chah-nulth claim the west coast portion of Vancouver Island from Port Renfrew north to the tip of Cape Cook. They also claim open access to the sea and its resources.* The bands included in the claim are:

Ahousaht	Opechesaht	Ucluelet
Clayoquot	Pacheenaht	Ehattesaht
Hesquiaht	Sheshaht	Kyoquot
Nitinat	Toquaht	Mowachart
Ohiaht	Uchucklesaht	Nuchatlat

The Nootka's main occupation was the harvesting of sea and river resources, including whale and seal hunting. Land hunting in the dense forests was a traditional occupation but of less importance than the sea. Today the main occupations are troller fishing, the related fish processing industry and logging. Port Alberni is the only shipping port of any consequence in the area. The topography has contributed to relative isolation from other Indian groups.

The Nuu-chah-nulth base their claim on traditional use and occupancy. They declare that "aboriginal interest in these territories and their natural resources has never been extinguished by treaty or superceded by law."

The basic philosophy of the Nuu-chah-nulth is to ensure that their rights and title are recognized and that a just settlement will ensure no private interests will be displeased. They intend to share resources on a consultative basis.

* Two of the bands of the Tribal Council are claiming aboriginal title to Meares Island. This is the Nuu-chah-nulth's position in a legal dispute with the Province which is due to commence after the Gittksan-Wet'suwet'en case has been heard.

* Although the claim submitted gives no indication of the area of the claim, provincial officials estimate it totals approximately 6,000 square miles.

7. *Haida Nation*
    (Combined band population approximately 1,600)
    (Claim accepted by Federal Government in 1983)

The Haidas of the Queen Charlotte Islands claim on aboriginal and occupational right to the land and water resources of the region. The claim encompasses all of the Queen Charlottes.*

The Haida Indians today comprise two bands, the Skidegate, located on the inlet between Graham and Moresby Islands, and the Masset, located on the north coast of Graham Island. Island communities include Queen Charlotte City, Skidegate, Port Clements, Masset, Tlell and Tasu.

The Haidas have a distinct language (from the Athapascan linguistic family), and a culture similar to other northwest coast groups. Survival was based on sea, river and forest resources. The Haida were famed for their large sea-going canoes and their expert development of symbolic wood carving. Today their economy is based on fishing at Masset and the forest industry at Skidegate.

* Although the claim submitted gives no indication of the area of the claim, provincial officials estimate it totals approximately 4,000 square miles.

* The British Columbia and Federal Governments signed a memorandum of understanding on July 11, 1987, creating a National Park Reserve of the South Moresby area of the Queen Charlotte Islands. Where comprehensive land claims have been accepted a National Park Reserve is established pending the settlement of the land claim.

8. *Heiltsuk Nation*
   (Heiltsuk Band population 1,495)
   (Claim submitted 1981, accepted by Federal Government 1984)

The Heiltsuk nation comprises the descendants of many ancient Heiltsuk-speaking tribal groups who used and occupied approximately 6,000 square miles of the central coast of British Columbia.

During the latter part of the 19th century, under the impact of European contact, these groups completed a process of amalgamation and settled primarily at two locations — Bella Bella on Campbell Island and Klemtu on Swindle Island. The majority settled at Bella Bella, becoming eventually the Bella Bella Band and recently changing their name to Heiltsuk. A smaller number settled at the more northern village of Klemtu. A neighbouring group of Southern Tsimshian-speakers, the Kitasoo, also settled at Klemtu and the name "Kitasoo" came to be that of the Band established there. In addition, through intermarriage and resettlement, people descended from or affiliated with the ancient Heiltsuk-speaking tribes are found today among the membership of the Nuxalk (formerly Bella Coola) and the Oweekeno (Rivers Inlet) Bands.

The ancient Heiltsuk-speaking tribal groups are said to have had clearly defined concepts of territorial ownership and occupancy. This is the basis of the claim of the Heiltsuk Band, among which pre-amalgamation tribal identities still remain strong.

The claim area extends from the southern tip of Calvert Island, north to Kelkane Inlet across from Butedale in Graham Reach and as far inland as the head of Dean Channel. It includes mainland, islands, and adjacent offshore resources. Ocean Falls and Namu lie within the claim area.

Although traditionally harvesting and managing a broad range of both sea and land resources, the current economic base of the claimant group is primarily fishing and the harvesting and development of other marine resources. The Heiltsuk Band proposes the construction of a fish processing plant, the organization of the fishing fleet under native council direction, and a native-controlled forestry operation.

The boundaries of the Heiltsuk claim overlap with those submitted by the Nuxalk, the Oweekeno, and the Council of the Tsimshian Nation.

9. *Naxalk Nation*
   (Population 830)
   (Claim accepted by Federal Government in 1983)

The Nuxalk Nation is commonly known as the Bella Coola Indians. They claim aboriginal title to approximately 6,000 square miles of central coastal B.C. around Burke and Dean Channels, and including offshore waters. Bella Coola and Hagensborg are within the claim area, the boundaries of which overlap those of the Heiltsuk Nation.

The Bella Coola Indians are a distinct cultural and linguistic group within the larger northwest coast culture. Their intermarriage with neighbouring Kwakiutl-speaking groups may be the basis for the overlapping claims. Salmon was the basis of the Bella Coola food supply and is still the main commercial activity. As well, oolachen oil was traded to other coastal groups.

The Nuxalk Nation proposes tripartite negotiations based on the principle of the continuance of native title. This title is said to include the land, minerals, trees, lakes, rivers, streams, the sea and other resources. The Indians seek resource royalties, compensation benefits, participation in resource management, and hunting and fishing rights. In their view development on Crown lands should be halted until agreement is reached on land claims.

10. *Nazko-Kluskus Bands*
    (Combined population 313)
    (Claim accepted by Federal Government in 1983)

The Nazko and the Kluskus bands have joined to pursue a formal claim to "an interest" of approximately 8,000 square miles in the rolling Interior Plateau of B.C., comprised of the valley in the Blackwater and Nazko Rivers lying between Prince George and Williams Lake.

The area appears to include the town of Quesnel, although the Quesnel Band has not joined in the claim at this point. The only Indian settlement of any size is Nazko Village.

The Nazko and Kluskus represent two of the five Southern Carrier bands. These Athapascan-speaking groups historically were flexible units which had divided and united as circumstances required. Hunting, fishing and gathering were traditional means of sustenance.

Today there is very little cash economy. Some ranching, and a little logging for mainly off-reserve residents, supplement the subsistence economy.

The bands are concerned about possible oil and gas discoveries and generally want a say in resource development within their traditional territory.

NOTE: The Nazko Band is also involved in cut-off lands negotiations with the federal and provincial governments.

11. *Kaska-Dena Council*
    (Combined population approximately 804)
    (Claim accepted by Federal Government in 1983)

The Kaska-Dena Council has submitted a claim based on traditional use and occupancy of more than 25,000 square miles of territory in the mountains far north of central B.C. The territory claimed stretches into the Yukon and Northwest Territories, but the Northwest Territories portion is the concern of the Ross River Kaska from the Yukon. The Council for Yukon Indians is negotiating on behalf of Yukon residents, while the Kaska-Dena are pursuing a recognized discrete claim to 17,000 square miles of Yukon Territory. The Kaska-Dena claim also extends into the Treaty No. 8 area. None of the Kaska-Dena claimants were ever signatories to the treaty.

The Kaska-Dena people reside in five communities:

Good Hope Lake	Muncho Lake
Lower Post	Fort Ware
Fireside	

The Fort Ware Band administers to the Fort Ware community, while the Liard River Band administers to the other four communitie.

The towns of Cassiar, Murcho Lake Park, Kwadaha Park and Tarlatui Park are within the area claimed, as is a sizeable section of the Alaska Highway.

The Kaska people speak an Athapascan language that can be understood by the neighbouring Tahltan Indians, whose comprehensive claim overlaps with the Kaska-Dena claim.

Because of the sub-arctic climate, agricultre is not practised. The economy was traditionally based on hunting, trapping and fishing and these are still the major activities, carried out on a seasonal basis within traditional family-controlled territories. About 25 percent of the people go to communities such as Cassiar, Prince George, Watson Lake and Fort St. John for part of the year for job opportunities.

12. *Carrier-Sekani Tribal Council*
    (Combined population 4,518+)
    (Claim accepted by Federal Government in 1983)

The Carrier-Sekani Tribal Council represents 13 bands with a very large aboriginal claim in north central B.C.* The bands are:

Broman Lake	Lake Babine	Stoney Creek
Burns Lake	Necoslie	Stuart Trembleur Lake
Cheslatta	Nee Tahi Bhun	Takla Lake
Fort George	Stallauo	Ingenika
Fraser Lake		

The territory claimed overlaps with the other Sekani claim (Kaska-Dena) and that of the Gitksan-Wet'suwet'en (Carrier). There is also overlap with the United Tahtan claim. Although the Ingenika band may reside within the Treaty 8 area, the band was not a signator to Treaty 8. Some of the larger non-Indian communities located within the claim area include: Prince George, Tumbler Ridge, Vanderhoof, Burns Lake, Fort St. James and Fraser Lake.

The bands involved are part of the Athapascan or Déné language grouping, and speak the Carrier and Sekani dialects. The Carrier peoples primary emphasis was on fishing with hunting and gathering playing a secondary role, while the Sekani on the other hand relied heavily on the hunting of Caribou, Moose, Bear, Procupine and Beaver with fishing playing the lesser role.

The forest industry, oil and gas, coal and electrical energy all have major developments in the claim area. Flooding caused by the building of the Bennett Dam and Alcan's Kenny Dam has greatly altered the composition and quality of wildlife habitat, thus impacting on the Indians' guiding and trapping activities.

Although not related to the claims process, a major economic breakthrough was the awarding of a 25 year Tree Farm Licence covering about 54,000 hectares to Tanizul Timber Limited, the business arm of the Stuart-Trembleur Lakes Band.

* Although the claim submitted gives no indication of the area of the claim, provincial officials estimate it totals approximately 68,000 square miles.

13. *Alkali Lake Band*
    (Population approximately 403)
    (Claim accepted by Federal Government in 1983)

The Alkali Lake Band of central interior B.C. claims aboriginal title and rights to two areas: one on the Cariboo Plateau surrounding the Alkali Lake reserves on the east side of the Fraser River; and the other on the west side of the Fraser River south of the Chilcotin River. The claim area is smaller, comparatively, than most of the other comprehensive claims.*

The Alkali Lake Band speaks the Shuswap language and is considered as one of the Fraser River Division groups of the Shuswap. Hunting, especially deer and moose, fishing for salmon, and gathering roots and berries formed the traditional modes of subsistence.

Today the band has established several co-operative ventures and is anxious to extend their economic development opportunities. There is logging both on and off-reserve with the result of enlargement of grazing land on-reserve.

Alkali Lake Band views their claim to aboriginal rights and self-government as part of a renewed spiritual, moral and cultural thrust, one that has seen the re-emergence of the teaching of the Shuswap language.

* Although the claim submitted gives no indication of the area of the claim, provincial officials estimate it totals approximately 1,750 square miles.

14. *Taku-Tlingit (Atlin Band)*
    (Population approximately 178)
    (Claim accepted by Federal Government in 1984)

The Taku-Tlingit of the Atlin Band claim aboriginal title (based on traditional use and occupancy) to more than 10,000 square miles in the mountainous northwestern corner of B.C. and extending into southern Yukon (about 1,000 square miles).

The small community of Atlin is the only non-Indian settlement of any size in the area. The claims of the United Tahltans and the Council of Yukon Indians overlap the Atlin claim.

The Atlin Band is part of the Inland Tlingit Indians. Members speak a dialect of the Tlingit language. Hunting, fishing, trapping and berry gathering all formed part of the Tlingit exploitation of their natural resources. Trading oolachen oil was carried on with other Indian groups. Mountain wool was woven into the distinctive Chilkat blanket, a mark of high prestige. The Inland Tlingit had a more informal political system than other northwest cultural groups.

The Taku-Tlingit moved to the interior of their territory in the 19th century to gather more pelts for trading and to maintain control over the trapping area (which was hotly contested by the Tahltans), and also to participate in the gold economy. Today trapping remains an important Taku-Tlingit economic activity.

Major industries in the area in order of importance are: mining, tourism, agriculture and fishing. Improved access roads would spur development further.

15. *Allied Tsimshian Tribes*
    (Approximate population 1,710)
    (Claim accepted by Federal Government in 1987)

Hereditary chiefs of nine Tsimshian tribes from the Port Simpson and Metlakatla Bands claim aboriginal title to the Lower Skeena River area to Terrace, and the lands and waters around Prince Rupert.* One reason for the filing of the claim was anticipated negotiations with Dome Petroleum on a proposed LNG plant in Port Simpson Harbour. This project foundered.

The claimants, the majority of whom belong to the Port Simpson Band, speak the Coast Tsimshian dialect, and belong to the Northwest Coastal culture. Evidence of Tsimshian occupation in the area dates back to at least 500 B.C.

Port Simpson, a creation of the fur trade, was originally located on the Naas River and named Fort Simpson. One of the nine tribes which soon grouped around the Fort gained control over the fur trade and established a monopoly.

Metlakatla was established in 1862 as a Christian village by missionary William Duncan. It became a tightly-controlled, self-sustaining Victoria village. Soon Thomas Crosby, a Methodist missionary, transformed Port Simpson into the same type of model community. It remains isolated, however, with no road access to Prince Rupert.

Commercial fishing, a fish cannery, logging and the Band Councils make up the main source of employment.

* Although the claim submitted gives no indication of the area of the claim, provincial officials estimate it totals approximately 4,000 square miles.

16. *Council of the Tsimshian Nation*
    (Population approximately 2,389 — including Metlakatla)
    (Claim accepted by Federal Government in 1987)

The Council of the Tsimshian Nation claims approximately 13,500 square miles including the watershed of the Skeena River, the North Coast of British Columbia and its adjacent islands and surrounding waters. The intention of this group was to make a representative claim on behalf of all Tsimshian people:

Southern Tsimshian — At Kelmtu, Hartley Bay and Kitkala
Lower Skeena Tsimshian — At Port Simpson and Metlakatla
Canyon Tsimshian — At Kitsumkalum and Kitselas

However, the Port Simpson Tsimshian (which includes nine tribes) did not sign this claim, probably because they had already initiated another claim with Metlakatla as the *Allied Tsimshian Tribes*. This has led to confusion and overlap, particularly as the Metlakatla Band is now signator to both claims. The Council of the Tsimshian Nation's claim includes the area claimed by the Allied Tsimshian Tribes and overlaps with the Nisga'a, Gitksan-Wet'suwet'en, Haisla and Heiltsuk claims as well.

The Tsimshian claim is based upon the area occupied by the Coast Tsimshian at the time of contact with Europeans. It includes Prince Rupert and Terrace and extends south below Klemtu.

The economy is heavily resource-orientated with fishing, forestry and mining the predominant industries. Major development potential includes the Port of Prince Rupert, Alcan's Kemano Completion Project, a liquified natural gas terminal and hydro development.

However, the state of the economy, the size of the local market and the distance from major population centres remain formidable obstacles.

17. *Nlaka'pamux Nation (Thompson Salish)*
    (Population approximately 3,608)
    (Claim accepted by Federal Government in 1987)

Eighteen Thompson, Nicola and Similkameen Indian Bands, memberof the Nlaka'pamux Tribal Council, claim 10,000 quare miles of the southern Interior of B.C., east of the coast range and centering around the Fraser, Thompson and Nicola Rivers. The Tribal Council says it acts on behalf of about 7,000 status and non-status Indians in the area. Merritt, Boston Bar, Spuzzum, Lytton, Manning Park and Spences Bridge and within the claim area. Bands include:

Ashcroft	Lytton	Shaka
Boothroyd	Nicomen	Lower Similkameen
Boston Bar	Nooaitch	Upper Similkameen
Coldwater	Lower Nicola	Siska
Cook's Ferry	Upper Nicola	Skuppah
Kanaka Bar	Oregon Jack Creek	Spuzzum

The Nlaka'pamux are Interior Salish Indians, with the dialect of the Upper Thompson Indians predominating. The economy and subsistence centred around hunting, trapping, fishing (salmon), gathering roots and berries, and trading with other Indians before contact and with non-Indians after contact.

The discovery of gold in the 1850s somewhat disrupted the pattern of traditional life. This was followed by missionaries and the railroad. Mining and forestry are extensively practised, and the bands have been involved in cattle ranching and farming from the early post-contact period. They are considered to be very successful ranchers and farmers.

18. *Kootenay Nation (Area Council)*
    (Population approximately 633)
    (Claim accepted by Federal Government in 1987)

The St. Mary's, Lower Kootenay, Tobacco Plains, Columbia Lake and Shuswap Indian Bands have empowered the Kootenay Indian Area Council to negotiate an aboriginal claim to approximately 27,500 square miles of southeastern B.C. Cranbrook, Kimberley, Nelson, Castlegar, Golden, Invermere and Fernie lie within the claim boundaries.

The Kootenay Indians were a semi-nomadic people with a subsistence economy based on hunting, gathering and fishing. They spoke a common, distinctive language unrelated to any other tribal language. The horse, introduced in the mid-18th century, extended their hunting range and soon became the dominant feature of their economy. In the early 19th century the fur trade brought about a shift in harvesting to desirable fur-bearing species. The area supports a great variety and quantity of big game species. Kootenay people are involved in hunting, guiding, outfitting, trapping, subsistence fishing and gathering of vegetables, fruits and other plants. The cutting of Christmas trees has added to the economy since the early 1930s.

CLAIMS REJECTED

1. *Musqueam Band*
   (Population approximately 526)
   (Claim submitted in 1977)

NOTE: This claim was rejected in its original form and has recently been resubmitted. Information on the new claim is not available.*

The Musqueam Band presented an aboriginal claim to its "traditional lands" which include most of Greater Vancouver including Stanley Park, Burrard Inlet and the University Endowment Lands. The Office of Native Claims rejected Musqueam's submission on the basis that most of the land had been patented, which "effectively superceded any Indian Title." The Musqueam subsequently pointed out that several other claims, including the Nisga'a, contained alienated lands but were accepted for negotiation. It is probably that the dimensions of the potential cost of settling the Musqueam claim was a major underlying reason for the initial rejection.

The Musqueam are Coast Salish people who spoke the Halkomelem language. Primarily fishermen, hunters and gatherers, the Musqueam moved in family groups according to season. Social and political organization was complex, with primary identification and loyalty belonging to the ancestral family.

From a combined sustenance-wage economy which developed after the arrival of the non-Indian, Musqueam Band members today depend mainly on wages and revenue from leases. Unemployment ranges as high as 70 percent. Much of Musqueam Indian Reserve #2 has been leased. Lessees include two golf courses, three housing developments and several market gardens. The Supreme Court decision in the "Guerin Case" resulted in lage settlement to the Musqueam based on the Department of Indian Affairs abrogation of fiduciary responsibility in negotiating a lease with a golf course.

* Although the claim submitted gives no indication of the area of the claim, provincial officials estimate it totals approximately 480 square miles.

CLAIMS UNDER REVIEW

1. *Kwakiutl First Nations*
   (Population approximately 3,476)
   (Claims submitted in 1984)

The aboriginal claim of the Kwakiutl First Nations is based upon sovereignty and aboriginal title. This includes the ability to make laws; the protection of Kwakiutl culture, and the recognition of the existence of Indian "nationhood."

The Southern Kwakiutl Indians who have joined together to present their aboriginal land claim comprise 15 Indian bands. They are:

Nimpkish	Kwakiutl	Cape Mudge
Tsawataineuk	Mamalillikulla	Tlowitsis-Mum-Tagila
Kwiksutaineuk	Tanakteuk	Kwiakah
Kwa-Wa-Aineuk	Tsulquate	Nuwitti
Quatsino	Comox	Campbell River

The territory claimed includes the upper northwestern side of Vancouver Island from Cape Cook Point; the whole eastern side above Comox; Smith Inlet, Bute and Knight Inlet on the heavily fjorded adjacent mainland. Port Hardy, Campbell River, Courtenay, Comox and Mt. Waddington are in the claim area.*

The Southern Kwakiutl belonged to the Northwest Coast culture. They were highly skilled carvers, and ceremonies played a large role in their complex society. Southern Kwakiutl occupied village sites in the claim area for several thousand years, although there was no sense of "nationhood" as a tribal unification concept, before the coming of the white man.

Fish and the forests, in particular salmon and cedar, were essential bases to the flourishing of the culture. With the coming of the white man, disease, especially small pox, took a great toll on the Southern Kwakiutl.

Today, fishing and logging still provide employment and sustenance to the people. A resurgence in the traditional arts of carving, traditional dances and cultural display continues to develop and define the Southern Kwakiutl's adaptation to contemporary life.

* Although the claim submitted gives no indication of the claim area, provincial officials estimate it totals approximately 18,000 square miles.

2. *Sechelt Band*
   (Population approximately 619)
   (Claim submitted in 1984)

The Sechelt Band claims approximately 2,200 square miles of the lower coast of British Columbia, including the Sechelt Peninsula, Jervis Inlet and surrounding area (see map attached). It is estimated that only about one-half of one percent of the land area is designated as agricultural land. The villages of Sechelt and Half-Moon Bay are located in the claim area.The Sechelt Band also has the unique distinction of establishing itself as a quasi-municipality by means of a federal statute (Sechelt Indian Band Self-Government Act, 1986).

In its comprehensive claim the Band has declared that in return for self-government legislation, it will agree to the extinguishment of aboriginal title to the traditional Sechelt territory. Further, it would "yield those specific aboriginal rights for which fair and appropriate provision has been made in the envisaged settlement."

This offer to agree to extinguishment is unique among B.C. comprehensive claims. What it amounts to is in fact an offer to treaty. The Sechelt Act would then become a contemporary version of a treaty.

The Sechelt Band belongs to the Coast Salish Group of Indians, with a dialect related to other Salish groups such as the Comox and Squamish. Fishing and hunting characterized the traditional culture. After the devastation of a small pox epidemic in 1862, Catholic missionaries persuaded survivors of the four original tribes to coalesce to establish a mission village. The Oblates entrenched their rigidly-controlled social order known as the "Durieu System" after the Order's Bishop on the Coast.

Today the logging industry, fishing and tourism form the basis for the economy. The Sechelt have become sophisticated business people who intend to continue developing their region's potential while retaining their identity and control.

229

3. *Homalco Band*
   (Population approximately 228)
   (Claim submitted in 1985)

The Homalco Band is situated in and around Bute Inlet. The claim area lies completely within the larger Kwakiutl First Nations claim. The Homalco people however are not Kwakiutl but Coast Salish, at the northern limits of Salish territory, and speak the Comox language. On Vancouver Island, Comox is considered the dividing line between Coast Salish and Kwakiutl peoples, while the Salish inhabit the mainland further north to a line above Bute Inlet.

Today only 90 Band members live on reserve while 138 live mainly in Campbell River and the Lower Mainland.

The Homalco claim was submitted in November of 1985. A review has not yet been completed.*

* Although the claim submitted gives no indication of the area of the claim, provincial officials estimate it totals approximately 1,250 square miles.

The Institute for Research on Public Policy
L'Institut de recherches politiques

A national, independent, research organization
Un organisme de recherche national et indépendant

Founded in 1972, The Institute for Research on Public Policy is a national organization whose independence and autonomy are ensured by the revenues of an endowment fund which is supported by the federal and provincial governments and by the private sector. In addition, the Institute receives grants and contracts from governments, corporations and foundations to carry our specific research projects.

The *raison d'être* of the Institute is threefold:

- To act as a catalyst within the national community by helping to facilitate informed public debate on issues of major public interest.
- To stimulate participation by all segments of the national community in the process that leads to public policy making.
- To find practical solutions to important public policy problems, thus aiding in the development of sound public policies.

The Institute is governed by a Board of Directors, which is the decision-making body, and a Council of Trustees, which advises the Board on matters related to the research direction of the Institute. Day-to-day administration of the Institute's policies, programs and staff is the responsibility of the president.

The Institute operates in a decentralized way, employing researchers located across Canada. This ensures that research undertaken will include contributions from all regions of the country.

Wherever possible, the Institute will try to promote public understanding of, and discussion on, issues of national importance with clarity and impartiality. Conclusions or recommendations in the Institute's publications are solely those of the author and should not be attributed to the Board of Directors, Council of Trustees, or contributors to the Institute.

The president bears final responsibility for the decision to publish a manuscript under the Institute's imprint. In reaching this decision, he is advised on the accuracy and objectivity of a manuscript by both Institute staff and outside reviewers. Publication of a manuscript signifies that it is deemed to be a competent treatment of a subject worthy of public consideration.

Publications of the Institute are published in the language of the author, along with an executive summary in both of Canada's official languages.

The Institute for Research on Public Policy
L'Institut de recherches politiques

A national, independent, research organization
Un organisme de recherche national et indépendant

Créé en 1972, l'Institut de recherches politiques est un organisme national dont l'indépendance et l'autonomie sont assurés grâce a des revenus provenant d'un fonds de dotation auquel souscrivent les gouvernements fédéral et provinciaux ainsi que le secteur privé. L'Institut obtient en outre des subventions et des contrats des gouvernements, des compagnies et des fondations afin de réaliser certains projets de recherche.

La raison d'être de l'Instute est triple:

- Servir de catalyseur au sein de la collectivité nationale en favorisant un débat public éclairé sur les principales questions d'intérêt général.

- Stimuler la participation de tous les éléments de la collectivité nationale à l'élaboration de la politique d'État.

- Trouver des solutions réalisables aux importants problèmes d'ordre politique afin de contribuer à l'élaboration d'une saine politique d'État.

Un Conseil d'administration, chargé de la décision, et une Commission de direction, responsable d'éclairer le Conseil sur l'orientation de la recherche, assurent la direction de l'Institut. L'administration courante des politiques, des programmes et du personnel relève du président.

L'Institut fonctionne de manière décentralisée et retient les services de chercheurs en divers points du Canada, s'assurant ainsi que toutes les régions contribuent aux recherches.

L'Institut cherche à favoriser, dans la mesure du possible, la compréhension et la discussion publiques des questions d'envergure nationale, controversées ou non. Il publie les conclusions de ses recherches avec clarté et impartialité. Les recommandations ou les conclusions énoncées dans les publications de l'Institut sont strictement celles de l'auteur et n'engagent aucunement le conseil d'administration, la commission de direction ou les bailleurs de fonds.

Le président assume la responsabilité ultime de publier un manuscrit au nom de l'Institut. Il jouit à cette fin des conseils du personnel de l'Institut et de critiques de l'extérieur quant à l'exactitude et l'objectivité du texte. Ne sont publiés que les textes qui traitent de façon compétente d'un sujet digne de la réflexion du public.

Les publications de l'Institut paraissent dans la langue de l'auteur et sont accompagnées d'un abrégé dans les langues officielles du Canada.